Exploring the Literature of Fact

Exploring the Literature of Fact

Children's Nonfiction Trade Books in the Elementary Classroom

BARBARA MOSS

THE GUILFORD PRESS
New York   London

KH

Printed in the United States of America

This book is printed on acid-free paper.

Last digit is print number: 9 8 7 6 5 4 3 2 1

Library of Congress Cataloging-in-Publication Data

Moss, Barbara, 1950–
   Exploring the literature of fact : children's nonfiction trade books in the
elementary classroom / Barbara Moss.
      p. cm.   —   (Solving problems in the teaching of literacy)
Includes bibliographical references and index.
   ISBN 1-57230-803-6 (cloth) — ISBN 1-57230-546-0 (pbk.)
   1. Literature—Study and teaching (Elementary)—United States. 2. Children's
literature—Study and teaching (Elementary)—United States. 3. Children—Books
and reading—United States. I. Title. II. Series.
LB1575.5.U5 M68 2003
372.64—dc21

                                                      2002012526

10/25/04

About the Author

Barbara Moss, PhD, is a professor at San Diego State University in the area of literacy education. She teaches courses in children's literature and content area reading for preservice and inservice teachers. A classroom teacher at the middle and high school levels for 10 years and a reading supervisor for 12 years, Dr. Moss has spoken at numerous local, state, and national conferences and has done many inservice programs on using nonfiction literature in elementary and middle grade classrooms. She has published in *The Reading Teacher, Language Arts, Reading Psychology,* and *Reading and Writing Quarterly*, and has coedited several International Reading Association publications.

Dr. Moss received her PhD from Kent State University in 1988. She has served as editor of *The Ohio Reading Teacher* and as a coeditor of *The Reading Teacher*. In 1997 she received an Elva Knight Grant from the International Reading Association, which helped to support portions of the research described in this book. Her research interests focus on content area reading and children's responses to nonfiction trade books.

Preface

Exploring the Literature of Fact: Children's Nonfiction Trade Books in the Elementary Classroom represents the melding of two areas of personal interest for me: content area reading and children's literature. This book is the culmination of more than a decade of reading, writing, discussing, and teaching about nonfiction literature to hundreds of preservice and inservice teachers.

An important goal of this book has been to illustrate that nonfiction trade books are literature and should be treated like literature in the classroom. They can prompt delight, wonder, and reflection in many of the same ways that fiction can. Individual children may be as passionate about particular nonfiction titles as fiction titles, if only given the opportunity to read them. The possibilities for using nonfiction extend far beyond the narrow confines of student inquiry projects, although this certainly is an important and valid use of nonfiction literature.

This book is intended not only to provide teachers with a guide for choosing the many wonderful nonfiction trade books available today but to give them concrete examples of ways to actually begin using them in the classroom. The ideas in this book represent current thinking about the importance of using literature in the classroom and helping students read and write about that literature in strategic ways. All of the ideas within the covers of this book have been field-tested in classrooms either by me or by classroom teachers I have known and worked with over the years. Through the descriptions of actual classrooms, I have tried to illustrate the many unique and creative ways teachers have incorporated nonfiction trade books into their classroom curricula.

In addition to providing glimpses of actual classrooms, this book includes the voices of students themselves, through their spoken and written responses to nonfiction. Their honest reactions to the literature of fact helps deepen the reader's understanding of the possibilities this genre holds for helping today's children gain the literacy skills necessary for the future.

No book is completed without the help of many dedicated friends and colleagues. I would like to express special thanks to my editor, Chris Jennison, for his unwavering support. I would also like to thank the proposal reviewers, Beth Roberts, Brenda Sabey, and Diane Tracey. I also wish to thank Zoë Abrahams for her help with creating the visuals. In addition, I wish to offer my sincere appreciation to the manuscript reviewers—Nancy Padak, Kent State University; Dorothy Leal, Ohio University; and Sharon Kletzien, West Chester University—for their careful reading of the text and their helpful feedback.

My gratitude also goes to Judy Hendershot, teacher and children's author extraordinare, whose love of literature and insights about its uses in the classroom have influenced this work in myriad ways. Judy and I collaborated on a 3-year study of sixth graders' responses to nonfiction, during which I was in her classroom once a week. We are grateful to the International Reading Association for their funding of an Elva Knight Grant to support that research during 1998–1999. I also wish to extend my appreciation to the many teachers who allowed me to describe the creative ways in which they use nonfiction in their classrooms. Thank you also to Mary Lou DiPillo of Youngstown State University, Susan Leone of the Mahoning County Office of Education, and Ruth Oswald of the University of Akron. Their dissertations and our collaborations related to the study of nonfiction in the classroom have illuminated my understanding of the many ways nonfiction can promote literacy learning in all subjects. I also wish to thank my mentors, Rich and JoAnne Vacca, who sparked my interest in content reading 20 years ago and continue to influence my thinking. Finally, I wish to thank my husband, Pat, for his patience and love.

I hope that through this book both novice and veteran teachers will feel my enthusiasm for the extraordinary nonfiction literature available today. I hope too that this book will prompt all teachers who believe in the power of literature to complement their use of fiction with the literature of fact and to discover the myriad possibilities it offers for enriching today's classrooms.

BARBARA MOSS

Contents

Exploring the Literature of Fact

Introduction

Today's children are different from those of the past. They are more sophisticated, less inhibited, and have different interests from children years ago. They have access to an array of amusements that children of earlier generations could not even imagine—television, computers, electronic games, and videos, to name just a few. In spite of the differences in the lives of today's children compared with those of the past, children's curiosity about the world around them remains constant. Today's children, just like those living long ago, are fascinated by the daily wonders of life on this planet. For them, the world is a kaleidoscope of images seen for the first time. From a preschooler watching an ant carrying food to its nest to the middle grader enthralled by the spectacle of a boa constrictor devouring a mouse, this sense of wonder and curiosity persists. It also provides the basis for many forms of learning. According to Betsy Hearne (1999), "In the matter of education, a child's own curiosity is the greatest tool. It starts long before school does and is a driving force in growing up" (p. 133).

Children don't leave their curiosity at the schoolroom door. They bring it into their classrooms, along with their fears, their fantasies, and their dreams for the future. This curiosity often sparks learning that persists long after the bell has rung—and sometimes continues throughout a lifetime.

Regardless of a child's area of interest, whether rocks, horses, dinosaurs, medieval weaponry, outer space, or art, nonfiction books can fuel this curiosity. These are the books that answer children's questions about the universe—about the people, places, and things children encounter in their daily lives. Too often, though, we teachers don't capitalize on youngsters' fascination with exploring facts. Instead, we fill our classrooms with a plethora of stories—fairy tales, fantasies, and realistic tales—ignoring the excitement for reading that information books might ignite (Moss, Leone, & DiPillo, 1997).

1

In the past decade, teachers have begun to discover the power of trade books to transform even the most reluctant readers into lovers of literature. But while teachers are using more and more trade books in their classrooms, the literature they choose is usually fiction. Today's children get little exposure to nonfiction in school either through basal readers or teacher read-alouds (Moss & Newton, 2002; Hoffman, Roser, & Battle, 1993). In fact, almost two-thirds of fourth graders interviewed as part of the 1994 National Assessment of Educational Progress (NAEP) reported *not* reading information trade books at school (Campbell, Kapinus, & Beatty, 1995).

If today's students are to become fully literate, they need to be comfortable with many types of texts. According to experts, available information is doubling every 5 years (Wurman, 1989). Surprisingly, most youngsters find it difficult to locate information independently from a single textbook (Dreher & Sammons, 1994), let alone select, analyze, and synthesize information from multiple resources. We pay little attention to teaching children to become competent readers of different types of texts, and we seem to assume that as children progress through the grades they will transfer their ability to read narrative into the ability to read non-narrative. (Littlefair, 1993).

If today's children are not just to survive but thrive in the Information Age, we must immerse them in the literatures of fiction *and* fact. Nonfiction trade books offer a meaningful, motivating, and natural way to make this happen. They can complement textbooks and the wonderful narrative literature already found in many classrooms. They offer rich opportunities for deepening children's understanding of text, which lead to increased enjoyment and improved understanding.

The purpose of this book is to offer teachers information about how nonfiction trade books can enhance classroom literacy instruction. Chapter 1 gives a rationale for using nonfiction and explains the various types of information books and biographies. It also focuses on representative multicultural nonfiction titles. Chapter 2 suggests ways to effectively select nonfiction for classroom use. Chapter 3 gives ideas for introducing nonfiction and motivating children to read from this genre; it also suggests ways to link nonfiction with fiction titles and the Internet. Chapter 4 suggests strategies designed to increase student comprehension of this genre. Chapter 5 focuses on ways teachers can promote response to nonfiction through discussion, writing, and drama. Chapter 6 examines the role of nonfiction in the content area classroom and suggests ways these books can contribute to content area inquiry.

An annotated bibliography of nonfiction titles appears at the end of each chapter. These listings describe books mentioned in each chapter and provide recommended grade levels for each title. These books were selected, first and foremost, on the basis of their quality. Many titles have won awards, have appeared on lists of notable books, or have been designated with starred reviews in *The Bulletin of the Center for Children's Books*, *The Horn Book*, or *Booklist*. In addition, an effort was made to include representative titles by noted nonfiction authors such as James Cross Giblin, Laurence Pringle, and Patricia Lauber, to name a few. Curricular considerations also influenced the selection of particular titles. Titles relevant to topics commonly addressed in the elementary school curriculum were selected over those that lacked such relevance. Young-adult titles have been included along with books for younger readers, reflecting the fact that books from this genre often hold great appeal for upper-elementary-grade readers. Unfortunately, many of the books mentioned in the bibliographies are, or soon will be, out of print. They are, however, still available through libraries and used book stores.

Books in various lists throughout the text are grouped by level and labeled "P" for primary, corresponding roughly to grades 1–3. Books labeled "I" for intermediate are suitable for better readers in third grade and for fourth graders. Books with the designation of "U" are for upper-grade readers, probably children in grades 5 and 6. These designations, however, are meant only as guidelines and not absolute levels.

I hope that this book will be a resource for teachers who want to move their literature instruction beyond the use of narrative to incorporate the rich resources of today's nonfiction trade books. I invite readers to use this book as a springboard for developing their own ways of making the reading and writing of non-narrative text an integral part of their classrooms.

REFERENCES

Campbell, J. R., Kapinus, B., & Beatty, A. S. (1995). *Interviewing children about their literacy experiences: Data from NAEP's integrated reading performance record at grade 4* (23-FR-05). Washington, DC: U.S. Department of Education.

Dreher, M. J., & Sammons, R. B. (1994). Fifth-graders search for information in a textbook. *Journal of Reading Behavior, 26,* 301–314.

Hearne, B. (1999). *Choosing books for children: A commonsense approach*. Chicago: University of Illinois Press.

Hoffman, J., Roser, N. L., & Battle, J. (1993). Reading aloud in classrooms: From the modal to a "model." *Reading Teacher, 46,* 496–505.

Littlefair, A. (1993). The "good book": Non-narrative aspects. In R. Beard (Ed.), *Teaching literacy, balancing perspectives* (pp. 126–139). London: Hodder & Stoughton.

Moss, B., Leone, S., & DiPillo, M. L. (1997). Exploring the literature of fact: Linking reading and writing through information trade books. *Language Arts, 74,* 418–429.

Moss, B., & Newton, E. (2002). An examination of the informational text genre in recent basal readers. *Reading Psychology, 23,* 1–13.

Wurman, R. S. (1989). *Information anxiety: What do to when information doesn't tell you what you need to know*. New York: Bantam.

CHAPTER ONE

Exploring the Nonfiction Genre

A 5-year-old Cambodian girl watches as her parents are killed and her family destroyed by the Khmer Rouge. She survives this nightmare, emigrates to the United States, and wins the 1997 Nobel Peace Prize for her efforts to create a land-mine-free world (*First They Killed My Father: A Daughter of Cambodia Remembers*; Ung, 2000).

A Washington elementary school bands together to save a polluted stream, hoping that the salmon will return (*Come Back Salmon: How a Group of Dedicated Kids Adopted Pigeon Creek and Brought It Back to Life*; Cone, 1992).

Firefighters in Idaho's Salmon National Forest race from a fire run wild into specially designed foil shelters that act like a shell. Although the shelters reach temperatures of 160 degrees, they allow the firefighters to escape angry fires and survive (*Fire in Their Eyes: Wildfires and the People Who Fight Them*; Beil, 2000).

These topics and more are typical of today's nonfiction for children. Though they sound like fictional narratives, they are factual accounts, products of extensive research and compelling storytelling. And these examples provide just a small sampling of the intriguing nonfiction titles available for today's elementary-grade readers. This has not always been the case though.

Until recently, children's nonfiction was the "stepchild" of children's literature. For many years it has been pushed aside as though it were socially inferior to real literature (Freedman, 1988). It received little attention from experts in the field. In the past 10 years, though, it has moved from the shadows into the spotlight. Why?

First of all, its quality has improved dramatically in the past 10 years. Today's books are much more attractive, interesting, and appealing than in the past. They combine wonderful book design with exquisite visuals and clear, interestingly written texts.

Second, nonfiction titles are getting more and more awards and prizes. The 1988 Newbery Medal, for example, went to a nonfiction work, *Lincoln: A Photobiography* (Freedman, 1987b). Three other nonfiction titles have won Newbery Honor Awards since then; they include two titles by Russell Freedman, *The Wright Brothers: How They Invented the Airplane* (1991) and *Eleanor Roosevelt: A Life of Discovery* (1993), and Jim Murphy's (1995) *The Great Fire*. Two biographies, *Bill Peet: An Autobiography* (Peet, 1989) and Peter Sis's (1996) *Starry Messenger*, were Caldecott Honor books in 1990 and 1997, respectively. *Snowflake Bentley* (Martin, 1998) captured the Caldecott in 1999, as did *So You Want to Be President* (St. George, 2000) in 2001.

Third, nonfiction is getting more attention in America's classrooms. While basal readers and textbooks are still the "bread and butter" of most classrooms, the literature-based movement has prompted some teachers to supplement these texts with real literature. At first, that literature was primarily fiction, but books from the nonfiction genre have begun to appear, especially in connection with content-related inquiries.

This has happened for at least a couple of reasons. First, teachers are becoming more aware of the need for children to be able to read expository, or non-narrative, text. Not surprisingly, as children progress through the grades, the need to effectively read this type of text increases. By the time they reach high school and adulthood, some 85–90% of what they read will be expository (Venezky, 1982). Secondly, teachers are discovering that children are often enthusiastic about nonfiction. For some children nonfiction offers a way into literacy that fiction does not.

This chapter provides basic information about the nonfiction genre. It examines the importance of informational literacy, the limitations of textbooks, and the advantages of nonfiction trade books. It also examines recent trends in nonfiction trade books and then focuses on the two major categories of nonfiction: information books and biographies. Following that discussion, the focus shifts to multicultural nonfiction, a relatively new but growing category of nonfiction.

THE IMPORTANCE OF INFORMATIONAL LITERACY

The ability to read and understand exposition, or text that explains or sets forth facts, is becoming increasingly critical in today's society. Venezky (1982) notes that by sixth grade more than 75% of students' school reading is expository, or non-narrative, material. He further notes that the literacy needs of adults center primarily on getting information from non-narrative text. It stands to reason that if students are to survive in the Information Age they must understand the language of information—exposition.

In spite of the importance of being able to read expository text, children in today's classrooms get limited exposure to well-written forms of this genre. All too often, children's exposure to nonfiction is limited to series books, or sets of books devoted to topics like Native American Tribes or the various states of the union. These series books generally lack the quality of nonfiction trade books, which are typically written by more experienced and knowledgeable authors (Patent, 1998). As the next section explains, children's nonfiction trade books, especially informational titles, can provide children with much needed exposure to effectively written expository text.

LIMITATIONS OF TEXTBOOKS

For many teachers, textbooks are essential classroom tools. Basal readers help them teach reading, and content area texts aid with instruction in science, social studies, mathematics, health, and many other subjects. Lately, though, both basal texts and content area textbooks have come under fire for their limitations. Basal readers, for example, contain primarily narrative, or story-type, text. Until very recently, fewer than 20% of basal selections at any level were nonfiction (Moss & Newton, 2002). So, if basal readers are the chief form of classroom reading material, students will not get much exposure to, let alone experience in, reading exposition.

Content area textbooks, while they do contain exposition, or nonstory text, have many weaknesses (Moss, 1991):

First, they are often written well above the level for which they are intended, sometimes as much as 3 or 4 years. They typically contain abstract, technical vocabulary, which make them even more difficult, especially for struggling readers.

Second, content area texts are often "inconsiderate"—their writing is often poorly organized and unclear. They do not use generally accepted patterns of exposition such as cause–effect, sequence, or comparison–contrast, but are often written in a descriptive mode, which makes retention of material difficult. In a recent analysis of a 1995 science text, Walpole (1998/99) found that the information was arranged in a highly complex, nonlinear way. Connections among ideas were not clearly stated, and signal words like "first," "second," and so on, were seldom used.

Third, content coverage in most content area texts is uneven. Typically, content area texts provide cursory examination of many topics rather than in-depth study of a few. These texts are often guilty of merely mentioning people or topics, rather than providing important background information about them. This results in students who have superficial knowledge of many topics, but lack deep understanding of any.

Fourth, the information in content area texts is sometimes inaccurate and often outdated. An edition of the television show *20/20* on April 2, 1999, focused on some of the problems with recent textbooks (Phillips, 1999). It reported that today's textbooks are rife with errors. In fact, it featured a concerned parent who found 113 errors in a recent edition of a best-selling science textbook. A further problem is that students in many schools are using outdated textbooks because of budget constraints. An Ohio principal recently complained that, according to science texts used in his school district, man had not yet landed on the moon!

Finally, content area texts are typically not motivating for children to read. Despite the increased visual appeal of recent textbooks, the writing continues to be boring—it lacks the life that skilled authors can bring to virtually any subject. In addition, textbook publishers seek to avoid controversy, which also contributes to bland, lifeless writing that may offer little to entice today's young readers.

ADVANTAGES OF NONFICTION

It is easy to see how the materials used with students in school may do little to further their understanding of expository text. If expository text is limited in basal readers and poorly written in content area texts, teachers clearly need to supplement these materials. Nonfiction trade books, used effectively, can fill the need for clearly written exposition even primary grade readers can understand. Written by authors experienced in making complicated concepts comprehensible, they give children the opportunity to explore the real world. They can address many disadvantages of textbooks and provide a motivating alternative to textbooks. They can do the following:

1. *Facilitate individualization of instruction.* By using nonfiction trade books, teachers can provide students with materials closer to their individual reading levels. Instead of having all students read the same textbook, students can read a variety of different books about the same topic (see Chapter 3).

2. *Familiarize children with terms and concepts associated with a topic.* Nonfiction literature can acquaint children with the technical vocabulary of a topic. In Byron Barton's (1982) *Airport*, for example, primary grade children are introduced to words like "fuel," "cargo hold," "cockpit," and "control tower." The large, detailed illustrations support understanding of these terms. From exposure to this technical vocabulary, children build ever-widening circles of understanding about a range of topics and discover how knowledge is organized, used, and related.

3. *Facilitate comprehension because they are written in user-friendly styles.* Instead of "baskets of facts," today's nonfiction trade books usually contain clearly organized, interesting content. Unlike textbooks, they let children hear the voice behind the information provided. Their authors speak personally to the reader through informal, engaging writing styles, rather than "textbookese" (see more in Chapter 2).

4. *Provide in-depth information on content-related topics ranging from people, to places, to scientific processes.* One recent trend in nonfiction is to examine a single topic in great depth. Today's titles explore topics like a day in the life of a Wampanoag boy (*Tapenum's Day: A Wampanoag Indian Boy in Pilgrim Times*; Waters, 1996), Washington's Revolutionary War travails during the battle at Trenton (*Crossing the Delaware: A History in Many Voices*; Peacock, 1998), and the mysteries of plate tectonics (*Our Patchwork Planet: The Story of Plate Tectonics*; Sattler, 1995). Through these types of trade books, children develop a rich context for understanding many aspects of a time, place, or phenomenon, thereby enhancing their schema.

5. *Give accurate, up-to-date information.* Nonfiction authors and illustrators take great pains to ensure accuracy of information. In a recent speech in Columbus, OH, Jim Murphy (1995) explained that *each* fact in his award-winning *The Great Fire* was checked for accuracy at least three times.

Nonfiction trade books are more current than content area textbooks, which are typically revised every 5–10 years. Current trade books reflect the latest developments in science and recent world events. They address timely topics like AIDS, homelessness, child abuse, and immigration.

6. *Motivate children to read.* Today's nonfiction trade books have both visual and content appeal. Their cover designs, attractive graphics, and effective illustrations can attract and hold the attention of the most unmotivated reader. Once dull and dry, today's nonfiction is well written and zeroes in on intriguing topics. Even the most reluctant sixth grader, for example, would find it hard to resist Gary Paulsen's (1996) autobiographical *Puppies, Dogs and Blue Northers: Reflections on Being Raise by a Pack of Sled Dogs.* This is the extraordinary story of the loving bond Paulsen had with his lead dog, Cookie, as he describes the birth and training of her pups, her skills as a lead dog for some 14,000 miles, and her ultimate retirement and death.

Figure 1.1 summarizes these advantages of nonfiction trade books.

Quality nonfiction has the potential to be an effective complement to fiction and content area textbooks. Early exposure to the language of nonfiction can help enhance children's understanding of exposition and may prevent the difficulties many students encounter with these texts later on. Nonfiction trade books can add richness and depth to children's learning by expanding children's general knowledge about the world we live in. The best nonfiction "leaves in the

Facilitate individualization of instruction.
Familiarize children with terms and topics associated with a topic.
Facilitate comprehension because they are written in user-friendly styles.
Provide in-depth information on content-related topics.
Give accurate, up-to-date information.
Motivate children to read.

FIGURE 1.1. Advantages of nonfiction trade books.

child's mind a residue of information about people, times, places, processes and heroes" (Montabello, 1972, p. 63). This information contributes to children's schemata about a vast array of topics.

Finally, nonfiction promotes exploration and stimulates thinking. Good nonfiction simulates direct experience; it makes children want to experience the discovery firsthand. In this way it can serve as a powerful motivator that compels children to make voluntary reading an important part of their lives.

TRENDS IN RECENT NONFICTION

Nonfiction literature for children has undergone a magical transformation over the past 20 years. There is no genre of children's literature that has changed as radically in recent years as nonfiction. While nonfiction used to be poorly written, today it is engaging. While content formerly focused largely on broad topics related to school curricula, today's nonfiction explores everything from cave paintings to how teddy bears are made. While books of the past contained dreary black-and-white line drawings or diagrams, today's nonfiction books contain an array of visuals, including color photographs and dazzling computer-generated maps, graphs, charts, diagrams, cutaways, and timelines.

This section of the chapter examines trends in nonfiction related to three areas: content and topics, writing, and book design and illustration. It examines a variety of titles representative of these trends, providing examples of books for children of all ages. It can, perhaps, help to explain why nonfiction has today gained an unparalleled prominence in the world of children's literature.

Today's nonfiction titles maintain a tight focus on a single aspect of a particular topic. They focus in on specific animals, historical events, or occurrences in nature. Text is, in short, designed to hold the attention of young readers. Titles in the "I Was There" series illustrate this trend. Virtually all of the books in this series focus on a specific person, event, or natural occurrence. They include *The Buried City of Pompeii: What It Was Like When Vesuvius Exploded* (Tanaka,

1997), *Graveyard of the Dinosaurs: What It's Like to Discover Prehistoric Creatures* (Tanaka, 1998), and *In the Time of Knights: The Real-Life Story of History's Greatest Knight* (Tanaka, 2000).

A second notable trend related to text content is the increasing popularity of picture-book biographies. These biographies include the stories of famous athletes, artists, musicians, writers, politicians, and many other subjects. Many of these biographies are appropriate for both young and older learners. The best of these biographies inform without overwhelming the learner and use visual features to complement the text. One of the finest of these titles, *Laura's Album: A Remembrance Scrapbook of Laura Ingalls Wilder* (Anderson, 1998), uses photographs and mementos of Wilder's life and writings to complement the compelling text.

Other trends relate to the types of writing found in today's nonfiction. While many, if not most, books still use an expository style, today's books may be written using a narrative, lyrical, or combination of literary styles. Informational storybooks (see the next section) are increasingly popular. Even in books that use exposition, a clear but tight conversational style prevails. *Frozen Man* (Getz, 1994), which describes the 1991 discovery of the 5,000-year-old "Iceman" in the Alps, illustrates this trend. In a mere 65 pages, Getz suspensefully unravels the mystery surrounding the Iceman's death. In this excerpt, he uses the available evidence to reconstruct the Iceman's last day:

> Sometime in late August or September he died. One key piece of evidence pointing to his time of death is a small berry found with his belongings. Scientists examined this fruit under a microscope and determined it was a type of plum called a sloe berry, which ripens in late August or early September. The Iceman had probably picked it as a snack as he walked. . . .
>
> He died lying on his left side. Archaeologists know this because the Iceman's left ear was neatly folded over. This would only have been possible had he lain on his left side, with his head raised and resting on something like a rock for a pillow.
>
> He died without a struggle. His body shows no signs of cuts or bruises. Xrays show no abnormally broken bones or damaged organs. . . .
>
> He didn't die from hunger. A piece of wild-goat meat, along with some berries, was found beside him.
>
> He wasn't frantic. The position in which the artifacts were found suggests the Iceman set them down neatly before he lay down.
>
> He wasn't cold. Somebody who was freezing would curl up, hugging his body for warmth. The Iceman stretched out. Scientists studying the body believe he died lying on his left side, with his arms straightened down along his body. His legs were slightly spread open.
>
> What killed the Iceman? (Getz, 1994, pp. 51–52)

Getz uses a conversational style to heighten the suspense surrounding the death of the Iceman. The author encourages interaction on the part of the reader by creating an air of mystery sure to appeal to young readers. Today's nonfiction authors promote interaction with their readers in other ways as well.

In many titles, for example, authors encourage active involvement through engagement with the text content. Often this involves learners in hands-on activities. In *The Piñata Maker/El Piñatero* (Ancona, 1994), George Ancona introduces children to Tio Rico, a Mexican piñata maker. The text, written in both English and Spanish, clearly explains the process of piñata making. At the end of the book the author provides instructions for children who wish to try their hand at this craft.

A third trend in recent nonfiction pertains to book design and illustration. Modern children's nonfiction is designed to engage today's visually oriented learners. Book designers and artists carefully consider the appearance of the cover as well as the content. Their challenge is to combine accuracy with imagination while extending and enlivening the messages of the author. An array of variables must be considered: shape and size of pages, placement of texts or labels, position on the page, media, page sequence, and typeface. The use of sidebars is increasingly popular; it allows authors to include information not addressed in the main text. All of these features must work together to create a book that is a meaningful blend of text and visual elements that appeal to the intended audience.

My Fellow Americans: A Family Album (Provensen, 1995), for example, teaches readers of all ages about the people who shaped America—warriors and patriots, writers, poets, entertainers, free spirits, and rogues—all grouped by subject. This uniquely visual presentation uses labeled pictures, slogans, and symbols to portray these members of the American family. Each grouping is accompanied by a pertinent quotation.

Aliki's (1999) *William Shakespeare and the Globe* also beautifully demonstrates the best in recent nonfiction illustration and book design. Her delicate, detailed, captioned illustrations complement the text, which introduces Shakespeare's life and times through the disciplines of history, architecture, biography, and archaeology. Landscapes, tiny portraits, maps, and diagrams imaginatively enhance the text. The contents page is arranged in five acts, and quotes from the Bard are strategically placed throughout the text. The back matter chronicles Shakespeare's works, dates in his life, words and expressions, and sites to visit.

Recent trends in nonfiction related to topic and content, writing, and book design and illustration have resulted in improving both the content and appearance of children's nonfiction trade books. These improvements have not only led to more publication of books from this genre but have succeeded in increasing the popularity of nonfiction with today's students, making books from this genre much more sought after than in the past.

UNDERSTANDING THE FORMS OF NONFICTION

Well-written nonfiction books fascinate children. To capitalize on that fascination, though, teachers must know the possibilities nonfiction offers by understanding the forms it can take. This section introduces the reader to these forms. The nonfiction genre includes two types of books: information books and biographies. Information books are books of facts and concepts about a subject or subjects, whereas biographies tell the stories of people's lives. The following subsection describes the different types of children's information books. The next subsection describes the various forms of biography. Figure 1.2 summarizes the diverse forms of information and biography. The third section will provide information about nonfiction trade books that address multicultural themes and topics.

Information Books

Information books explain or inform children about a topic or concept. The best information book authors, however, are like the best teachers—they don't just give information. They take facts and weave them into interesting forms that engage readers. They create books children can understand, but they still care about accuracy of content. They are sensitive to readers' needs but do not talk down to them. Like good teachers, the best authors encourage and extend children's thinking. Like good teachers, these authors inspire; they prompt children to explore their own world more completely or seek out more information on a particular topic.

Today's information books examine an array of topics from AIDS to zebras. They can be used in any or all subject areas including language arts, mathemat-

Types of information books	Types of biographies
Concept books	Cradle to grave biographies
Nature identification books	Partial biographies
Life cycle books	Single biographies
Experiment and activity books	Collective biographies
Books based on primary sources	Autobiographies
Photographic essays	
Craft and how-to books	
Informational storybooks	

FIGURE 1.2. Types of nonfiction books.

ics, science, social studies, health, art, and music. They provide information at levels appropriate to first graders or eighth graders, on familiar, simple topics or unfamiliar, sophisticated ones; *I Love Guinea Pigs* (King-Smith, 1994), for example, teaches young children about an animal familiar to all. This book grabs primary graders from the first page, which begins:

> There's a silly old saying that
> if you hold a guinea pig up
> by its tail, its eyes
> will drop out.
> Well of course they wouldn't,
> even if you could—which you couldn't,
> because guinea pigs don't have tails.
> And they aren't pigs either.
> They're rodents—like mice and rats and squirrels. (pp. 1–2)

Other nonfiction titles tackle more serious topics. *Kennedy Assassinated! The World Mourns: A Reporter's Story* (Hampton, 1997) describes the events of that terrible day in November 1963 and their aftermath. The author, a young reporter in Dallas covering the story, compared the experience to being in the eye of a tornado as the tempestuous winds of history surrounded him.

All information books are not alike; each type has unique features and purposes. The types of information books include concept books, nature identification books, life cycle books, experiment and activity books, books based on original documents and journals, photographic essays, craft and how-to books, and information storybooks. They address myriad subjects including the arts, animals, mathematics, architecture, sex, the life cycle, man-made or woman-made objects, language, zoology, and many others.

Concept books explore abstract ideas through concrete examples. They are typically written for young children. Aliki (1993) has written and illustrated a number of excellent concept books including *Communication*, which provides simple lessons about talking and listening.

Nature identification books broaden children's understanding of the world around them. *The Red-Eyed Tree Frog* (Cowley, 1999), for example, teaches primary graders about the adventures of a rain-forest-dwelling animal through fabulous photographs and engaging text. The compelling story line captivates young readers, while three or four pages of back matter provide information about the factual basis of the story.

Life cycle books trace animal or plant growth from birth to adulthood. They are often, but not always, picture books. *The Life and Times of the Honeybee* (Micucci, 1997) provides fascinating and amusing facts about the life cycle, work, and social organization of honeybees. The finely detailed illustrations effectively support and reinforce the text.

Leonardo da Vinci for Kids: His Life and Ideas (Herbert, 1998) contains 21 activities designed to help older children understand Leonardo's major discoveries through activities like determining the launch of a catapult, drawing animals, creating maps, and exploring human proportions. *These experiment and activity books* give children hands-on explorations relevant to many different school subjects.

Books based on primary sources such as photographs and documents include well-researched works like *The Perilous Journey of the Donner Party* (Calabro, 1999), told through the eyes of 12-year-old Virginia Reed, a member of the ill-fated party. Numerous historical photographs and reproductions of art and artifacts bring the plight of the travelers into sharp relief. The author even reproduces a complete letter from Virginia Reed to her cousin detailing their terrible trials on the trip to California.

Photographic essays are increasingly popular. *How Is a Crayon Made?* (Charles, 1988) uses captivating color photographs to illustrate the manufacturing of crayons. This book, sure to be popular with elementary grade children, effectively demonstrates the stages in the process by which crayons ultimately arrive on the desks of youngsters.

Craft and how-to books teach steps in a process. This category includes cookbooks for children, along with titles that provide directions for everything from pop-up books to planting a garden. Books for younger children like Tomie de Paola's (1976) *Things to Make and Do for Valentine's Day* describe simple procedures for creating crafts, projects, and recipes. How-to books for older children, like Lee J. Ames's (1986) *Draw 50 Cars, Trucks and Motorcycles*, provide step-by-step instructions for drawing each type of vehicle.

More and more books bring different genres together under a single cover. *Informational storybooks* blur the lines between genres; they combine information with a story line. These hybrid, or "infotainment," books entertain at the same time they inform. The immensely popular Magic School Bus books clearly achieve this goal. *The Magic School Bus Inside the Human Body* (Cole, 1989), for example, combines fact with fantasy by describing a teacher, Miss Frizzle, who takes her class on an incredible journey through the human body. Another example of this genre includes *How to Dig a Hole to the Other Side of the World* (McNulty, 1990). In this book a child takes an imaginary journey to the earth's core and discovers what's inside.

Dateline: Troy (Fleischman, 1996), a sophisticated book for older readers, crosses genre lines in ways that make it difficult to categorize. In this book, author Paul Fleischman narrates the story of the Trojan War through modern-day newspaper headlines positioned next to text about specific sections of the myth.

In this way the author draws interesting parallels between the past and the present.

Biographies

Biographies are the other major category of nonfiction. Biographies, like information books, are factual, providing information about individual lives. In the case of autobiography, individuals tell the stories of their own lives. At the same time, human lives, with their triumphs and tragedies, their victories and defeats, are stories. Biographies and autobiographies tell those stories. As Denise M. Wilms (1978) notes: "When biography is working, it sparks your interest—even when you thought you had none in the first place. It's a human encounter, it's literary people watching, and that's what makes it many people's favorite reading. When it comes to this basic fascination, children are no different from adults" (p. 136).

Biographies let children identify with people of the past and present. Children can see others' lives as models in terms of achievement and career goals, or they may learn about courage and tenacity in the face of adversity and difficulty.

In the past, children's biographies extolled American heroes like George Washington, Thomas Jefferson, Benjamin Franklin, and Abraham Lincoln. These historical figures are still popular subjects of children's biographies, but today's authors don't idealize them. Modern authors portray the heroes of today and yesterday, but present them "warts and all."

Jean Fritz creates biographies with real "kid appeal." Her unique blend of humor, history, and unexpected details "that give the past a pulse" (Fritz, 1990, p. 25) make her books tremendously appealing to children. For example, in *And Then What Happened, Paul Revere?* (Fritz, 1973) she explains how Paul Revere forgot his spurs on his way to his famous ride. She describes how Paul Revere tied a note to his wife around his dog's neck and sent the dog home. The dog returned with the spurs tied around its neck. These footnotes to history give icons of the past a much more human dimension.

Today's biographies include world leaders, explorers and adventurers, inventors and scientists, authors and artists, and ordinary people who have done extraordinary things. Diane Stanley's *Cleopatra* (1994), for example, focuses upon its subject's intelligence rather than her beauty. It portrays a shrewd woman who lives by her wits. Jeanette Winter's (1991) *Diego* is a superb beginning biography of Diego Rivera, world-renowned Mexican artist. Written in both English and Spanish, this title features miniature paintings bursting with color reminiscent of Rivera's work.

The life stories of important scientists have been told in at least two outstanding books for children. *Snowflake Bentley* (Martin, 1998), the 1998 Caldecott Medal winner, describes the life of Wilson Bentley, who spent his life studying and photographing snowflakes. Books for older readers profile scientists like William Beaumont (*Dr. Beaumont and the Man with a Hole in His Stomach*; Epstein & Epstein, 1978), who studied digestion through experiments on Alexis St. Martin, a man whose stomach contained a hole created by a gunshot wound.

Biographies run the gamut in terms of difficulty and sophistication. *Cradle-to-grave* picture-book biographies like *George Washington* (Giblin, 1992) are ideal for children in grades 2–4, whereas longer titles like *Sky Pioneer: A Photobiography of Amelia Earhart* (Szabo, 1997) are suitable for older readers. The latter title traces Amelia Earhart's life while celebrating her daring and skill as an aviator. The oversized photos and large-print quotations make it ideal for large-group sharing.

Partial biographies focus on a particular time or specific event in a subject's life. *Home Run: The Story of Babe Ruth* (Burleigh, 1998) examines Ruth's years in baseball by focusing on a single moment when he hits a home run. Reproductions of luminous oil paintings by Mike Wimmer portray the power and majesty of Babe's swing. Tiny baseball cards appearing on each page examine topics like "Babe's Best Year" and his career as a pitcher. These *single biographies* focus upon the life of one individual, whereas *collective biographies* describe several different subjects whose lives are connected in some way. *Lives of the Artists: Masterpieces, Messes (and What the Neighbors Thought)* (Krull, 1995) gives lighthearted, amusing glimpses of well-known artists including Rembrandt van Rijn, Pablo Picasso, Marc Chagall, and Salvador Dali.

Autobiographies let individuals tell their own life stories. In *Ryan White: My Own Story* (White & Cunningham, 1992) Ryan White, a teenager with AIDS, described how he suffered with this terrible disease both physically and emotionally while dealing with the prejudice and fear created by his illness.

Authors and illustrators, too, share their lives through autobiographies. Tomie de Paola's (1999) *26 Fairmount Avenue*, for example, describes the ups and downs of the year his family built a new home. *Bill Peet: An Autobiography* (Peet, 1989) traces Peet's life and work as an artist for Walt Disney and later as a creator of many popular children's books.

The focus of this section of the chapter has been to familiarize teachers with the forms of nonfiction trade books by providing an overview of the various categories of books, both information and biography, available today. It described each of these forms, as well as providing examples of books reflective of each type. The next section examines nonfiction titles with a multicultural focus.

MULTICULTURAL NONFICTION

By the year 2020, one of every two students in this country will be a person of color (Banks, 1991). Because these children represent a variety of cultures, diversity has become the norm in today's classrooms. As these children begin school, they bring knowledge of the world that is unique to their cultural background. Their concepts of family, morality, rules, time, sex roles, dress, safety, and values reflect their own unique cultural heritage.

If children from different backgrounds are to work together productively and effectively, we must teach them to understand and value the cultural backgrounds of their peers. A commonly suggested means for achieving this goal is through classroom use of multicultural children's literature. Multicultural literature focuses upon people of color—African, Asian, Native American, and Latino, to name a few.

The best of these books reveal the experiences of members of parallel cultures with authenticity and accuracy. Most often, however, the multicultural literature recommended for classroom use is from the picture-book and/or folktale genre. This literature is certainly valuable and is more plentiful than that of many other genre. Yet, Miller-Lachman (1992) and others caution against exclusive use of multicultural folktales. This may give children a sense that the group being studied lived "long ago and far away" and may lack "here and now relevance" (Lewis, 1992). Limiting children's exploration of a country or ethnic group to its folklore may also give children a distorted view of a group or culture. After reading a number of folktales from Africa, for example, a child may conclude that the entire continent is filled with wild animals and all the people live in remote villages (Miller-Lachman, 1992).

Multicultural nonfiction, which includes all of the types of information books and biographies mentioned in the previous section, can provide a window on the real lives of people living in diverse cultures that fiction cannot. Multicultural nonfiction can provide accurate, up-to-date views of children living in other cultures. It can also provide teachers with a vast array of books that are relevant to both the past and the present.

Tom Feelings's (1995) *Middle Passage*, for example, depicts the terrible passage of slaves from Africa to America. *The Journey: Japanese Americans, Racism and Renewal* (Hamanaka, 1990) portrays the tragedy of 120,000 Japanese Americans interned during World War II, providing text that accompanies a huge mural. Both books give today's readers glimpses of what it would have been like to be a member of a parallel culture in times past.

Through encounters with memorable children who actually live today, youngsters may develop greater empathy for the circumstances of other children. Books like Janet Bode's (1995) *New Kids in Town: Oral Histories of Immigrant Teens*, for example, can help all young people understand the many difficulties associated with immigration to the United States. In this book, 11 teenagers describe how they escaped war, poverty, and repression to build new lives in America.

Multicultural nonfiction literature, both information books and biographies, can further multicultural understanding in many ways. Figure 1.3 illustrates the ways multicultural nonfiction books can achieve this goal and lists books relevant to each example.

The virtual explosion in the publication of high-quality nonfiction literature in the past 10 years has resulted in more and higher-quality multicultural nonfiction. Violet Harris (1997) has identified the increase in quality nonfiction depicting the African American experience as an important trend in children's literature depicting blacks. A similar improvement in the quality and quantity of recent nonfiction representing other cultural groups can be noted as well.

The next subsection examines multicultural nonfiction literature related to particular cultural groups including Africans and African Americans, Asian and Asian Americans, Native Americans and Latinos and Latino Americans. These groups are clustered into categories for discussion purposes only; each group contains subgroups that differ greatly from one another in terms of language, race, country of origin, customs, and so on. The titles mentioned here provide a sampling of books available related to each cultural group. Many other titles are discussed in later chapters.

African and African American

While there are more books published on Africans and African Americans than any other group, the number of nonfiction books is still limited. Biographies about well-known black Americans are, however, relatively plentiful, and those describing more ordinary people are becoming more popular. Informational titles addressing a wide range of topics are becoming increasingly common.

Information books can provide learners with accurate information about modern Africa. An excellent book for older students entitled *No More Strangers Now: Young Voices from a New South Africa* (McKee, 2000) contains first-person stories about the lives of 12 South African teenagers living under Apartheid. Ogbo: *Sharing Life in an African Village* (Onyefulu, 1996) is a photoessay describing daily life in eastern Nigeria. The *ogbo* is an age group, and members of each are responsible for one another for life. The author's description of the village provides an insider's view of customs, work, play, and community. *Learning to Swim in Swaziland: A Child's-Eye View of a Southern African Country* (Leigh, 1993) simply but accurately describes the experiences of an 8-year-old American girl during her year in that country.

Other information books provide glimpses of Africa in the past. *Cat Mummies* (Trumble, 1996), for example, describes the discovery of thousands of

Goal	Book titles
Contribute to students' self-esteem and awareness.	*The Lost Garden* by Lawrence Yep (1991) *A Boy Called Slow: The True Story of Sitting Bull* by Joseph Bruchac (1995) *Day of the Dead: A Mexican-American Celebration* by Diane-Hoyt Goldsmith (1994a)
Help children of parallel cultures appreciate the contributions of their ancestors.	*The Pueblo Storyteller* by Diane Hoyt Goldsmith (1994b) *In Search of the Spirit: The Living National Treasures of Japan* by Sheila Hamanaka (1999) *We Were There Too!: Young People in U.S. History* by Phillip M. Hoose (2001)
Contribute to development of respect across cultures.	*Children Just Like Me* by Barnabas Kindersley, Susan Copsey, & Anabel Kindersley (1995) *Children from Australia to Zimbabwe: A Photographic Journey Around the World* by Maya Ajmera, Anna Rhesa Versola, & Marian Wright Edelman (2001) *Teammates* by Peter Golenbock (1992)
Enhance student identification with members of parallel cultures.	*Through My Eyes* by Ruby Bridges (1999) *Family Pictures* by Carmen Lomas Garza (1990) *The Land I Lost: Adventures of a Boy in Vietnam* by Quang Nhuong Huynh (1982)
Illuminate the history of various parallel cultures in this country and abroad.	*Now Is Your Time!: The African American Struggle for Freedom* by Walter Dean Myers (1991) *The Journey: Japanese Americans, Racism and Renewal* (1990) by Sheila Hamanaka *The People Shall Continue* by Simon J. Ortiz (1988)
Provide up-to-the-minute portrayals of everyday lives of youngsters from parallel cultures living today.	*No More Strangers Now: Young Voices from a New South Africa* edited by Tim McKee (2000) *A Young Painter: The Life and Paintings of Wang Yani* by Zheng Zhensun & Alice Low (1991) *Voices from the Fields: Children of Migrant Farm Workers Tell Their Stories* by S. Beth Atkins (1993)

FIGURE 1.3. Promoting multicultural understanding with nonfiction.

cat mummies in the Egyptian desert. Along the way the author takes the reader back to early Egyptian civilization, describing the sacred role of cats in that culture that resulted in their mummification.

Biographies teach about the lives of Africans in both the past and the present. *Shaka: King of the Zulus* (Stanley & Vennema, 1988) uses unique illustrations and effective text to describes the life and rise to prominence of Shaka, a military genius who became king of the Zulu people. Walter Dean Myers's (1999) *At Her Majesty's Request: An African Princess in Victorian England* details the remarkable story of an orphaned African princess, Sarah Forbes Bonetta, who was given to Queen Victoria as a gift. Myers based this true account on letters he found in a rare bookshop in London.

Biographies also describe the lives of present-day leaders. *Mandela: From the Life of the South African Statesman* (Cooper, 1996) is a picture book biography detailing Nelson Mandela's childhood, political activism, and rise to the presidency of South Africa.

Information books with African American themes span a variety of age levels and topics. Diane Hoyt-Goldsmith's (1993) *Celebrating Kwanzaa,* a photoessay appropriate for young children, provides a clear picture of the rituals of this holiday. The author spent the holiday with a Chicago family, and the book is the story of that family's celebration.

Many information books for older children address the struggle for equality. Walter Dean Myers's (1991) first nonfiction book, *Now Is Your Time!: The African-American Struggle for Freedom* presents the African American experience as the effort of a people who have made important contributions to the development of the United States. Milton Meltzer's (1984) *The Black Americans: A History in Their Own Words* recounts the experiences of blacks from the time of slavery to the present day, using the actual words of those who lived through these events. *A Long Hard Journey: The Story of the Pullman Porter* by Patricia McKissack and Fred McKissack (1989) traces the history of the first African American labor union.

Biographies of African Americans appropriate for younger children include *Rosa Parks: My Story* (Parks & Haskins, 1992), which details the story of the woman whose quiet courage spearheaded the civil rights movement in this country. *Ragtime Tumpie* (Schroeder, 1989) is a beautifully illustrated fictionalized biography of the childhood of legendary performer Josephine Baker. The *joie de vivre* of this young girl is captured through the brilliant illustrations that are full of movement.

Biographies of African Americans for older readers are fairly plentiful. Titles about black Americans from the past and present include *Sorrow's Kitchen: The Life and Folklore of Zora Neal Hurston* (Lyons, 1990) and *Let It Shine!: Stories of Black Women Freedom Fighters* (Pinkney, 2000). Biographies of more recent heroes and heroines include the story of Ruby Bridges (*Through My Eyes*; Bridges, 1999), who was the first black child to attend a white school in New Orleans, LA, and Rudine Sims Bishop's (1990) *Presenting Walter Dean Myers,* one of a very few biographies of an author of black children's and young adults' literature.

Asian and Asian American

While there are far fewer books addressing the Asian and Asian American experience, books about this group are increasing. *Look What Came from China* (Harvey, 1999) details inventions, holidays, and customs of China in a format accessible for primary-grade children. *In Search of the Spirit: The Living National Treasures of Japan* (Hamanaka, 1999) presents portraits of six prominent artists who engage in traditional Japanese crafts that began to disappear after World War II. These "Living National Treasures" include a kimono artist, bamboo weaver, puppet master, sword maker, Noh actor, and potter.

Excellent biographies for older children include *Gandhi* (Fisher, 1995) and *A Young Painter: The Life and Paintings of Wang Yani* (Zhensun & Low, 1991). The first title is a picture book biography examining the life of the great Indian leader, focusing on his efforts to champion Indian rights in South Africa. The second title describes the child prodigy Wang Yani, a Chinese teenager who began painting at age 3 and was the youngest artist to have a one-person show at the Smithsonian Institution.

Information books about Asian Americans include Ashabranner and Ashabranner's (1987) *Into a Strange Land*. This unusual book describes the experiences of young refugees, most from Southeast Asia, who have come alone to America. It describes the horrors these youth experienced as they left their homelands, and well as the difficulties they encountered in attempting to adjust to a new, unfamiliar culture. A number of recent nonfiction books for older readers address the Japanese internment during World War II. Jerry Stanley's (1994) *I Am an American* focuses on this time in history, describing the experiences of a single family.

Lawrence Yep, a Chinese American, is one of the most outstanding children's authors living today. Most of his books focus on Asian American themes in this country. In his autobiography, *The Lost Garden* (Yep, 1991), he describes his 1950s childhood as a boy coming of age in San Francisco. In this excellent memoir he describes how he often felt out of place as a Chinese American and how writing empowered him to explore his own identity.

Excellent biographies for young children about Asians Americans include *Hoang Anh: A Vietnamese-American Boy* (Hoyt-Goldsmith, 1992). This title describes the life of a young Vietnamese boy living in California. It carefully details how the boy remains a member of two cultures, practicing Buddhism and speaking Vietnamese while also enjoying American pastimes such as football and roller skating. *The Land I Lost: Adventures of a Boy in Vietnam* (Huynh, 1982) details a Vietnamese American boy's memories of his childhood in Vietnam and a world that is gone forever.

Native American

Native American information titles can help youngsters understand what it means to be member of these little-understood cultures. These titles can also combat the frequent stereotype that Native Americans are a people of the past rather than of the present. Through these books students can learn about the lives of such diverse people as Maria Tallchief, a world-renowned dancer (*Tallchief: America's Prima Ballerina*; Tallchief, 1999, describes her ascent from her early years on an Oklahoma Osage reservation to the world stage), and Crazy Horse, the great Sioux chief (*Life and Death of Crazy Horse*; Freedman, 1996).

Two excellent nonfiction books explore different aspects of Native American arts. In *Pueblo Storyteller* (Hoyt-Goldsmith, 1994b) April Trujillo, a young Cochiti Pueblo girl, describes the process her grandparents use today to make clay storyteller sculptures that represent the oral tradition of the Pueblos. *Arctic Memories* (Ekoomiak, 1990) is an artistic tribute to the Inuit people. This elegant book contains color reproductions of fabric artworks illustrating life in the Inuit culture.

Books that provide the perspectives of those within the Native American culture can be especially useful in the classroom. *The People Shall Continue* (Ortiz, 1988) describes the westward expansion of European Americans from the viewpoint of Native Americans, a perspective not often explored through children's literature. Virginia Driving Hawk Sneeve's (1996) *The Cherokees* is an excellent book for older readers. Its evenhanded treatment explores the customs, tragedies, and accomplishments of the Cherokees in the past and present.

An excellent biography for younger children is *A Boy Called Slow: The True Story of Sitting Bull* (Bruchac, 1995). This book combines sensitive text with mythical illustrations that describe how a young Lakota boy labeled "slow" by others performs a brave deed that earns him respect and a new name. Written by Joseph Bruchac, a member of the Abenaki tribe, the book captures the essence of a culture that almost disappeared.

An interesting biography of a Native American woman is *The Flight of Red Bird: The Life of Zitkala-Sa* (Rappaport, 1999). Zitakala-Sa, or Red Bird, was born in 1876 to a Sioux mother and a white father. As a child she was forced to give up her life on the reservation and become "civilized" by attending boarding school. Later she reclaimed her heritage and became an advocate for Native Americans during the early 20th century. Another highly acclaimed work is Russell Freedman's (1987a) collective biography *Indian Chiefs*. This superbly documented and researched presentation of the lives of prominent Indian chiefs is based on primary-source documents and authentic photographs.

Latino and Latino American

Nonfiction books about Latinos can help children learn about this group, the largest parallel culture in this country. Information books are relatively few in number. They include the excellent *Bananas: From Manolo to Margie* (Ancona, 1990), a book for young readers. This book explains how bananas are grown in Honduras and make their way to the United States. It provides a glimpse of the people of Honduras and their work. Caroline Arnold's *South American Animals* (1999) introduces younger readers to the varied regions and wildlife of South America. Stunning photographs add drama to the presentation.

An excellent biography for older readers, *Under the Royal Palms* (Flor Ada, 1998), describes the Cuban childhood of renowned author Alma Flor Ada. This remarkable book captures the sights, sounds, and smells of the author's native land while describing an array of memorable family members. Latino biographies for younger readers are especially limited. As already noted, *Diego* (Winter, 1991) is written in both Spanish and English. This easy-to-read biography represents a culturally conscious treatment of the life of the famous Mexican muralist Diego Rivera that focuses mainly on his earlier years.

Information books about Latino Americans are more plentiful, with most focusing on Mexican Americans. Nonfiction books for younger children include *Hector Lives in the United States Now: The Story of a Mexican American Child* (Hewitt, 1990), a photo documentary about the life of Hector, a Mexican American boy living in Los Angeles. The family has come to this country illegally and is deciding whether or not to apply for citizenship as a result of the 1982 amnesty law.

Nonfiction titles for older readers include books about holidays such as the Day of the Dead. Diane Hoyt-Goldsmith's (1994a) *Day of the Dead: A Mexican-American Celebration* takes the reader to a present-day Day of the Dead celebration in Sacramento, CA. It also provides an extensive history of the holiday, along with a description of how masks related to this holiday are made; it includes a glossary of terms and an index.

Family Pictures (Garza, 1990) provides an intimate glimpse of the childhood of author Carmen Lomas Garza in Kingsville, TX. In this work she describes everyday experiences and events along with special occasions in her life. Each experience is accompanied by a reproduction of a richly detailed painting.

Voices from the Fields: Children of Migrant Farm Workers Tell Their Stories (Atkin, 1993) is a powerful book describing the lives of 10 Mexican American children of migrant farm workers. The author interviewed each of the children, and the diverse stories are told largely in their own words. One child is a gang member, one is an unmarried teenaged mother, and one is making plans to attend college to become a physician. The author skillfully portrays the transience and uncertainty of their lives, as well as the strong, loving bonds that tie them to their families.

SUMMARY

Nonfiction trade books have enormous potential as a complement to the textbooks that often dominate classroom instruction. To most effectively use the nonfiction genre in the classroom, teachers need awareness of the enormous diversity and varied purposes of today's nonfiction trade books. When teachers have a clear understanding of the books found in this genre, they are better able to select books for classroom use. Most importantly, understanding of the types of nonfiction helps the teachers familiarize students with the myriad possibilities this genre has to offer.

Nonfiction books are divided into two broad categories: information books and biographies. Information books address myriad topics, take many forms, and are geared toward children of all ages from preschool through high school. Their purpose is to inform, explain, or describe facts related to a particular subject. Biographies serve a different function. While they too are factual, they are designed to provide facts about an individual life and are most frequently arranged in chronological order. Multicultural nonfiction provides information about parallel cultures. Both information books and biographies can help students appreciate these cultures and the contributions of members of those cultures.

REFERENCES

Banks, J. A. (1991). *Teaching strategies for ethnic studies.* Boston: Allyn & Bacon.

Freedman, R. (1988). Newbery acceptance speech. *Journal of Youth Services in Libraries, 1*, 421–427.

Fritz, J. (1990). The teller and the tale. In W. Zinsser (Ed.), *Worlds of childhood: The art and craft of writing for children* (pp. 23–46). Boston: Houghton Mifflin.

Harris, V. (1997). Children's literature depicting blacks. In V. Harris (Ed.), *Using multiethnic literature in the K–8 classroom* (pp. 21–58). Norwood, MA: Christopher-Gordon.

Lewis, J. Y. (1992, November). *Authenticity of cultural portrayal.* Paper presented at the National Council of Teachers of English Fall Conference, Louisville, KY.

Miller-Lachman, L. (1992). *Our family, our friends, our world: An annotated guide to significant multicultural books for children and teenagers.* New Providence, NJ: Reed.

Montabello, M. (1972). *Children's literature in the curriculum.* Dubuque, IA: Brown.

Moss, B. (1991). Children's nonfiction trade books: A complement to content area texts. *Reading Teacher, 45,* 26–32.

Moss, B., & Newton, E. (2002). An examination of information literature in recent basal readers. *Reading Psychology, 23,* 1–13.

Patent, D. H. (1998). Science books for children: An endangered species? *The Horn Book, 74,* 309–314.

Phillips, H. (Producer). (1999, April 2). Book report. In *20/20.* New York: American Broadcasting Company.

Venezky, R. (1982). The origins of the present day chasm between adult literacy needs and school literacy instruction. *Visible Language, 16,* 113–136.

Walpole, S. (1998/99). Changing texts, changing thinking: Comprehension demands of new science textbooks. *Reading Teacher, 52,* 358–369.

Wilms, D. M. (1978). An evaluation of biography. *Booklist, 75,* 218–220.

CHILDREN'S BOOKS

In all lists of children's books, numbers in parentheses represent recommended grade levels.

Ajmera, M., Versola, A. R., & Wright Edelman, M. (2001). *Children from Australia and Zimbabwe: A photographic journey around the world.* Watertown, MA: Charlesbridge. (2–5)
> Texts and photographs describe the lives of children living in nations arranged alphabetically from Australia to Zimbabwe.

Aliki. (1993). *Communication.* New York: Greenwillow Books. (1–3)
> This simple concept book uses easy-to-follow drawings to convey the principles of communication.

Aliki. (1999). *William Shakespeare and the Globe.* New York: HarperCollins. (4–6)
> Aliki traces the life of Shakespeare and the history of the Globe Theatre.

Ames, L. J. (1986). *Draw 50 cars, trucks and motorcycles.* Illustrated by the author. New York: Doubleday. (4–6)
> This author provides children with step-by-step information on drawing a variety of vehicles.

Ancona, G. (1990). *Bananas: From Manolo to Margie.* Boston: Houghton Mifflin. (1–3)
> This photoessay traces bananas grown in Honduras from the banana fields to American grocery stores.

Ancona, G. (1994). *The piñata maker/El piñatero.* New York: Harcourt Brace. (1–3)
> The author portrays how an elderly Mexican man makes traditional piñatas.

Anderson, W. (1998). *Laura's album: A remembrance scrapbook of Laura Ingalls Wilder.* New York: HarperCollins (4–6)
> The fascinating compilation of letters and mementos of the beloved author's life is sure to please her many fans.

Arnold, C. (1999). *South American animals.* New York: Morrow. (1–3)
> The author examines the habitats and wildlife of South America.

Ashabranner, B., & Ashabranner, M. (1987). *Into a strange land.* New York: Dodd, Mead. (4–6)

This nonfiction book describes the experiences of Southeast Asian refugee children as they seek to adjust to life in this country.

Atkin, S. B. (1993). *Voices from the fields: Children of migrant farm workers tell their stories*, New York: Little, Brown. (5–6)

Children of migrant workers describe their lives and hopes for the future.

Barton, B. (1982). *Airport.* New York: Crowell. (1–2)

The author presents a child's eye view of a trip to the airport.

Beil, K. M. (2000). *Fire in their eyes: Wildfires and the people who fight them*. New York: Scholastic.

This interesting book describes the work of firefighters and smokejumpers who put their lives on the line to control wildfires in the West.

Bishop, R. S. (1990). *Presenting Walter Dean Myers.* New York: Twayne. (5–6)

This title describes the life of Walter Dean Myers, an African American author of children's and young adults' literature.

Bode, J. (1995). *New kids in town: Oral histories of immigrant teens.* New York: Scholastic. (5–6)

Eleven teenaged immigrants describe their struggles to come to this country.

Bridges, R. (1999). *Through my eyes.* New York: Scholastic. (4–6).

Ruby Bridges describes her experiences as the first black child to attend public school in New Orleans, LA.

Bruchac, J. (1995). *A boy called slow: The true story of Sitting Bull.* New York: Philomel. (1–3)

The story of the boy who grew up to be Sitting Bull is told through sensitive text and magnificent illustrations.

Burleigh, R. (1998). *Home run: The story of Babe Ruth.* Illustrated by Mike Wimmer. New York: Silver Whistle. (3–6)

An unusual biography with illustrations reproducing glowing oil paintings portrays a moment in the life of the Babe.

Calabro, M. (1999). *The perilous journey of the Donner party.* Boston: Houghton Mifflin. (5–6)

This book based upon primary source letters and photographs details the trials of the Donner party.

Charles, O. (1988). *How is a crayon made?* New York: Simon & Schuster. (4–6)

Beautiful color photographs trace the process by which a box of crayons is created.

Cole, J. (1989). *The magic school bus inside the human body.* Illustrated by Bruce Degens. New York: Scholastic. (3–5)

Ms. Frizzle's class takes a fantastic field trip that gives them a look at the major body organs and how they work.

Cone, M. (1992). *Come back, salmon: How a group of dedicated kids adopted Pigeon Creek and brought it back to life.* San Francisco: Sierra Club Juveniles. (5–6)

The inspiring true story of how school children of Everett, WA, worked with their teachers to clean up Pigeon Creek and reclaim it as a salmon spawning ground.

Cooper, F. (1996). *Mandela: From the life of the South African statesman.* New York: Philomel. (1–3)

The author creates an easy-to-read biography of Nelson Mandela's life.

Cowley, J. (1999). *Red-Eyed Tree Frog*. Photography by Nic Bishop. New York: Scholastic. (1–3)

Stunning colorful photos combine with arresting text to create this science book for early readers.

de Paola, T. (1976). *Things to make and do for Valentine's Day*. New York: Watts. (1–3)

This book provides suggestions for crafts, projects, and recipes children can create for this popular holiday.

de Paola, T. (1999). *26 Fairmount Avenue*. New York: Putnam. (1–3)

This beloved author's first chapter book portrays the year his family built a new home.

Ekoomiak, N. (1990). *Arctic memories*. New York: Holt. (1–3)

Text in both Inuit and English describes a vanished way of life.

Epstein, S., & Epstein, B. (1978). *Dr. Beaumont and the man with a hole in his stomach*. Illustrated by Joseph Scrofani. New York: Coward, McCann & Geoghegan. (4–6)

The biography of an egotistical doctor who made significant discoveries about digestion from experiments on a man with an exposed stomach.

Feelings, T. (1995). *The middle passage: White ships/black cargo*. New York: Dial. (5–6)

This wordless picture book portrays the terrible passage of slaves from Africa to the New World.

Fisher, L. E. (1995). *Gandhi*. New York: Atheneum. (5–6)

Fisher examines the life of Mohandas K. Gandhi in this picture book for older readers.

Fleischman, P. (1996). *Dateline: Troy*. Needham Heights, MA: Candlewick. (5–6)

This unusual book recounts the story of the Trojan War by juxtaposing modern newspaper headlines with events from the story.

Flor Ada, A. (1998). *Under the royal palms*. New York: Atheneum. (5–6)

Flor Ada describes her childhood in Cuba through lyrical text and memorable characters.

Freedman, R. (1987a). *Indian chiefs*. New York: Holiday House. (5–6)

Freedman profiles six famous Indian chiefs in this well–documented and re-searched book. (5– 6)

Freedman, R. (1987b). *Lincoln: A photobiography*. New York: Clarion. (5–6)

This Newbery Medal Book provides a fascinating view of Abraham Lincoln, his family, and his times.

Freedman, R. (1991). *The Wright brothers: How they invented the airplane*. New York: Holiday House. (5–6)

Freedman focuses on the events leading to the first successful flight and the Wright brothers' improvements on their invention.

Freedman, R. (1993). *Eleanor Roosevelt: A life of discovery*. New York: Clarion. (5–6)

This carefully researched biography details the public life and times of this ex-traordinary social reformer.

Freedman, R. (1996). *The life and death of Crazy Horse*. New York: Holiday House. (5–6)

Freedman's excellent biography describes the strengths and weaknesses of this great chief.

Fritz, J. (1973). *And then what happened, Paul Revere?* Illustrated by Margot Tomes. New York: Coward, McCann & Geoghegan. (2–4)

Fritz's lighthearted prose makes the life and times of Paul Revere come alive.

Garza, C. L. (1990). *Family pictures*. San Francisco: Children's Book Press. (2–5)
The author describes her life as a child in Brownsville, TX.

Getz, D. (1994). *Frozen man*. New York: Holt. (4–6)
This account of the 1991 discovery of the Iceman in the Italian Alps explains how the age of the body was determined, as well as providing information about how humans lived in his time, some 5,000 years ago.

Giblin, J. C. (1992). *George Washington: A picture book biography*. Illustrated by Michael Dooling. New York: Scholastic. (2–4)
This easy-to-read cradle-to-grave biography also discusses legends, monuments to Washington, and Mount Vernon.

Golenbock, P. (1992). *Teammates*. Illustrated by Paul Bacon. New York: Harcourt Brace.
Describes the enduring friendship between Jackie Robinson, the first black major league baseball player, and Pee Wee Reese, his white teammate. (2–4)

Hamanaka, S. (1990). *The journey: Japanese Americans, racism and renewal*. New York: Orchard. (5–6)
This book, depicting the plight of Japanese Americans interned in World War II, is based upon a mural.

Hamanaka, S. (1999). *In search of the spirit: The living national treasures of Japan*. New York: Morrow. (5–6)
Features six major artists engaging in traditional Japanese crafts and provides information on the processes they use to create their art.

Hampton, W. (1997). *Kennedy assassinated! The world mourns: A reporter's story*. Cambridge, MA: Candlewick. (5–6).
A young United Press International (UPI) reporter recounts the events of Kennedy's assassination.

Harvey, M. (1999). *Look what came from China*. (1–3)
Presents information on food, sports, holidays, and customs of China.

Herbert, J. (1998). *Leonard da Vinci for kids: His life and ideas*. Chicago: Chicago Review Press. (5–6)
This unique book contains 21 activities that help children understand the life and times of Leonardo.

Hewitt, J. (1990). *Hector lives in the United States now: The story of a Mexican-American child*. Illustrated by Richard Hewitt. New York: Lippincott. (3–5)
Hector has always lived in the United States, but his family is thinking of moving back to Mexico.

Hoose, P. M. (2001). *We were there too! Young people in U.S. history*. New York: Farrar Straus & Giroux. (4–6)
Short biographies of dozens of young people demonstrate the active role young people have taken in shaping events in American history.

Hoyt-Goldsmith, D. (1992). *Hoang Anh: A Vietnamese-American boy*. Photography by Lawrence Migdale. New York: Holiday House. (4–6)
Hoang Anh describes life as a bicultural child in America.

Hoyt-Goldsmith, D. (1993). *Celebrating Kwanzaa*. New York: Holiday House. (5–6)
A Chicago family celebrates this African holiday.

Hoyt-Goldsmith, D. (1994a). *Day of the Dead: A Mexican-American celebration*. Photography by Lawrence Migdale. New York: Holiday House. (3–6)
This photoessay describes a Day of the Dead celebration in Sacramento, CA.

Hoyt-Goldsmith, D. (1994b). *Pueblo storyteller*. Photography by Lawrence Migdale. New York: Holiday House. (3–6)
> April Trujillo from Santa Fe, NM, describes how her grandparents create clay storyteller sculptures.

Huynh, Q. N. (1982). *The land I lost: Adventures of a boy in Vietnam*. New York: Harper & Row. (5–6)
> A young Vietnamese-American boy reminisces about his homeland and a way of life that he feels is gone forever.

Kindersley, B., Cropsey, S., & Kindersley, A. (1995). *Children just like me*. London: Dorling Kindersley. (2–5)
> Features information about children in thirty countries, describing their homes, friends, schools, families, and cultures.

King-Smith, D. (1994). *I love guinea pigs*. Cambridge, MA: Candlewick. (K-2)
> Provides information about guinea pigs and how to care for them.

Krull, K. (1995). *Lives of the artists: Masterpieces, messes (and what the neighbors thought)*. San Diego, CA: Harcourt Brace Jovanovich. (4–6)
> Brief, entertaining vignettes provide an introduction to 21 well-known artists.

Leigh, N. K. (1993). *Learning to swim in Swaziland: A child's-eye view of a southern African country*. New York: Scholastic. (2–4)
> An 8-year-old girl describes her life in Swaziland over a 1-year period.

Lyons, M. E. (1990). *Sorrow's kitchen: The life and folklore of Zora Neale Hurston*. New York: Alladin. (5–6)
> Presents the extraordinary life story of the author of *Their eyes were watching God*.

Martin, J. (1998). *Snowflake Bentley*. Illustrated by Mary Azarian. Boston: Houghton Mifflin. (3–6)
> This Caldecott Award winner details the life of Wilson Bentley, who became an expert on snowflakes.

McKee, T. (Ed.). (2000). *No more strangers now: Young voices from a new South Africa*. New York: DK Publishing. (5–6)
> Readers encounter the voices of South African teens as they reflect on life under Apartheid.

McKissack, P., & McKissack, F. (1989). *A long hard journey: The story of the Pullman porter*. New York: Walker. (5–6)
> The McKissacks outline the history of the African Americans who worked as Pullman porters.

Meltzer, M. (1984). *The black Americans: A history in their own words*. New York: Crowell. (5–6)
> Meltzer's excellent work covers three and half centuries of black life in the United States.

McNulty, F. (1990). *How to dig a hole to the other side of the world*. Illustrated by Marc Simont. New York: Harper & Row. (3–6)
> In this book a child takes an imaginary journey through the earth.

Micucci, C. (1997). *The life and times of the honeybee*. New York: Ticknor & Fields. (4–6)
> Portrays the life cycle and other interesting facts about the world of the honeybee.

Murphy, J. (1995). *The great fire*. New York: Scholastic. (5–6)

Firsthand descriptions by people who lived through the 1871 fire in Chicago.

Myers, W. D. (1991). *Now is your time!: The African-American struggle for freedom*. New York: HarperCollins. (5–6)

Myers outlines the efforts of African Americans to attain freedom throughout history.

Myers, W. D. (1999). *At her majesty's request: An African princess in Victorian England*. New York: Scholastic. (4–6)

This title describes the life of an orphaned African princess who became Queen Victoria's protégée.

Onyefulu, I. (1996). Ogbo: *Sharing life in an African village*. New York: Harcourt Brace. (2–4)

This photoessay explores cultural customs in an African village.

Ortiz, S. (1988). *The people shall continue*. Illustrated by S. Graves. San Francisco: Children's Book Press. (4–6)

This book portrays the Native American point of view about the coming of the Europeans and is accompanied by colorful paintings.

Parks, R., & Haskins, J. (1992). *Rosa Parks: My story*. New York: Dial. (4–6)

This simple biography tells the story of the woman who started the Montgomery bus boycott.

Paulsen, G. (1996). *Puppies, dogs and blue northers: Reflections on being raised by a pack of sled dogs*. New York: Scholastic. (5–6)

This moving book describes Paulsen's love affair with his lead dog, Cookie.

Peacock, L. (1998). *Crossing the Delaware: A history in many voices*. Illustrated by Walter Krudop & Walter Lyon. New York: Atheneum. (4–6)

The author uses three voices—a straight narrative, excerpts from actual writings, and the voice of a fictional soldier writing letters to his sister—to re-create the weeks preceding the American troops' crossing of the Delaware River with General George Washington.

Peet, B. (1989). *Bill Peet: An autobiography*. Illustrated by the author. Boston: Houghton Mifflin. (3–6)

Bill Peet tells the story of his life through entertaining text and illustrations.

Pinkney, A. D. (2000). *Let it shine!: Stories of black women freedom fighters*. New York: Gulliver. (5–6)

This inspirational collective biography describes the lives of 10 strong black women who fought to make their voices heard.

Provensen, A. (1995). *My fellow Americans: A family album*. San Diego, CA: Browndeer Press. (2–6)

This uniquely visual book portrays Americans of the past through captions, slogans, labels, and other visual forms,

Rappaport, D. (1999). *The flight of Red Bird: The life of Zitkala-Sa*. New York: Puffin. (5–6)

This book describes the life of a young Sioux girl caught between her native culture and the white culture.

Sattler, H. R. (1995). *Our patchwork planet: The story of plate tectonics*. Illustrated by Guilio Maestro. New York: Lothrop, Lee & Shepard Books. (5–6)

This engaging title explains the theory of plate tectonics through helpful analogies and smoothly written text.

Schroeder, A. (1989). *Ragtime Tumpie*. Illustrated by Bernie Fuchs. Boston: Little, Brown. (2–4)

   This biography describes the life of Josephine Baker.

Sis, P. (1996). *Starry messenger: A book depicting the life of a famous scientist, mathematician, astronomer, philosopher Galileo Galilei*. Illustrated by the author. New York: Farrar, Straus & Giroux. (3–5)

   This beautifully illustrated work describes the life and work of the man who contended that the earth was not the center of the universe.

Sneeve, V. D. H. (1996). *The Cherokees*. New York: Holiday House. (5–6)

   This book describes the history of the Cherokee tribe, as well as present day accomplishments.

Stanley, D., & Vennema, P. (1988). *Shaka: King of the Zulus*. New York: Morrow. (2–4)

   This picture book biography describes the life of the great Zulu warrior, Shaka.

Stanley, D. (1994). *Cleopatra*. Illustrated by the author. New York: Morrow Junior Books. (3–5)

   This interesting biography portrays Cleopatra as a strong, clever ruler.

Stanley, J. (1994). *I am an American: A true story of the Japanese internment*. New York: Crown. (5–6)

   Describes the plight of a Japanese American family interned during World War II.

St. George, J. (2000). *So you want to be president?* Illustrated by David Small. New York: Philomel. (4–6)

   A creative and witty examination of the characteristics of past and recent Presidents,

Szabo, C. (1997). *Sky pioneer: A photobiography of Amelia Earhart*. Washington, DC: National Geographic Society. (5–6)

   Amelia Earhart's sense of daring and adventure is captured in this cradle-to-grave biography.

Tallchief, M. (1999). *Tallchief: America's prima ballerina*. New York: Viking. (5–6)

   Describes the ascent of Maria Tallchief from an Oklahoma reservation to the world stage.

Tanaka, S. (1997). *The buried city of Pompeii: What it was like when Vesuvius exploded*. New York: Hyperion/Madison. (3–6)

   Tells the story of the disaster at Pompeii through enticing visuals and text.

Tanaka, S. (1998). *Graveyard of the dinosaurs: What it's like to discover prehistoric creatures*. New York: Hyperion/Madison. (3–6)

   Describes the work of paleontologists who have discovered prehistoric creatures throughout the world.

Tanaka, S. (2000). *In the time of knights: The real-life story of history's greatest knight*. New York: Hyperion/Madison. (3–6)

   This book tells the true story of William Marshal the Earl of Pembroke, born in 1146, who became the Regent and Mareschal of England and Protector to Prince Henry, the heir to the throne.

Trumble, K. (1996). *Cat mummies*. Illustrated by L. Kubinyi. New York: Clarion. (4–6)

   The author explains the sacred role of cats in Egypt and their mummification.

Ung, L. (2000). *First they killed my father: A daughter of Cambodia remembers*. New York: HarperCollins. (6)

A precocious young girl watches her life become a nightmare as the Khmer Rouge take over the Cambodian government in April 1975.

Waters, K. (1996). *Tapenum's day: A Wampanoag Indian boy in Pilgrim times.* Photography by Russ Kendall. New York: Scholastic. (4–6)

This companion book to *Sarah Morton's Day* and *Samuel Eaton's Day* examines the life of a Native American boy living in the 1620s.

White, R., & Cunningham, A. M. (1992). *Ryan White: My own story.* New York: Dial. (5–6)

This poignant book profiles a courageous young man struggling with a deadly illness that creates fear and prejudice among the public.

Winter, J. (1991). *Diego.* Illustrated by the author. Translated by Amy Prince. New York: Knopf. (1–2)

This bilingual (English and Spanish) biography of Diego Rivera is illustrated in the style of Rivera's work.

Yep, L. (1991). *The lost garden.* Englewood Cliffs, NJ: Julius Messner. (5–6)

This autobiographical memoir of one of the foremost Chinese American children's authors in this country helps us to understand the experiences that have shaped his writings.

Zhensun, Z., & Low, A. (1991). *A young painter: The life and paintings of Wang Yani.* New York: Scholastic. (4–6)

This profusely illustrated work describes the life of Wang Yani, a gifted Chinese painter.

CHAPTER TWO

Choosing Nonfiction Trade Books

On a recent visit to a school near Canton, OH, I met Kevin, a gifted second grader. Kevin was passionate about animals. According to his teacher, virtually all of the books he read in and out of school were nonfiction relating to this topic. During a classroom visit, I asked him about his interest in nonfiction. During our brief encounter, he clutched a book entitled *Animals of the Rainforest*. Kevin explained his fascination with facts in this way: "I like information. Stories just tell you something silly like bears with clothes on. This gives more information than stories. It makes you smarter. Everything you think about is in this book."

Teachers are beginning to realize that there are more and more Kevins in our schools. For the Kevins in today's classrooms stories are not enough—they want something more. Nonfiction sates these youngsters' curiosity at the same time it offers a "way in" to the world of books. It provides a meaningful and worthwhile alternative to the stories that constitute such a large part of the primary curriculum.

Fortunately for Kevin, his teacher understood and nurtured his love of nonfiction. She carefully identified books designed to appeal to his interests and level of maturity. She did not force Kevin to read imaginary stories exclusively, but allowed him the freedom to explore books that fulfilled his "need to know."

This chapter explores the kinds of decisions teachers make as they select nonfiction books for classroom use. It examines the following questions: How can teachers select excellent nonfiction books from such an overwhelming number of choices? What resources can aid with the selection process? How can teachers match specific children with books that address their interests? In addition, a section briefly addresses special considerations relevant to selecting multicultural nonfiction.

GUIDELINES FOR BOOK SELECTION

More children's nonfiction trade books are published each year than books in any other genre; some 2,500 of the 5,000 books published each year are nonfiction. Because most teachers are far more familiar with children's fiction than nonfiction, selecting nonfiction can be a challenge. Most of the time teachers select nonfiction books for one of two reasons: (1) their relevance to the curriculum or (2) their potential use for student report writing. When a teacher plans a unit on plants, for example, she will select a variety of books related to this topic. If later in the year her students do reports on different states, she may select books students can use to complete this task.

Book selection should, ideally, extend beyond concern for these two issues and recognize the many uses for nonfiction in the classroom. Teachers also need to recognize that for some students nonfiction is pleasure reading. As one sixth-grade girl reported: "Before [my teacher] told me about nonfiction, I read strictly fiction books. Every time I heard the word nonfiction I thought of reports. Now I know nonfiction can be just as fun as fiction."

Nonfiction titles selected for classroom use should address a range of topics of interest to learners at a particular level. The literary quality of a book should be the primary consideration when selecting any title. Children need consistent exposure to the *best* books that this genre offers, not just those that relate to a particular thematic unit. When evaluating nonfiction trade books for classroom use, teachers should consider the five A's: (1) the *authority* of the author, (2) the *accuracy* of the text content, (3) the *appropriateness* of the book for children, (4) the literary *artistry*, and (5) the *attractiveness* of the book (Moss, 1995). This section will discuss these criteria for evaluating nonfiction and provide examples to illustrate each one.

Authority

The best nonfiction authors speak with authority about their topics of choice. Some authors are experts in the areas about which they write, but most are not. Virtually all authors conduct exhaustive research about their subjects and document that research in their books. They consult experts in various fields to ensure accuracy and credit those experts in the preliminary pages of the book. For example, on the copyright page of *Flute's Journey: The Life of a Wood Thrush* Lynn Cherry (1997) lists more than 20 different experts she consulted, including naturalists, ornithologists, biologists, educators, and conservationists.

Accuracy

Outstanding nonfiction provides information that is clear, correct, and up to date. Maps, graphs, charts, and other information should also be clear, accurate, and current. Good nonfiction authors distinguish between facts and theories and avoid anthropomorphism, that is, attributing human thought and speech to animals. While animals that talk and think like humans are appropriate to the fantasy genre, they are not acceptable in nonfiction.

The accuracy of today's biography also extends to the way famous Americans are presented. For many years, children's biographies presented idealized versions of American heroes. Today's biographies of people like George Washington and Abraham Lincoln are generally not reverential; they present heroes of the past in a realistic way. This excerpt from *Lincoln: A Photobiography* (Freedman, 1987) demonstrates this trend:

> [Lincoln's] untidiness followed him home from the office. He cared little for the social niceties that were so important to his wife. He was absent-minded, perpetually late for meals. He was away from home for weeks at a time. And he was moody, lapsing into long, brooding silences. (p. 41)

How can teachers know if the information in a book is accurate? First of all, they can read reviews appearing in sources like *The Horn Book*, *Bulletin of the Center for Children's Books*, or *New York Times Review of Books*. Because experts in a particular field often write them, reviews in sources like these can help teachers assess the accuracy of even the most sophisticated books. For example, David Macaulay's (1988) *The Way Things Work* and his updated version, *The New Way Things Work* (Macauley & Artley, 1998), explain how more than 400 different machines function. A review in the *New York Times Review of Books* by Mario Salvadori, a professor emeritus of civil engineering and architecture at Columbia University, crowned the original work "a superb achievement" and noted only one minor inaccuracy in the entire book.

A second way to check for accuracy is to compare text information with that in an encyclopedia. Finally, teachers can consult local experts who can verify the accuracy of the information provided. The science teacher down the hall or the history professor at a local university can readily determine whether or not the information presented is correct.

Accuracy is only the beginning, though; the best authors distinguish between facts and theories and opinions. Good authors, for example, identify supposition or conjecture by using qualifying phrases. Terry Carr (1991) does this skillfully in *Spill!: The Story of the* Exxon Valdez when she enumerates the many birds and otters that perished from the oil spill:

By the end of the first summer after the spill, rescue workers had counted about 30,000 dead birds. Wildlife biologists estimated, though, that this number is only 10 to 30 percent of the toll, meaning that between 90,000 and 270,000 birds have probably died and disappeared in the waters of the sound. They also counted 1,016 dead sea otters. The toll in both otters and birds could increase as the years pass. (p. 53)

Carr notes the actual number of birds killed at the beginning of the passage, but continues to indicate matters of conjecture by using words like *estimated*, *probably*, and *could* to qualify her statements. In this way young readers are not misled, but rather are informed about the possible consequences of this disaster.

Appropriateness

Nonfiction books must be appropriate to their audience. They must not talk down to children but should respect them. Direct address and concrete details that promote reader involvement appeal to primary graders. In *I Want to Be an Astronaut* (Barton, 1988), the child narrator speaks directly to other children, stating the desire to be an astronaut and live in space. The speaker provides concrete examples of what he will do in space—have ready-to-eat meals, sleep in zero gravity, and help fix a satellite.

Clear organization helps all readers, but particularly older ones, grasp the author's intent. Books that incorporate typical patterns of exposition, which include sequence, cause–effect, problem–solution, enumeration, description, and comparison–contrast are easier for children to understand (see Chapter 4) than those that ignore these structures.

Chapter titles and headings enhance children's understanding of these patterns. Most of the time headings appear in books for older children, but they are sometimes found in books for younger readers as well. Gail Gibbons's (1995) *The Reasons for Seasons*, an information picture book appropriate for second or third graders, provides a simple introduction to the basic astronomy behind each of the seasons. Large-print headings titled "Spring," "Summer," "Autumn," and "Winter" alert young readers to the sequential pattern of the text.

Literary Artistry

While conveying information is a major purpose of nonfiction, the best books of this genre are more than "baskets of facts." The best nonfiction is literature; it uses a range of literary devices that help make information come alive. As Russell Freedman (1992) notes:

The basic purpose of nonfiction is to inform, to instruct, hopefully to enlighten. But that's not enough. An effective nonfiction book must animate its subject, infuse it with life. It must create a vivid and believable world that the reader will enter willingly and leave only with great reluctance. A good nonfiction book should be a plea-sure to read. It should be just as compelling as a good story. (p. 3)

To create this believable and vivid world, authors use a variety of literary devices. These include (1) letting readers hear the "voice" behind the information, (2) combining narrative techniques with expository ones such as poetry and prose, (3) creating comparisons using metaphors and similes, and (4) using "hooks" at the beginning of a book or chapter. This literary artistry is just one feature that distinguishes excellent nonfiction from textbooks or encyclopedias.

Voice

Generally the best children's authors are teachers. They convey passion about their subject and pass it on to their readers. To illustrate this, comparing this textbook treatment of the Pilgrim's Thanksgiving with one found in a children's trade book can be instructive. Consider this account of the Pilgrim experience as described in a second grade social studies text:

> The Pilgrims celebrated the first Thanksgiving in America. At harvest, the Pilgrims planned a feast to thank God for their food. They invited their Indian friends.
> Men hunted ducks and geese for the feast. Children gathered nuts and berries. Women made cornbread, fish stew, and other food. Indians brought deer meat. Everyone helped, and everyone celebrated together. (Armento, Nash, Salter, & Wixson, 1991, pp. 106–107)

This textbook description, while accurate, gives a bare-bones view of the Pilgrim experience. It tells children the facts but clearly lacks voice. We cannot hear the person behind the writing. It does nothing to make the past come alive. The writing is clear but pedestrian.

Leonard Weisgard's *The Plymouth Thanksgiving* (1967) provides children a more lively view of the Pilgrim experience:

> For three days, the women cooked. The women baked. The women worked and prepared. And the children helped. Tables were prepared out of doors alongside rough-hewn benches. Fires blazed. . . . When the day of the feast arrived, so did the Indians. Some in feathers. Some in furs. Some in animal skins. Ninety-one Indians came . . . . As their contribution to the feast, Massasoit presented five freshly killed deer to the Pilgrims.

With clear, simple sentences and vivid details Weisgard helps the child, or any reader, visualize the first Thanksgiving. Readers see the women and children preparing the feast, a description many children can relate to since they've helped with these preparations themselves. They can easily imagine the Indians coming to the feast in their panoply of apparel. Most importantly, readers feel the author's interest in the subject and hear his voice; rather than dryly reciting the facts, he *shows* readers the Pilgrims and his interest in the events of their lives.

Style

Today's nonfiction authors don't use a "one size fits all" approach to writing, but select literary styles that fit the subjects of their texts. This is especially evident in children's biographies. In the past, biographies began with the inevitable that so-and-so was born in such and such a place in such and such a year. Today's biographers capture children's interest in their subjects in the first paragraph. Nowhere is this done more effectively than in Andrea Davis Pinkney's (1998) *Duke Ellington: The Piano Prince and His Orchestra*. Pinkney adopts a slang-filled "jazzy" style in this exuberant treatment of the life of this musical giant. The first sentence sets the tone for the rest of the book, asking readers if they have heard of this jazz immortal born with the name of Edward Kennedy Ellington.

Combining Poetry and Prose

Bugs (Parker, 1987) introduces a variety of common insects through two-page spreads with rhymed riddles on the left side and labeled diagrams and descriptions on the right. The humorous rhymes grab readers' attention, while the descriptions offers information about the characteristics, habits, and natural environment of many different bugs.

Metaphors and Similes

Metaphors and similes create comparisons that help children link new concepts to more familiar ones. In *Heartbeats, Your Body, Your Heart* (Silverstein & Silverstein, 1983), for example, the authors compare red blood cells to ferry boats that carry cargoes of oxygen or carbon dioxide. They compare heart valves to trapdoors that prevent blood from flowing backward through the heart. By comparing scientific features to familiar objects, the authors help young readers understand the complex functions of the heart.

Hooks

Hooks, which refer to a story, anecdote, or example, help draw youngsters into nonfiction. Most often, hooks appear on the opening pages of a book. For example, Sally Ride and Susan Okie (1986) hook the reader's attention at the beginning of *To Space and Back*: "Launch morning. 6 . . . 5 . . . 4 . . . The alarm clock counts down. 3 . . . 2 . . . 1 . . . Rring! 3:15 a.m. Launch minus four hours" (p. 1). The interesting comparison of the countdown with the ringing of an alarm clock captures the readers' attention, draws them into the text, and makes them want to read on.

Attractiveness

Attractiveness, or "kid appeal," is essential in nonfiction trade books. Interesting appearances grab young readers' attention by sparking their interest and enthusiasm for information. Print size, text arrangement, and placement of information on the page can make the difference between a book that children pick up again and again or leave on the shelf.

Today's children, bombarded by visual images on the television and computer screen, expect materials with dramatic visual impact. Today's nonfiction does not disappoint; in fact, many books provide a visual feast. Well-known artists like Steven Kellogg, Tomie de Paola, and Aliki use illustration to both inform and entertain. Illustrators of nonfiction use a range of media, including watercolors, pen and ink, oils, and acrylics. Photography is increasingly common and gives the reader the sense of "being there."

Layouts clearly influence children's responses to nonfiction. Innovative pop-up formats are increasingly common and extremely popular. Some noteworthy examples include *The Human Body* (Miller & Pelham, 1983), which depicts parts of the body in three-dimensional relief, and *Strange Animals of the Sea* (J. Pinkney, 1987), which shows various forms of sea life including coral, hermit crabs, goosefish, and sharks. Dorling Kindersley Publishing, the creator of the Eyewitness books, has pioneered a distinctive layout with a museum look. These books use clearly organized text, much white space, and interesting and varied placement of objects on the page to entice young readers.

Selecting Multicultural Nonfiction

Selecting and evaluating multicultural nonfiction involves assessing the quality of a work as a work of nonfiction as well as a representation of the multicultural experience. For that reason, evaluation of multicultural nonfiction extends beyond consideration of the criteria described above to consider issues unique to multicultural literature.

It is essential that multicultural nonfiction meet the criteria of the five A's: it must have authority, accuracy, appropriateness, literary artistry, and attractiveness. Multicultural nonfiction books should, first and foremost, represent quality literature. They should be held to the same standards as other literature in terms of their literary quality.

Multicultural nonfiction works should possess authority. The best nonfiction authors speak with authority about their topics of choice. A perennial concern about authors of multicultural literature is the question of whether the author must be an "insider," or member of the culture, to accurately portray it. This issue too relates to the authority of authors and their ability to accurately portray the culture. Most experts agree that it is possible for members of majority cultures to take on the perspective of the insider, but only if they have had much contact with the culture being portrayed.

Miller-Lachman (1992) suggests that nonfiction with African American themes should be written from an Afrocentric rather than Eurocentric viewpoint. She points out that the McKissacks approach their material from such a view. In *Frederick Douglass: The Black Lion* (McKissack & McKissack, 1987) for example, they note that had the British won the Revolutionary War, Douglass (1817–1895) would no longer have been a slave in 1838, when he escaped to the North. This would have been so because in 1833 Great Britain abolished slavery in her Western Hemisphere colonies, long before emancipation. Such perspectives illustrate clearly the point of view of African Americans rather than European Americans.

Accuracy is a crucial consideration when evaluating multicultural nonfiction. It is essential that authors scrupulously check the information in nonfiction books. In addition, accuracy requires that multicultural books avoid stereotyping in both text and illustration. This means that authors must avoid the tendency to create "cultural conglomerates," suggesting that a given portrayal of a group represents all members of the group. There is great diversity within each of these cultural groups, and children should be aware of this. We, and students, must realize that cultural experiences differ from place to place and from individual to individual.

When judging multicultural nonfiction, cultural authenticity is as critical a concern as factual accuracy. Language patterns, religious beliefs, types of music, family relationships, social mores, attitudes, values, and holidays must be portrayed correctly. Illustrations, too, must be culturally authentic. People of color should be shown with varying skin hues, a range of hair colors, textures, and styles, and a variety of facial features.

In addition, specific details within illustrations should correctly reflect the culture of the group. For example, illustrators Leo and Diane Dillon present many glimpses of daily rural life in Africa in books like the Caldecott-winning *Ashanti to Zulu: African Traditions* (Musgrove, 1976). Members of different African groups are shown gathering food, cooking, eating, praying, farming, carving, and dancing.

By considering authority, accuracy, appropriateness, literary artistry, and attractiveness, teachers can make informed choices about the nonfiction titles they use in their classrooms. Thinking about these criteria can help teachers go beyond selecting books based solely on topics of study and move them to consider the variety of factors that in combination create excellence in children's nonfiction. Figure 2.1 summarizes the five A's for evaluating nonfiction. It also offers questions related to each category that teachers can use as they consider books for classroom use.

RESOURCES FOR NONFICTION BOOK SELECTION

A vast array of resources can help teachers pick interesting nonfiction titles for children of every age. *Eyeopeners II: Children's Books to Answer Children's Questions about the World Around Them* (Kobrin, 1995) lists more than 5000 nonfiction titles arranged by category. The *School Library Journal, Booklist, Horn Book, Bulletin of the Center for Children's Books*, and *Reading Teacher* regularly review children's nonfiction titles. *Booklinks,* an American Library Association publication, not only reviews nonfiction titles but provides features about nonfiction authors, ways to use nonfiction in the classroom, and much more. It also groups books of all genre by age-appropriate themes including the Holocaust, the Civil War, counting, and others relevant to the school curriculum. It provides grade level designations and information about paperback availability for every book listed.

Criteria	Questions to ask
Authority	Does the author identify and credit experts consulted during the research process?
Accuracy	Is text content accurate? Are maps, graphs, charts, and other visual information presented clearly? Does the author distinguish between facts and theories?
Appropriateness	Is information presented in ways appropriate to the intended audience? Does the author show respect for the reader? Is information effectively organized?
Literary artistry	Does the book have literary artistry? Does the author use literary devices to make information come alive? Is the author's style engaging?
Attractiveness	Is the appearance and layout of the book likely to entice readers?

FIGURE 2.1. The five A's for evaluating nonfiction trade books.

Online resources like the Children's Literature Web Guide (*www.acs. ucalgary.ca/~dkbrown*) list annual winners of various awards, including the Orbis Pictus Award for Outstanding Nonfiction for Children, established in 1990 by the National Council of Teachers of English to honor the best nonfiction book of the year. This award was named for the first nonfiction book published for children, *Orbis Pictus*, which was written by John Comenius and published in 1657. Another important award is the *Boston Globe–Horn Book* Award for nonfiction.

The American Library Association has established a third award for outstanding nonfiction—the Robert F. Sibert Award (see *www.ala.org/alsc/sibert.html*). The first recipient of the award was Marc Aronson (2000) for the book *Sir Walter Ralegh and the Quest for El Dorado*. This extraordinary biography of Ralegh (aka Raleigh), which also won the *Boston Globe–Horn Book* Award for nonfiction for 2000, traces the triumphs and tragedies of his life as a soldier, sailor, explorer, and schemer. It goes beyond the traditional biography, however, to provide a vivid portrait of the Elizabethan age and its politics, literature, and religion.

Annual lists of "best books" that include nonfiction are available from a variety of sources. The American Library Association identifies "notable books" (available online at *www.ala.org/alsc/notablebooks_terms.html*) annually. YALSA (Young Adult Library Services Association) also includes nonfiction titles in its listing of the year's best.

The American Library Association website includes nonfiction book reviews from *Booklist,* a journal that reviews adult, young-adult, and children's books. A second source for reviews and lists of award-winning books is the *Bulletin of the Center for Children's Books* (available online at *www.lis.uiuc.edu/puboff/bccb*). This site contains reviews of recent nonfiction titles along with lists of Bulletin Blue Ribbon winners for the past several years.

Another important resource for teachers seeking motivating nonfiction titles is the Children's Choices Award list. This is the only award that recognizes children's own book preferences, both fiction and nonfiction, rather than those of teachers or other adults. More than 10,000 children nationwide vote on their favorite books from hundreds provided by publishers. Selected nonfiction titles from selected Children's Choices Award lists appear in Figure 2.2. The books are categorized by age level and content area. These titles, because they were selected by children, can be good choices for classroom purchase.

While most of the aforementioned resources include titles with multicultural themes, other resources can provide guidance for the selection of multicultural nonfiction. *Our Family, Our Friends, Our World: An Annotated Guide to Significant Multicultural Books for Children and Teenagers* (Miller-Lachman, 1992) includes annotated listings of fiction and nonfiction books focused on

Primary grades		
Hands	Lois Ehlert	Language arts
Crayon Counting Book	Pam Munoz Ryan & Jerry Pallotta	Mathematics
Tiger, Tiger Growing Up	Joan Hewett, Illustrated by Richard Hewett	Science
Look to the North: A Wolf Pup Diary	Jean Craighead George	Science
Puppy Love	Dick King Smith	Science
What's Faster Than a Speeding Cheetah?	Robert E. Wells	Science, mathematics
Monster Math	Grace Maccarone, Illustrated by Marge Hartelius	Mathematics
Christopher Columbus: From Vision to Voyage	Joan Anderson	Social studies

Intermediate grades		
The Last Princess: The Story of Princess Ka'culani of Hawai'i	Fay Stanley, Illustrated by Diane Stanley	Social studies
Nine O'Clock Lullaby	Marilyn Singer Ill. by Frane Lessac	Social studies
Shadow Theater: Games and Projects	Denny Robson & Vanessa Bailey	Language arts, drama
Merry Go Round: A Book about Nouns	Ruth Heller	Language arts
Talking with Artists	Pat Cummings	Art, language arts
Fly Traps!: Plants That Bite Back	Martin Jenkins, Illustrated by David Parkins	Science
Doesn't Fall Off His Horse	Virginia A. Stroud	Social studies
Sharks	Seymour Simon	Science
Baseball Super Stars	David Gowdey, Illustrated by Sam Whitehead	Physical education

Upper grades		
Spill!: The Story of the Exxon Valdez	Terry Carr	Science, social studies
Secrets of Vesuvius: Exploring the Mysteries of an Ancient Buried City	Sara Bisel	Science, social studies
Mistakes That Worked	Charlotte Foltz Jones, Illustrated by John O'Brien	Science, social studies
Incredible Cross Sections	Richard Platt, Illustrated by Stephen Biesty	Science, social studies
Jackie Robinson: Baseball's Civil Rights Legend	Karen Mueller Coombs	Social studies, physical education
The Librarian Who Measured the Earth	Kathryn Lasky	Mathematics
Rosa Parks: My Story	Rosa Parks	Social studies
The Story in a Picture: Children in Art	Robin Richmond	Art

FIGURE 2.2. Selected nonfiction from Children's Choices Award lists.

parallel cultures within the United States and Canada, as well as native cultures in Asia, Central America, Africa, and other regions. *Multicultural Literature for Children and Young Adults, 1980–1990* (Kruse & Horning, 1991) and *Multicultural Literature for Children and Young Adults, Vol. 2. 1991–1996* (Kruse, Horning, & Schliesman, 1997) list multicultural titles from all genre recommended by the Cooperative Children's Book Center at the University of Wisconsin.

Award-winning children's books about people of color represent another resource for identifying quality multicultural nonfiction titles. The Coretta Scott King Awards are given annually for books honoring African American authors and illustrators of outstanding books for children and young adults. Nonfiction titles are frequently among the books recognized through this award. Nonfiction titles have, on occasion, been given the Pura Belpre Award, which honors Latino authors and illustrators whose work best portrays, affirms, and celebrates the Latino cultural experience in children's books.

MATCHING READERS WITH BOOKS

Book selection does not occur in a vacuum. While the 5 A's are important, teachers can't select books without remembering the children who will read them! The key to matching readers with books is knowing the students—their interests, background experiences, and levels of reading development. A solid knowledge of the books available and the individual characteristics of students will make the process of matching books and readers much easier.

Nonfiction Preferences

While research is limited, several studies suggest that some children prefer nonfiction to fiction. A recent study by Kletzien (1998) found that elementary school children enjoy and would choose to read information text almost half the time. This was particularly true for boys and for children in first, second, and third grades.

Yet, this study does not tell us much about the kinds of nonfiction children enjoy. Very little research has focused specifically on this question, but teachers and children themselves can give some insights. Young children often enjoy books on familiar topics like pets, firemen, trucks, or bugs because they can draw on their prior knowledge about these everyday subjects. Kletzien (1998) suggests that developmentally these younger children are in a stage of exploring the world and trying to figure out "how things work." This may account for the appeal of nonfiction to younger children.

In Ruth Oswald's second grade, for example, children studied crickets for 2 weeks. They read *Chirping Crickets* (Berger, 1998), *Grasshoppers and Crickets* (Greenaway & Fairclough, 1999), and several other titles. They observed crickets' behaviors, recorded information about their habits, and wrote books about crickets as a culminating activity (see Chapter 6).

While many young children enjoy reading about the familiar, others have more exotic interests. Some children with consuming passion for a topic become "experts" on, say, rocks, elephants, or the solar system. They absorb information from television and other sources that give them unexpected depth and breadth of knowledge. Isaac, a third-grade immigrant child from a nonliterate home, was just such a child. Isaac struggled with literacy learning for several years. Despite this, he had a vast amount of knowledge about elephants and other factual topics. Ultimately, nonfiction books about volcanoes, samurai, planets, and how-to experiments provided a "way into" literacy for Isaac (Caswell & Duke, 1998).

Older boys prefer books about adventure, science, sports, and other kinds of information, whereas older girls generally prefer mysteries, romance stories, fairy tales, and books about home and school life and animals (Johnson & Greenbaum, 1982). Children may also be interested in books that explore subjects like war, children of the past, space exploration, sports figures, and world events. Sixth graders in Judy Hendershot's room, for example, enjoyed titles like *Immigrant Kids* (Freedman, 1980), *Journey to the Planets* (Lauber, 1993), and *Secrets of Vesuvius* (Bisel, 1990).

A recent classroom study by a fourth-grade teacher in Ohio found that average and below-average readers preferred nonfiction to fiction. They made statements like "I like to read about what really happens" and "I like learning about real people." These children expressed preferences for books on topics like sports and dinosaurs.

Assessing Student Interests and Background

In order to get at children's reading interests, teachers often use interest inventories. Too often, though, these informal assessments reflect a bias toward stories, not even giving children the chance to express preferences for nonfiction topics. By using a survey specifically designed to tap students' interests in real-life topics, teachers can more easily match children with nonfiction books that will intrigue them. The primary-grade interest inventory shown in Figure 2.3 asks children for information about their favorite school subjects, their hobbies, and other areas of interest typically addressed through nonfiction books. The interest inventory in Figure 2.4 was created for upper-grade students. It asks older students about people and things they would like to read

1. What is your favorite book?

   _____

2. What are your favorite subjects?

   _____

3. What do you like to do best?

   _____

4. What do you want to be when you grow up?

   _____

5. What hobbies do you have?

   _____

6. Do you take any lessons in music, dancing, or art?

   _____

7. Would you like to learn about the things below? Circle the ones that interest you:

Jungle animals	Dancing	Football
Bugs	Space	Baseball
Pets	Oceans	Gymnastics
Trucks	Rocks	Crafts
Firemen	Motorcycles	Art
Sewing	Music	Dolls
Ice skating	Horses	Birds
Dinosaurs	Soccer	Snakes

8. What else would you like to learn about this year? Name three things:

   _____

   _____

   _____

FIGURE 2.3. Primary nonfiction interest inventory.

1. What nonfiction books have you read in the past?

   _____

2. What were these books about?

   _____

3. What is the title of your favorite book?

   _____

4. What made this book your favorite?

   _____

5. What three things would you like to learn about this year?

   _____ _____ _____

6. What are your two favorite hobbies?

   _____ _____

7. Name three well-known people you would like to learn about:

   _____ _____ _____

8. What are your favorite sports?

   _____

9. What are your favorite school subjects?

   _____

10. What magazines do you have at home?

   _____

11. Circle the topics that would be of the most interest to you:

Music	Art	Sports
World War II	Scientific discoveries	Famous artists
The solar system	The outdoors	Sports
Antarctica	Native Americans	Mummies
The Holocaust	Civil rights	Disasters
Famous athletes	Animals	Mathematics
Games	Inventions	Immigrants
Civil war	Famous artists	Famous dancers
The Alamo	Finding your ancestors	Children in the past

12. What other topics would you like to read about?

   _____

   _____

   _____

FIGURE 2.4. Upper grade nonfiction interest inventory.

about, along with other questions designed to tap interest in nonfiction. These surveys are best used in concert with teacher observation and other informal means of determining student interest. They can provide teachers with information that can help in grouping children for nonfiction literature study, selecting nonfiction read-alouds, or identifying topics for nonfiction book displays (see Chapter 3).

Considering Students' Reading Abilities

As noted earlier, reading nonfiction is different from reading fiction (this will be discussed further in Chapter 4). Because they contain specialized vocabulary and less familiar text structures, nonfiction trade books are almost always more difficult for children than fiction. For this reason, it is important to consider the reading ability of the child along with the reading level of the book.

Book publishers often assign reading levels to trade books that appear in the lower-right-hand corner of the back of the book. RL2, for example, means that the book is at the second-grade reading level. These levels must be viewed with caution because they are often misleading. For example, Gail Gibbons's (1989) *Monarch Butterfly*, which the publisher designates at a second-grade reading level, contains the following terms: chrysalis, abdomen, and metamorphosis. While this book is perfectly suitable for reading aloud at the second- or even first-grade level, most second graders would have difficulty reading it independently.

Nonfiction books for the youngest readers should be designed in ways that make information accessible to them. Emergent readers need books with predictable text and simple language. They need illustrations that support and provide clues to understanding the text. They need books with a limited number of words per page so they are not overwhelmed with text. Other features that make nonfiction titles accessible for younger readers include the following (Moore, 1998, pp. 84–85):

- Books that make it easy for young children to point and read
- Simple vocabulary and sentence structures
- Illustrations that make text information explicit
- Large-print size and generous spaces between words
- Consistent page layouts that make it easy to distinguish print from illustrations.

Matching Books to Readers: Using Leveled Books in Guided Reading, K–3 (Pinnell & Fountas, 1999) is an indispensable resource for teachers who need help matching children in grades 1–4 with appropriate books, both fiction and nonfiction. The authors provide lists of books arranged on a gradient of difficulty from A to R designed for use during guided or independent reading. Non-fiction titles range from simple books for beginning readers to more sophisticated and complex titles for older children. Information about the author/series, the number of words, and the publisher is included.

Fountas and Pinnell's (2001) *Guiding Readers and Writers Grades 3–6* provides lists of books appropriate for upper-grade readers. More mature readers need books with clear explanations and effective writing. While older readers can handle heavier vocabulary and concept loads, they still need textual supports such as glossaries, pronunciation guides, clear headings, and appropriate captions. Older readers may still encounter difficulties understanding graphs, charts, maps, and other visual matter. The varied layouts of recent nonfiction may cause even sophisticated readers to wonder what they should read first on a page. For example, many teachers have reported that children have difficulty knowing what to read first in the Magic School Bus books. There is no substitute for careful teacher guidance in this area.

SUMMARY

The selection of nonfiction trade books should involve consideration of each book's relevance to the curriculum and its "interestingness" to children. Most importantly, however, it should involve consideration of the book's quality. Evaluation of books can be based upon the five A's: (1) the authority of the author, (2) the accuracy of the content, (3) the appropriateness of the book for children, (4) the literary artistry, and (5) the book's attractiveness—all are important considerations when selecting books. Particular attention should be given to the literary artistry of the book and the extent to which the book uses a range of strategies including voice, metaphors and similes, and hooks to engage young readers.

Effective book selection also requires consideration of readers themselves. Teachers need to consider children's interests and levels of reading development as they select nonfiction titles. Children's interests in nonfiction change as they mature, and teachers need to explore those interests with their own students. Resources like the nonfiction reading inventories provided in this chapter can help teachers identify books likely to be motivating to children.

REFERENCES

Armento, B., Nash, G. B., Salter, C. L., & Wixson, K. K. (1991). *Some people I know.* Boston: Houghton Mifflin.

Caswell, L., & Duke, N. K. (1998). Non-narrative as a catalyst for literacy development. *Language Arts, 75,* 108–117.

Fountas, I. C., & Pinnell, G. S. (2001). *Guiding readers and writers Grades 3–6: Teaching comprehension, genre and content literacy.* Portsmouth, NH: Heinemann.

Freedman, R. (1992). Fact or fiction. In E. B. Freeman & D. G. Person (Eds.), *Using non-fiction trade books in the elementary classroom: From ants to zeppelins* (pp. 2–10). Urbana, IL:National Council of Teachers of English.

Johnson, C. S., & Greenbaum, G. R. (1982). Girls' and boys' reading interests: A review of research. In E. M. Sheridan (Ed.), *Sex stereotypes and reading: Research and strategies* (pp. 35–48). Newark: DE: International Reading Association.

Kletzien, S. B. (1998). *Information text or narrative text?: Children's preferences revisited.* Paper presented at the National Reading Conference, Austin, TX.

Kobrin, B. (1995). *Eyeopeners II: Children's books to answer children's questions about the world around them.* New York: Scholastic.

Kruse, G. M., & Horning, K. T. (1991). *Multicultural literature for children and young adults, 1980–1990.* Madison: Wisconsin Department of Public Instruction.

Kruse, G. M., Horning, K. T., & Schliesman, M. (1997). *Multicultural literature for children and young adults, Vol. 2, 1991–1996.* Madison: Wisconsin Department of Public Instruction.

Miller-Lachman, L. (1992). *Our family, our friends, our world: An annotated guide to significant multicultural books for children and teenagers.* New Providence, NJ: Reed.

Moore, P. (1998). Choosing quality nonfiction literature: Aspects of selection for emergent readers. In R. A. Bamford & J. V. Kristo (Eds.), *Making facts come alive: Choosing quality nonfiction literature* (pp. 75–89). Norwood, MA: Christopher-Gordon.

Moss, B. (1995). Using children's nonfiction trade books as read alouds. *Language Arts, 72,* 122–126.

Pinnell, G. S., & Fountas, I. C. (1999). *Matching books to readers: Using leveled books in guided reading, K–3.* Portsmouth, NH: Heinemann.

CHILDREN'S BOOKS

Aronson, M. (2000). *Sir Walter Ralegh and the quest for El Dorado.* (5–6)
    This Newbery Medal Honor book traces the triumphs and tragedies of Ralegh's (or Raleigh's) extraordinary life, while providing rich historical context for the time period.

Barton, B. (1988). *I want to be an astronaut.* New York: Crowell. (K–2)
    A young child reflects upon what it would be like to travel in space.

Berger, M. (1998). *Chirping crickets.* New York: Harper Trophy. (K–2)
    This book provides information about the purpose of the cricket's chirping sound, as well as about its anatomy, mating habits, and life cycle.

Bisel, S. C. (1990). *Secrets of Vesuvius.* New York: Scholastic. (5–6)
    This book explains how an anthropologist "reads" the bones of those killed in 79 A.D. at Herculaneum to reconstruct their lives.

Carr, T. (1991). *Spill!: The story of the* Exxon Valdez. New York: Watts. (4–6)
    This book describes the effect of the oil spill created by the *Exxon Valdez* on the surrounding environment, as well as the cleanup efforts.

Cherry, L. (1997). *Flute's journey: The life of a Wood Thrush*. New York: Harcourt Brace. (3–5)

This book traces the migration of a Maryland Wood Thrush to Costa Rica and back.

Freedman, R. (1980). *Immigrant kids*. New York: Dutton. (4–6)

With authentic photographs and fascinating text, Freedman describes the lives of immigrant children in the late 1800s and early 1900s.

Freedman, R. (1987). *Lincoln: A photobiography*. New York: Clarion. (4–6)

This Newbery Medal book provides a fascinating view of Abraham Lincoln, his family, and his times.

Gibbons, G. (1989). *Monarch Butterfly*. New York: Holiday House. (1–3)

This beautifully illustrated book explains the life cycle of the Monarch Butterfly.

Gibbons, G. (1995). *The reasons for seasons*. New York: Holiday House. (2–3).

Clear illustrations and simple text introduce students to the astronomy behind each of the seasons.

Greenaway, T., & Fairclough, C. (1999). *Grasshoppers and crickets*. Orlando, FL: Raintree/Steck-Vaughn. (K–2)

This simple book descries the physical characteristics, behavior, and life cycle of grasshoppers and crickets.

Lauber, P. (1993). *Journey to the planets*. New York: Crown. (5–6)

Lauber takes readers on a guided tour of the nine planets of the solar system, describing their history, composition, and characteristics.

Macauley, D. (1988). *The way things work*. Illustrated by the author. Boston: Houghton Mifflin. (4–6)

This classic work describes in detail how more than 400 machines work.

Macauley, D., & Ardley, N. (1998). *The new way things work*. Boston: Houghton Mifflin. (4–6)

An update of the original (above), this new edition contains a section on re-lated to inventions of the digital age.

McKissack, P., & McKissack, F. (1987). *Frederick Douglass: The black lion*. New York: Children's Press. (4–6)

Describes the amazing life of this great African American statesman.

Miller, J., & Pelham, D. (1983). *The human body*. New York: Viking. (4–6)

The functions of various parts of the human body are described through three-dimensional pop-up illustrations.

Musgrove, M. (1976). *Ashanti to Zulu: African traditions*. Illustrated by Leo Dillon & Diane Dillon. New York: Dial. (1–3)

Explains some traditions and customs of African tribes from A to Z.

Parker, N. (1987). *Bugs*. Illustrated by J. Wright.New York: Morrow. (4–6)

Simple rhymes introduce information on various types of insects.

Pinkney, A. D. (1998). *Duke Ellington*. New York: Scholastic. (2–4)

A beautifully illustrated, lively biography of the jazz great.

Pinkney, J. (1987). *Strange animals of the sea*. Washington, DC: National Geographic Society. (3–6)

Describes a wide variety of marine animals through three-dimensional pop-up illustrations.

Ride, S., & Okie, S. (1986). *To space and back*. New York: Lothrop, Lee & Shepard Books. (3–6)

> Fantastic color photographs and lively readable text help explain life as an astronaut to young readers.

Silverstein, A., & Silverstein, V. (1983). *Heartbeats: Your body, your heart*. Illustrated by Stella Aurora Ormai. New York: Lippincott. (3–6)

> This book describes the workings of the human heart and associated information in simply stated, understandable text.

Weisgard, L. (1967). *The Plymouth Thanksgiving*. Illustrated by the author. New York: Doubleday. (1–3)

> The clearly written picture book describes the first Thanksgiving.

CHAPTER THREE

Bringing Nonfiction into the Classroom

Photographer Nic Bishop produced the illustrations for *The Red-Eyed Tree Frog* (Cowley, 1999), which won the *Boston Globe–Horn Book* Award for the best picture book of 1999. This nonfiction title for young children depicts a tiny tree frog's quest for food and its close encounter with a hungry boa snake. With painstaking care, this talented artist created the stunning action photography that makes this book come alive. In his acceptance speech for the award, he reflected on his own bittersweet childhood experiences with books both in and out of school:

> When I reached back into my own childhood, I remembered that my bookshelf was filled only with nonfiction titles. As a young boy, I was always more enchanted by the natural world than the imagined. At school, I would rarely read past page three of a fiction story before I was glancing out of the window, my mind drifting to the world outside. Certainly, I was one of those children who didn't respond to reading fiction. (Bishop, 2000)

As Bishop notes, nonfiction is the recreational reading of choice for some children. Outside of school, these children, like Bishop, may love reading because they can choose books of interest to them. In school, however, they may be reluctant readers—mainly because their book choices are constrained by lack of access to nonfiction. As Vardell and Copeland (1992) note: "Although our everyday lives are filled with observations about the world around us, we often neglect the opportunity to engage children in learning about that world. We introduce our children to great storybooks and novels, forgetting the fascination of facts" (p. 76).

Many children get little or no opportunity to read nonfiction in their classrooms. Duke (1999) examined the uses of informational texts in early-grade classrooms. To gather information for her study, she visited 20 different first-grade classrooms for four full days during one school year. She collected information about the types of texts on classroom walls and other surfaces, in classroom libraries, and in written language activities. She found a scarcity of informational texts in these classrooms—children averaged only 3.6 minutes per day interacting with this type of text. Furthermore, only 9.8% of the books in the classroom libraries were informational.

This chapter explores ways teachers can make nonfiction literature a natural part of classroom literacy learning experiences. The first section of this chapter focuses on reading nonfiction aloud. It provides a rationale, gives suggestions for selection and planning of nonfiction read-alouds, and recommends interesting formats for this activity. The second section suggests ideas for making nonfiction part of the classroom reading environment. It recommends ways to incorporate nonfiction literature into sustained silent reading time and classroom libraries. It also suggests ways teachers can pique interest in nonfiction through displays, centers, book talks, author visits, and technology. The last section of the chapter identifies five ways teachers can organize the classroom for more formal study of nonfiction literature.

READING NONFICTION ALOUD

Teachers often express concerns about how to begin to use nonfiction in the classroom. Reading nonfiction aloud is an easy way to get started in using this genre. Reading aloud is a familiar, comfortable activity for both teachers and students. Most importantly, it is of inestimable value for students of all ages. This section offers a rationale for reading nonfiction aloud and suggestions for selecting and planning nonfiction read-alouds. It also recommends effective read-aloud formats and identifies and discusses a number of excellent nonfiction read-aloud titles.

Why Read Nonfiction Aloud?

Daily reading aloud is the simplest, least expensive, and most often recommended practice for improving student's reading achievement. The link between reading aloud and academic success has been well established. Reading aloud to children exposes them to new words, new expressions, and new concepts. It helps them internalize the structures of written language used to create every text genre. It promotes familiarity with language that serves children well as they read and write independently. According to Chambers (1995), as children listen to prose of all kinds, they unconsciously absorb the rhythms, structures, and cadences of the various forms of written language. They are developing understanding of how print "sounds." It is only through hearing words in print being spoken that children discover their "color, their life, their movement, and drama" (Chambers, 1995, p. 130).

Narrative literature is usually the preferred genre for teacher read alouds. A 1993 survey of teacher read-aloud practices in 537 elementary schools validates this point (Hoffman, Roser, & Battle, 1993). While the identified titles included excellent fantasy and realistic fiction, none of the most frequently read books at any grade level were nonfiction.

Why should teachers expand the read-aloud "canon" to include nonfiction? What are the benefits of reading nonfiction aloud?

First, nonfiction read-alouds draw children into the magic of the real world—of predators and prey, of planets and space exploration, of other times, lands, and lives. Exposure to nonfiction read-alouds has the ripple effect of a pebble tossed into a pond. It expands children's knowledge, which adds to their schema about an infinite number of topics. This in turn ultimately enhances comprehension. It teaches children concepts and terms associated with topics, places, and things they may never encounter in real life (Moss, 1995).

Second, reading nonfiction aloud sensitizes children to the organizational patterns found in nonstory text. Children of all ages are well aware of the structure of story. Even so, they have little knowledge of common non-narrative patterns like cause–effect, problem–solution, description, and enumeration. By hearing nonfiction read aloud, children begin to internalize these structures. Consequently, they become better able to comprehend these structures as they read and model them in their own writing.

Third, nonfiction read-alouds provide excellent links to fictional texts. For example, after hearing the adventures of *Babe: The Gallant Pig* (King-Smith, 1983), children would probably enjoy another book by the same author, *All Pigs Are Beautiful* (King-Smith, 1995), which provides information about pigs. These experiences can lead to discussions about similarities and differences in the two genre, ways the information in each book complements the other, and the process the author used to create each book.

Nonfiction read-alouds can also provide powerful connections to curricular content. Listening to titles like *Red Scarf Girl: A Memoir of the Cultural Revolution* (Jiang, 1997) during a social studies unit on China can personalize a distant and unfamiliar culture in a way that no textbook can. This moving memoir describes how Ji Li Jiang, a young teenager in the 1960s, gradually becomes disillusioned with the Chinese government she has been taught to revere. Her life unravels as the Cultural Revolution and its propaganda destroy the lives of many innocent people, including her family. An excellent student and class leader, she is denounced for her intelligence and family background. Government officials search her home, steal precious family possessions, and imprison her father. Ultimately she must choose between her family and the revolutionary government in power. Her story offers much to think about in terms of the role of government, the power of propaganda, and the conflict between political and family considerations.

Finally, and most importantly, nonfiction read-alouds whet children's appetites for information. As Seymour Simon, a noted nonfiction author, states, "I'm more interested in arousing enthusiasm in kids than in teaching facts. The facts may change, but the enthusiasm for exploring the world will remain with them the rest of their lives" (personal communication, 2001). Through this enthusiasm, children may feel compelled to learn more about areas of intense personal interest, which can lead to further silent, independent reading of this and other genres.

Selecting and Planning Read-Alouds

What is the best way to select nonfiction titles appropriate for reading aloud? First, consider the quality of the book in terms of the five A's discussed in Chapter 2: (1) the authority of the author, (2) the accuracy of the text, (3) the appropriateness of the book for children, (4) the literary artistry, and (5) the appearance of the book (Moss, 1995).

Another essential factor to consider is the author's voice. Does the book's author speak to readers? Can children "hear" the person behind the information, or do they just hear fact piled upon fact? It's important also to select books that "ignite the imagination, as if children were indeed fires to be lit" (Carr, 1987, p. 710). Overly technical books or those overloaded with unfamiliar concepts will put off even the most enthusiastic listeners.

A third consideration pertains to children's interests and curricular relevance. Knowing the students, their interests, and their background experiences is the key to successful read-aloud selection. The interest inventory in Chapter 2 can help teachers identify topics that their students will enjoy hearing about. Teachers who not only know their students but also know what they want to know, can locate books that captivate children of any age.

Although all nonfiction read-alouds need not relate to the curriculum, many titles can boost children's understanding of subjects like science, social studies, health, art, music, or mathematics. Nonfiction read-alouds can provide interesting in-depth information on almost any classroom topic, as well as current issues such as the environment, cultural diversity, global warming, or AIDS.

Suggested Read-Aloud Titles

Figure 3.1 lists examples of good primary-, intermediate-, and upper-grade nonfiction read-alouds. Many of the primary titles listed contain captivating illustrations that provide support for text information. In *Growing Vegetable Soup* (Ehlert, 1987), for example, the brightly colored collage illustrations of the various vegetables are sure to captivate kindergarten and first-grade listeners. Lynn Cherry's (1992) *A River Ran Wild,* a book suitable for reading aloud to older primary graders, traces the history of the Nashua River from the settlement of its valley by Indians 7,000 years ago until its recent reclamation. Each double-spread illustration depicts a period or topic mentioned and is bordered with tiny illustrations of wildlife, artifacts, or scenes of the Nashua River area in north central Massachusetts and southern New Hampshire.

Many of the upper-grade read-alouds listed contain photographs, maps, and primary source documents that lend authenticity to text information. In *Into the Mummy's Tomb: The Real-Life Discovery of Tutankhamun's Treasures,* for example, author Nicholas Reeves (1992) uses maps of Egypt, cutaway diagrams of

Book title	Author	Level
Kites Sail High	Ruth Heller	Primary
Growing Vegetable Soup	Lois Ehlert	Primary
A River Ran Wild	Lynn Cherry	Primary
Home Run	Robert Burleigh	Primary
Diego	Jeanette Winter	Primary
Look to the North: A Wolf Pup Diary	Jean Craighead George	Primary
This Is The Way We Eat Our Lunch: A Book about Children Around the World	Edith Baer	Primary
Turn of the Century	Ellen Jackson	Intermediate
Leonardo da Vinci	Diane Stanley	Intermediate
Come Back, Salmon	Molly Cone	Intermediate
And Then What Happened, Paul Revere?	Jean Fritz	Intermediate
Through My Eyes	Ruby Bridges	Intermediate
Christmas in the Big House, Christmas in the Quarters	Patricia & Frederick McKissack	Upper grades
Lincoln: A Photobiography	Russell Freedman	Upper grades
Into the Mummy's Tomb: The Real-Life Discovery of Tutankhamun's Treasures	Nicholas Reeves	Upper grades
The Case of the Mummified Pigs and Other Mysteries in Nature	Susan E. Quinlan	Upper grades
In My Hands: Memories of a Holocaust Rescuer	Irene Gut Opdyke & Jennifer Armstrong	Upper grades
I Was a Teenage Professional Wrestler	Ted Lewin	Upper grades

FIGURE 3.1. Recommended nonfiction read alouds.

Tut's pyramid and tomb, and dramatic color photographs that help youngsters appreciate the splendor of these treasures.

Formats for Nonfiction Read Alouds

All too often, classroom read-aloud experiences are isolated and unrelated to other classroom work. Nonfiction read-alouds could be easily correlated to classroom content. In classrooms where teachers use inquiry units (see Chapter 6), for example, read alouds can introduce, culminate, or extend units of study. During a unit on the presidency, for example, Julie Allison read *So You Think You Want to Be President?* (St. George, 2000) aloud to her fifth-grade class. Full of interesting and amusing anecdotes, this Caldecott Medal winner explores the characteristics of Presidents present and past. It also examines the advantages and disadvantages of the presidency from a child's point of view. Advantages include having a swimming pool, a movie theater, and not having to eat broccoli, while disadvantages include having to dress up, be polite, and do lots of homework.

Nonfiction read-alouds could be linked with books from other literary genre on similar or related topics. Many elementary teachers, for example, read *Charlotte's Web* (White, 1952) aloud. *Spider Watching* (French, 1996), a Candlewick Press nonfiction title, perfectly complements *Charlotte's Web*. Left-hand pages of the book define scientific terms and spiders' physical characteristics, while right-hand pages tell a story of a young girl who overcomes her initial fear of spiders. Children can compare the contents of each book by using a Venn diagram. They might consider the purposes of each author and the ways each book achieved those purposes. From these experiences children develop understanding of the imaginative forms of fiction and the creative shaping of facts required for writing nonfiction.

Teachers might read aloud different books about the same person, place, or event. An intermediate-grade teacher could read *Abraham Lincoln* (D'Aulaire & D'Aulaire, 1939), F. N. Monjo's (1973) *Me and Willie and Pa: The Story of Abraham Lincoln and His Son Tad*, and Myra Cohn Livingston's (1993) poem *Abraham Lincoln: A Man for All the People—A Ballad*. In this way, children can examine different authors' points of view about this extraordinary man's life. The first title, an early Caldecott Medal winner, is an "idealized" version of Lincoln's life. It avoids mention of the assassination, since this fact was considered too harsh for inclusion in a children's book in the 1930s. The second title provides glimpses of life in the White House through the eyes of Lincoln's son Tad. It is narrated in first person in the vernacular of a youngster living in the 1860s. The third work, a narrative poem, uses Lincoln's own words to portray his life. Following these readings, children could compare the form of each book, the points of view each author took toward its subject, and the information each chose to include or exclude.

Most books mentioned so far in this section are best read in their entirety. Many nonfiction titles, however, are not appropriate for cover-to-cover reading. For this reason, teachers may want to model reading aloud "bits and pieces" of books. Dotty Lane, a first-grade teacher in Columbus, OH, often reads small, interesting sections of "browser" books like the Eyewitness Junior series aloud. After these short readings, she closes the book. In this way, she demonstrates the use of nonfiction for reference purposes and presents the idea that not every book must be read from cover to cover (Kamil & Lane, 1997).

Reading picture captions only is another form of "bits and pieces" reading aloud that can provide a sneak preview of a book. The lengthy captions for the pictures and documents in *Anne Frank: Beyond the Diary* (van der Rol & Verhoeven, 1993), for example, connect artifacts back to the diary itself. Beneath a photo of Otto Frank glued inside Anne's diary, the author explains that Anne was particularly attached to her father, who provided her with love and support during the long days of hiding from the Nazis in occupied Amsterdam.

Brief vignettes from other works like Kathleen Krull's (1993) *Lives of the Musicians: Good Times, Bad Times (and What the Neighbors Thought)* make great 5-to 10-minute read alouds. Music teachers could read one of her brief, amusing vignettes about Mozart, Beethoven, or other musicians at the beginning of class. Other great books for "bits-and-pieces" read-alouds for older children include *Guinness World Records 2000* (Kynaston, 2000) or *Amazing but True Sports Stories* (Hollander & Hollander, 1990).

Reading nonfiction aloud lets teachers capitalize on children's natural curiosity about a wide range of topics. It can heighten student interest in the world around them and provide an opportunity for in-depth exploration of curricular topics that textbooks cannot provide. In addition, it builds familiarity with this genre by exposing children to the language and organizational patterns of expository text. Most importantly, it puts nonfiction on a more equal footing with fiction; it demonstrates to children that nonfiction is as acceptable—and as engaging—as fiction.

MAKING NONFICTION PART OF THE CLASSROOM READING ENVIRONMENT

This section suggests ways to expand the literary canon by making nonfiction part of the reading environment in elementary classrooms. First, it explores ways to infuse nonfiction into uninterrupted sustained silent reading time and into the classroom library. Then it recommends strategies to promote nonfiction reading through book displays, book talks, author visits, and technology. Finally, it provides ideas for organizing the classroom for nonfiction literature study.

An important goal of most school reading programs is to create lifelong readers. This goal, unfortunately, has proven elusive. Studies repeatedly show that most students do little out-of-school reading. At the same time, research consistently shows that those youngsters who read out of school are better readers. According to the *National Assessment of Educational Progress 1994, Reading Report Card for the Nation and the States* (Campbell, 1996), students who reported reading for fun at least once a week had higher average reading proficiency scores than those of students who reported never or hardly ever reading for fun.

In addition to making nonfiction acceptable in the classroom, teachers hold the key to making this genre accessible to their students. By broadening student choices to include nonfiction, teachers may find this genre an untapped resource with great potential for motivating the many reluctant readers in our elementary classrooms.

Evidence for this point comes from the voices of students themselves. In interviews with unmotivated seventh-grade readers, Kylene Beers (1990) asked students to identify activities that motivated them to read. They mentioned the following: (1) choosing their own books, (2) having teachers read entire books aloud, (3) comparing books to movies, (4) reading illustrated books, (5) doing art activities related to books, and (6) reading nonfiction materials.

Uninterrupted Sustained Silent Reading

Many teachers use uninterrupted sustained silent reading (USSR) as a way to encourage voluntary reading. During USSR students and teachers take time to read self-selected books without interruption. Most of the time, USSR is scheduled at the same time every day. Depending on the age of the students, USSR may last from 10 minutes to as long as an hour.

The purpose of sustained silent reading is to let students practice reading and read for their own purposes and pleasure. It is an excellent way to encourage student reading within and beyond the classroom. During USSR, students should be asked to read materials other than their textbooks. Students should be given free choice of other reading material (within reason, of course), rather than being required to select from a list of "approved" books, and this choice should be extended to include nonfiction.

Classroom Libraries

A well-stocked classroom library is an essential feature for promoting reading in and out of the classroom. If students are to have the opportunity to locate books by favorite authors, to answer their own research questions, or to simply find a book on a topic they love, they need plenty of books close at hand. In order to address the range of tastes in a particular classroom, it is essential that the classroom library provide a wide array of choices.

As experienced teachers will attest, it takes time and effort to build a good classroom library. Nonfiction books should be a part of even the smallest classroom libraries. Most classroom collections are dominated by what Aiden Chambers calls the "Holy Three"—fiction, poetry, and drama. Every classroom library should also contain nonfiction titles appropriate to the age and interests of the students. About half of the collection should be devoted to engaging information books and biographies, and this percentage should increase as children move through the grades. Some books should be pertinent to classroom topics of study, while others should have a broader appeal. Students can use these nonfiction library books for voluntary reading, inquiry study, reference, or browsing.

Recent nonfiction titles make motivating reading for students of all ages. They address dozens of topics with something of interest for every student. Because of this, they would make excellent choices for classroom libraries. For young dog lovers, Jean Craighead George's (2000) delightful *How to Talk to Your Dog* teachers young children how to communicate with their favorite dog in its own language. First-person accounts of students' own lives connect older students to their peers through titles like *Seen and Heard: Teenagers Talk About Their Lives* (Kalergis, 1998). Titles like *The New Way Things Work* (Macaulay & Ardley, 1998) fuel the curiosity of children and adults alike who stay awake at night wondering how their computers—and thousands of other inventions—work.

Where can teachers get nonfiction books for their classroom libraries? How can teachers with limited budgets bring these books into their classrooms? First, they can contact their school or community library. Some public libraries will loan books to teachers for classroom use. Second, teachers can purchase books at garage sales, library sales, or book fairs. Many titles can be acquired for minimal cost in this way. Third, they can involve their students in buying paperbooks from clubs like Scholastic and Trumpet. These book clubs regularly feature outstanding nonfiction titles and award bonus points that can be used to purchase more titles. Finally, many teachers have obtained small grants from foundations, corporations, or parent–teacher organizations (PTOs). Check with your building administrator to identify sources like these for adding nonfiction to your classroom library.

Displaying Nonfiction Books

Once books are in place, teachers need to make them enticing to children. Simply arranging books in rows on shelves is much less effective than creating book displays. Like department store displays, decorative book displays make books prominent and stimulate interest. They may have a real influence on the mental set of people who see them (Chambers, 1995).

Just as department stores use attractive displays to sell merchandise, teachers can use displays to sell children on books and reading. Packing crates, easels, chairs, and cardboard boxes can be used to showcase books of all kinds. Bent coat hangers can hold pages open to an interesting photograph or section. Displays can focus on nonfiction holiday books, units of study, or works of a particular author. Nonfiction series titles like the "I Was There" books, which include *On Board the* Titanic: *What It Was Like When the Great Liner Sank* (Tanaka, 1996a) and *The Disaster of the Hindenberg: The Last Flight of the Greatest Airship Ever Built* (Tanaka, 1996) make excellent displays. Other displays might feature Orbis Pictus Award winners, nonfiction *Reading Rainbow* titles, or "our favorite nonfiction books." Some displays can last until children take the books; others may be suitable for classroom reading only.

A book display might focus on a unit of study like weather. It could include actual or student-made weather instruments along with nonfiction books like Seymour Simon's *Storms* (1991), and *Lightning* (1997), or Patricia Lauber's (1996) *Hurricanes: Earth's Mightiest Storms*. Fiction titles like *Cloudy with a Chance of Meatballs* (Barrett, 1982) or poetry like Arnold Adoff's (1977) *Tornado!: Poems* could complement the nonfiction choices.

A uniquely nonfiction display might focus on Orbis Pictus Award-winning, honor, and notable books (see Appendix A for a listing). The teacher could give a brief history of the award and showcase a reproduction copy of *Orbis Pictus* (*The World in Pictures*). Written in 1657, this book by John Comenius was the first illustrated nonfiction book for children. A display of Orbis Pictus winners for primary graders could include *The American Family Farm: A Photoessay* (Ancona, 1989), *To the Top of the World: Adventures with Arctic Wolves* (Brandenburg, 1993), *Hopscotch around the World* (Lankford, 1992), *Dinosaur Dig* (Lasky, 1990), *Everglades* (George, 1995), and *Hottest, Coldest, Highest, Deepest* (Jenkins, 1998). Children might create written reviews of the books that could be added to the display later.

Nonfiction books can easily become natural additions to the total classroom environment. If the classroom has an aquarium, the *ASPCA Pet Care Guide for Kids: Fish* (Evans & Caras, 1993) could be placed beside it for student reference. If the teacher is reading Cynthia Rylant's fictional *A Blue-Eyed Daisy* (1985), he or she might have Rylant's (1989) autobiography, *But I'll Be Back Again*, available as well. If upper-grade students are reading *Surviving Hitler: A Boy in the Nazi Death Camps* (Warren, 2001), a display featuring Holocaust-related titles might promote further reading. Titles like *Four Perfect Pebbles* (Perl & Lazan, 1999) or the autobiographical *No Pretty Pictures* (Lobel, 1998) could teach interested students about survivors of that terrible time in history.

Another way to incorporate nonfiction naturally is to create centers based on how-to and activity books. For example, *Walter Wick's Optical Tricks* (Wick, 1998) or *A Drop of Water* (Wick, 1997) could be placed in such a center, along with materials necessary for completing the science activities and experiments explained in each book. Books like Lee J. Ames and Warren Budd's *Draw 50 Buildings and Other Structures* (1987) or *How to Make Super Pop-Ups* (Irvine, 1992) might entice artistically inclined students to create something. *Look What I Did with a Leaf* (Sohi, 1993) teaches children ways to create pictures of animals by combining various types and sizes of leaves. Students could read about different artists and their styles in books like *What Makes a Monet a Monet?* (Muhlberger, 1993) and then use art supplies to imitate that style.

Book Talks

Book talks offer another surefire way to ignite children's interest in nonfiction. From book talks children learn just enough about a book to determine whether it appeals to them. Book talks can take many forms. Sometimes teachers provide a brief summary of the book; other times they read a short excerpt. Guidelines for giving book talks include (1) reading the book before telling students about it, (2) preparing the program in advance and collecting the books that will be presented, (3) considering the students and their interests, and (4) keeping the program brief. The most important component of a book talk is an enthusiastic teacher!

"Teaser" book talks are a good way to pique children's interest in books and may entice them to read for pleasure. Caroline Feller Bauer (1993) in her *New Handbook for Storytellers* suggests "booktalking" by reading only the first few lines of a title. The following examples provide a sampling of the possibilities:

He is the Babe. He has always loved this game. This baseball. But what he does not know yet is this: He will change this game he loves. Forever. (*Home Run: The Story of Babe Ruth*; Burleigh, 1998)

At the age of eight, I left school and was given a job in the mines. I found it pretty hard getting out of bed at five-thirty every morning. The first two months, the road to work wasn't bad, but with the coming of snow, I found that I was much too small to make my way to work alone. Many times I was forced to wait by the side of the road for an older man to help me through the snow. Often I was lifted to the shoulders of some fellow miner and carried right to the colliery. (*Growing Up in Coal Country*; Bartoletti, 1998, p. 1)

April 24, 1990. For decades, astronomers had waited for this day. The Hubble Space Telescope, a scientific instrument that some said was one of the greatest inventions of Twentieth-Century science, lay safely tucked inside the cargo bay of space shuttle

Discovery, waiting to be launched into orbit 370 miles above the earth. Once there, free from the distortions caused by earth's atmosphere, the great observatory would peer into the farthest edges of the universe, seeking answers to questions scientists have asked for centuries. How old is the universe? How big is it? How are stars born? How do they die? Do black holes really exist? Have planets formed around other stars, the way our solar system formed around our Sun? . . . (*Close Encounters: Exploring the Universe with the Hubble Space Telescope*; Scott, 1998, p. 4)

> Wherever you are when you open this book
> I bet you can see a wall, if you look.
> Could you build a wall?
> No problem at all!
> Put brick on brick.
> Mortar makes it stick.
> Neat and slick. Make it straight.
> That looks great!
> Oh, but wait. . . . (*What is a Wall, After All?*; Allen, 1993, pp. 6–8)

Learning about Nonfiction Authors

Another way to heighten student enthusiasm for nonfiction is through in-depth study of a particular nonfiction author. Author studies involve students in reading several books by a single author and exploring the connection between the author's life and his or her work. Such experiences give children the opportunity to examine the writer's craft, deepen their understanding of the author's style, and examine the author's work as a whole. They also help students to view the author as a person and develop awareness of the decisions authors must make as they craft their works.

An important outcome of an author study is that students develop an awareness of the techniques authors use to share information. Children begin to appreciate how authors research a topic. They develop understanding of the need to sift through mounds of information to select facts that can be shaped into a meaningful form. Becoming acquainted with authors as researchers is as important as knowing and responding to them as writers and illustrators (Hancock, 2000). In this way, authors become models for children as they conduct their own research in preparation for writing reports, newspaper articles, or their own nonfiction books (see Chapter 6).

Picture-book author studies are increasingly common in the primary grades, with the works of writers like Marc Brown, Eric Carle, and Tomie de Paola among the most popular. Nonfiction author studies are far less common, but can be equally rewarding. Author studies focused on writers like Gail Gibbons, Diane Stanley, or Jim Murphy can extend content area learning as well as literary understanding. Meaningful author studies can readily be incorporated into the curriculum at virtually any grade level.

When selecting an author for classroom study, teachers will first want to familiarize themselves with the books of authors suitable for their grade level. Second, they will want to consider the appropriateness of the books to their students' abilities and interests. Third, they will want to determine the availability of the author's works. Are the author's books still in print? Are several titles available for purchase in paperback? Fourth, are the books sufficiently interesting and varied that they will hold students' interest? Do they lend themselves to meaningful and worthwhile lessons appropriate to the curriculum?

Figure 3.2 lists authors suitable for nonfiction author study at the primary-, intermediate-, and upper-grade levels. Not surprisingly, many of these authors write children's fiction as well as nonfiction. These recognized authors have written many high-quality children's nonfiction titles on an array of topics at the designated levels. The third column of the chart lists examples of each author's nonfiction works.

It is essential, however, that teachers examine an author's body of work to get a real flavor for his or her areas of interest and expertise. Authors like Melvin Berger, Millicent E. Selsam, and Seymour Simon are noted for outstanding science-related nonfiction. Other authors like Milton Meltzer and Jim Murphy write mostly about events of the past. Patricia and Frederick McKissack have written on a multitude of topics, but their most recent books address people and events from African American history. Some authors like Jean Fritz and Diane Stanley specialize in biographies of people from the past.

Learning activities related to an author study will vary by grade level but can involve an array of reading, writing, speaking, and listening experiences. Teachers often involve students in strategy lessons involving comparison of different titles (see Chapter 4), creative dramatics, literature circle discussions (see Chapter 5), inquiry research related to text content (see Chapter 6) or writing letters to or e-mailing favorite authors. *The Author Studies Handbook: Helping Students Build Powerful Connections to Literature* (Kotch & Zackman, 1999) offers many additional suggestions for implementing author studies in the classroom.

No author study would be complete without familiarizing students with the author's own life. When students are really engaged in a book, they feel that the author is speaking directly to them. For this reason, young people often find it fascinating to learn about their favorite authors. The reference work *Something about the Author* (Gale Research, 1986) contains biographical information about hundreds of authors. It is available in most public libraries.

Some nonfiction authors such as Lois Ehlert (1996; *Under My Nose*), Patricia McKissack (1997; *Can You Imagine?*) and Lawrence P. Pringle (1997; *Nature!:*

Level	Author	Selected books
Primary	Lois Ehlert	Growing Vegetable Soup
		Red Leaf, Yellow Leaf
Primary	Joanna Cole	Magic School Bus Series
Primary	Gail Gibbons	My Baseball Book
		Gulls, Gulls, Gulls
Primary	Bruce McMillan	Eating Fractions
		Whale Watching
Primary	David Adler	Lou Gehrig: The Luckiest Man
Primary	Jean Fritz	And Then What Happened, Paul Revere
		Why Not, Lafayette?
Primary	Byron Barton	I Want to be An Astronaut
		Airplanes
Primary	Melvin Berger	Do All Spiders Spin Webs? Questions and Answers about Spiders
		Look Out for Turtles
Primary	Millicent Ellis Selsam	How Kittens Grow
		How Puppies Grow
Primary	Arthur Dorros	Ant Cities
		A Tree Is Growing
Intermediate	Aliki	William Shakespeare and the Globe
		Communication
Intermediate	Jim Arnosky	All About Alligators
		Crinkleroot's Guide to Knowing Animal Habitats
Intermediate	James Cross Giblin	The Amazing Benjamin Franklin
		Thomas Jefferson
Intermediate	Kathryn Lasky	The Librarian Who Measured the Earth
		Interrupted Journey: Saving Endangered Sea Turtles
Intermediate	Ann McGovern	The Secret Soldier: The Story of Deborah Sampson
		If You Lived 100 Years Ago
Intermediate	Diane Stanley	Leonardo da Vinci
		Cleopatra
Intermediate	Betsy & Giulio Maestro	Coming to America: The Story of Immigration
		The Story of Money
Intermediate	Dorothy G. Patent	Slinky, Scaly, Slithery Snakes
		Prairie Dog
Intermediate	Seymour Simon	Sharks
		Lightning
Upper Grades	Leonard Everett Fisher	The Oregon Trail
		Galileo
Upper Grades	Russell Freedman	Give Me Liberty!
		Eleanor Roosevelt
Upper Grades	Jean Craighead George	One Day in the Desert
		A Wolf Cub Diary
Upper Grades	Patricia Lauber	Hurricanes
		Seeing Earth from Space
Upper Grades	David Macaulay	Castle
		Mill
Upper Grades	Jim Murphy	Blizzard!
		Long Road to Gettysburg
Upper Grades	Lawrence Pringle	Dolphin Man: Exploring the World of Dolphins
Upper Grades	Jerry Stanley	I Am an American: A True Story of Japanese Internment
		Big Annie of Calumet: A True Story of the Industrial Revolution
Upper Grades	Patricia & Frederick McKissack	Black Hands, White Sails: The Story of African American Whalers
		Sojourner Truth: Ain't I A Woman

FIGURE 3.2. Suggested nonfiction authors for author study.

Wild and Wonderful) have written captivating autobiographies. In addition, videotapes can introduce students to favorite nonfiction authors like Aliki, Jean Fritz, and Arthur Dorros. Information about purchasing videotapes of visits with these authors and others is available on the Internet at *www.libraryvideo.com*.

Furthermore, many nonfiction authors have websites that describe their lives, their books, their interests, and their travel schedules. Links to web pages about almost all of the authors listed in Figure 3.2, for example, can be found at one or more of the websites shown in the accompanying tabulation.

Website	Title	Address
Scholastic	Author Studies	*www2.scholastic.com/ teachers/authorsandbooks/ authorstudies/ authorstudies.jhtm*
Internet School Library Media Center	Index to Authors and Illustrators Main Page	*falcon.jmu.edu/~ramseyil/*
Kay Vandergrift	Learning about the Author and Illustrator Pages	*www.scils.rutgers.edu/ ~kvander/AuthorSite/ index.htm/*
HarperCollins	Meet the Author	*www.harperchildrens.com/ hch/author*
Houghton Mifflin Education Place	Authors and Illustrators Main Page	*www.eduplace.com/kids/ hmr/mtai/index.html*

The ultimate culminating activity for an author study is an author visit. Author visits let students interact with writers on a personal level and provide role models and inspiration to aspiring young authors. Many nonfiction writers regularly make school visits and present programs to students and/or teachers. Betsy and Giulio Maestro, for example, speak to students about the process they use to create an illustrated nonfiction book They also provide teacher workshops. Many schools arrange to have the author's books available for student purchase. Authors are often willing to autograph these books for students, which provides them with a lasting memento of the author's visit.

Third-grade teacher Ellen Calvo involved her students in an author study centered around Gail Gibbons. To introduce the author's life and work, Ellen showed students Gail Gibbons's website. She obtained a small number of copies of the authors' many nonfiction picture books and introduced them to her students through book displays, book talks, and read-alouds. Students met as a class for guided reading experiences centering on titles like *The Milk Makers* (Gibbons, 1985) and *Monarch Butterfly* (Gibbons, 1989). During these experiences they examined the many nonfiction features found in Gibbons's books and listed these on chart paper. Students also shared their observations about the illustrations found in these texts, and recorded their own questions about the topics addressed.

Over time, the children began to develop understanding of the different text structures the author used to organize each book. Ellen introduced simple graphic organizers on large sheets of chart paper, and the children worked together to complete them. Children compared titles using Venn diagrams and completed organizers depicting series of events using books like *From Seed to Plant* (Gibbons, 1991).

Students then visited the school library to conduct a book search for Gail Gibbons's books. They read these books independently, and they shared them with small groups or the entire class on a daily basis. In addition, students chose books for partner reading several times each week. Following these experiences, they recorded what they learned about topics addressed in their books in learning logs.

As the author study progressed, students began to create lists of the different topics addressed in Gail Gibbons's work. Ellen explained to her students how authors conduct research about nonfiction topics, and she showed students how to locate information about the author's research within the covers of the book. This resulted in a class chart entitled "How the Author Created the Book." A variety of minilessons introduced children to the research process in preparation for the completion of research projects later in the year.

As students became more and more immersed in the author's books, they began to notice the many visual features she uses to make difficult concepts comprehensible. The children quickly developed the ability to identify visual features like labeled diagrams, cross sections, and flow charts, as well as many others. After several minilessons, Ellen involved the students in writing letters to Gail Gibbons.

Ellen culminated the unit with a classroom celebration. Parents were invited to attend the celebration, during which children read aloud "fascinating facts" they had learned from the authors' books. Small groups of students presented short readers' theater presentations they had written based on specific titles. In addition, a number of children assumed the role of class "experts," giving presentations on topics related to information contained in Gibbons's many books.

Technology

Visual media, especially television and the Internet, are extraordinary resources for encouraging reading about the real world. Many adults lament the impact of the media on children's reading habits, suggesting that television and the Internet may replace books in children's lives. James Cross Giblin, a noted children's nonfiction author, contends that visual media may well not replace books but instead may stimulate children to learn more about topics of interest. In "More Than Just the Facts: A Hundred Years of Children's Nonfiction" (Giblin, 2000) he states:

> Television in many instances has whetted the public's appetite for informational books. One librarian after another has told me that when a television program focuses on a particular subject—say a National Geographic special on elephants—libraries experience a run on books about elephants in the weeks that follow. I have a hunch that something similar may happen in the case of the Internet. After obtaining a summary of the desired information on a screen, the young person will turn to a book for a more in-depth treatment of the subject—a book that does not require an electrical outlet or battery to operate, and that can be transported easily to any place the young person wants to sit and read it. (p. 423)

Reading Rainbow, the popular Public Broadcasting Service television program, has an established reputation as an effective motivator of children's reading. The series featured several episodes centered on excellent nonfiction books appropriate for children in first through sixth grades. In the episode featuring *Bugs* (Parker, 1987), for example, host LeVar Burton takes children to visit bugs and insects at the Cincinnati Zoo's Insect World and to Mexico to see where Monarch Butterflies migrate for the winter. Other episodes focused on nonfiction titles include *Chickens Aren't the Only Ones* (Heller, 1994), *Desert Giant: The World of the Saguaro Cactus* (Bash, 1989), *Germs Make Me Sick!* (Berger, 1995), *Summer* (Hirschi, 1991), and *Mummies Made in Egypt* (Aliki, 1987). Teachers' guides for these and other *Reading Rainbow* programs are available on the World Wide Web at *www.gpn.unl.edu.rainbow*.

The World Wide Web offers a powerful means of introducing or extending nonfiction-related topics. Its sound and video capabilities provide extraordinary opportunities for linking nonfiction literature with other resources including art, music, and primary-source documents. These resources can engage children in simulations of historical events, virtual visits to places that span the globe, and late-breaking world events. Just as important, they offer children the chance to communicate with the wider world in ways that are not possible with other media. Through e-mail, for example, children can correspond with content area experts, underwater explorers like Robert Ballard, or even the President of the United States.

Web sites can effectively complement information found in nonfiction books. For example, after reading Seymour Simon's (1997) *Lightning*, youngsters can visit the website "Lightning Information and Safety" *www.azstarnet. com/anubis/zaphome.htm*, which was written and illustrated by a young girl who was actually struck by lightning. She provides factual information about lightning and her own experience, along with links to other related sites. Or a teacher might introduce *The Story of the White House* (Waters, 1992) through the White House website *www.whitehouse.gov*. This site contains fascinating facts about the executive mansion, including sections about children and pet occupants. It also gives children e-mail access to the President. The National Aeronautics and Space Administration's website *www.nasa.gov* contains up-to-the-minute videoclips from the Hubble Space Telescope that effectively complement information in *Close Encounters: Exploring the Universe with the Hubble Space Telescope* (Scott, 1998). After reading this book, students could question experts at the "Ask a Science/Math Expert" site located at *www.njnie.dl.stevens-tech.edu/curriculum/aska/science.html* where experts in chemistry, astronomy, earth science, and other areas respond to e-mailed questions. Figure 3.3 displays other examples of nonfiction books and companion websites.

ORGANIZING THE CLASSROOM FOR NONFICTION LITERATURE STUDY

As teachers become more familiar with nonfiction, they will identify many books relevant to their curricula and their students' lives. Excellent nonfiction can complement textbook material or become a resource for students as they conduct inquiry projects (more on this in Chapter 6). Equally important, excellent nonfiction can stand on its own as literature and can be studied just as fictional literature can.

One of the most challenging aspects of using literature in the classroom—whether fiction or nonfiction—is grouping children for instruction. The grouping pattern of choice depends upon teacher and student goals and purposes for using the literature. The following section explains four grouping models and provides examples that illustrate ways to group students for nonfiction literature study. Chapter 4 extends this information by suggesting strategies teachers can use to support student understanding as they engage in nonfiction literature study.

Whole-Group/Single-Book Model

Sometimes teachers want all students in a class to have a common reading experience centered on the same book. On these occasions they may use a whole-group model where all students read the same book. Fifth-grade science teacher Ken Blake wanted to extend his textbook's treatment of outer space and space travel. He decided to involve his students in reading Sally Ride and Susan Okie's (1986) *To Space and Back*.

Since this was the first time he had used literature to supplement the textbook, he decided to use the whole-group/one-book model. He purchased 25 pa-

Book title	Website
Anderson, W. *Laura's Album: A Remembrance Scrapbook of Laura Ingalls Wilder*	A Worldwide Web Guide to Laura Ingalls Wilder *worldwideguide.net/guides/index.cfm?guide;0=1*
Maestro, B. *Coming to America*	Ellis Island Foundation *www.ellisisland.org*
Gibbons, G. *Sunken Treasure*	The *Atocha* Home Page *www.ocf.berkeley.edu/~mars/atocha.htm*
Sky Pioneer: A Photobiography of Amelia Earhart	Amelia Earhart Web Page *www.ellensplace.net/eae_intr.html*
Anne Frank: Beyond the Diary	Anne Frank Online *www.annefrank.com*
Ryan, P. M. *The Flag We Love*	Betsy Ross Home Page *www.ushistory.org/betsy/*
Giblin, J. C. *The Amazing Life of Benjamin Franklin*	Benjamin Franklin: Glimpses of the Man *www.fi.edu/franklin/*
Aliki. *Shakespeare and the Globe*	Shakespeare's Globe *www.rdg.ac.uk/globe/oldglobe/oldglobe_index.htm*
Kuskin, K. *The Philharmonic Gets Dressed*	Energy in the Air: Sounds of the Orchestra *tqjunior.thinkquest.org/5116*
Bial, R. *Underground Railroad*	National Geographic Online Presents the Underground Railroad *www.nationalgeographic.com/features/99/railroad*
Coerr, E. *Sadako and the Thousand Paper Cranes*	Pieces and Creases: A Fun Guide to Origami *tqjunior.thinkquest.org/5402*
Berger, M. *Do Stars Have Points? Questions and Answers about Stars and Planets*	Space Kids *www.spacekids.com*

FIGURE 3.3. Nonfiction books and companion websites.

perback copies of the book. Each student read the book and participated in large-group discussions about a variety of topics, including everyday life in a space capsule. Students also compared information in their textbook to that found in Ride and Okie's book.

This model can be equally effective at the primary level. As a springboard to a classroom study of insects, second-grade teacher Bea Rebenack used *Ant Cities* (Dorros, 1987) with her students. Since this was one of her students' first exposures to informational text, Bea engaged her students in a "walk-through" of the book. She used a shared reading experience to focus their attention on understanding the ways that information books differ from stories (see Chapter 4). After reading, children recorded two facts about ants in their journals.

Whole-Group/Complementary Books

It can often enrich student study of a topic to pair a work of fiction or poetry with a work of nonfiction on the same or related topics. Such pairings can help students develop different perspectives about a particular time, person, or phenomenon. An easy to implement format is for the entire class to read two different books, one fiction and one nonfiction.

Judith Hendershot's sixth-grade language arts class read and discussed the poignant Newbery winner *Out of the Dust* (Hesse, 1997). This compelling novel introduced these sixth graders to Billie Jo, a young girl who faced a life of suffering in the 1930s Oklahoma Dust Bowl. They then read *Children of the Dust Bowl*, Jerry Stanley's (1992) nonfiction account of how the Okie children built their own school with the help of Leo Hart. After reading both titles, students explored the similarities and differences in the two genres and extended their understanding and appreciation of each. They reflected upon how reading each one had influenced their reading of the other. They deepened their understanding of the Depression era, as well as what it meant to be a child living during that time.

Figure 3.4 lists fiction and poetry titles that can be effectively paired with nonfiction titles at the primary-, intermediate-, and upper-grade levels. Some examples pair stories with factual treatments of the same person or topic. *Pedro's Journal* (Conrad, 1991), for example, is a fictionalized account of Columbus's voyage of 1492/93, narrated by Pedro, a cabin boy on the *Santa Maria*. *Westward with Columbus* (Dyson, 1992) recounts how in the summer of 1990 the author retraced Columbus's route aboard a replica of the *Niña*. In other examples, a work of fiction is paired with a biography of its author. Reading *The Call of the Wild, and Other Stories* (London, 1960) and *Jack London: A Biography* (Dyer, 1997), for example, may provide students with new perspectives on London's life and work.

Pairing two nonfiction works can deepen student understanding of each book. Each year, for example, Bonnie Pratt's sixth graders read an excerpt from *Anne Frank: The Diary of a Young Girl* (Frank, 1967) in their literature anthology. This year they followed that reading with the nonfiction title *Anne Frank: Beyond the Diary* (van der Rol & Verhoeven, 1993). This book contains photographs of artifacts that extend readers' understanding of Anne Frank's experience of hiding out in the "secret annex" in Nazi-occupied Amsterdam. Heartbreaking photographs of the diary and the Nazi's typewritten list of Frank family

Fiction/poetry title	Nonfiction title
Primary	
Bunting, E. *How Many Days to America*	Lawlor, R. *I Was Dreaming to Come to America*
Lindbergh, R. *A View from the Air*	Burleigh, R. *Flight: The Journey of Charles Lindbergh*
Livingston, M. *A Circle of Seasons*	Gibbons, G. *Seasons of Arnold's Apple Tree*
Yolen, J. *Letting Swift River Go*	Wick, W. *A Drop of Water*
Polacco, P. *Just Plain Fancy*	Bial, R. *The Amish*
Van Allsburg, C. *Just a Dream*	Cherry, L. *A River Ran Wild*
Rylant, C. *Poppleton in Fall*	Ehlert, L. *Red Leaf, Yellow Leaf*
	Sohi, M. *Look What I Did with a Leaf!*
DePaola, T. *The Art Lesson*	Cummings, P. *Talking with Artists*
Wilder, L. *Little House on the Prairie*	Erickson, P. *Daily Life in a Covered Wagon*
Peet, B. *Cyrus the Unsinkable Sea Serpent*	Peet, B. *Bill Peet: An Autobiography*
Conrad, P. *Pedro's Journey*	Dyson, J. *Westward with Columbus*
King-Smith, D. *Babe, the Gallant Pig*	King-Smith, D. *All Pigs are Beautiful*
White, E. B. *Charlotte's Web*	McNulty, F. *The Lady and the Spider*
	French, V. *Spider Watching*
Zolotow, C. *The Seashore Book*	Parker, S., & King, D. *Eyewitness Books: Seashore*
Oppenheimer, J. *Have You Seen Birds?*	Ehlert, L. *Feathers for Lunch*
McPhail, D. *Lost!*	McPhail, D. *In Flight with David McPhail: A Creative Biography*
Van Allsburg, C. *Two Bad Ants*	Dorros, A. *Ant Cities*
Cole, J. *Give a Dog a Bone: Stories, Poems, Jokes and Riddles about Dogs*	Selsam, M. *How Puppies Grow*
Martin, B. *Brown Bear, Brown Bear*	Wallace, K. *Bears in the Forest*
Intermediate	
Paterson, K. *Park's Quest*	Ashabranner, B. *Always to Remember*
Hamilton, V. *The House of Dies Drear*	Bentley, J. *"Dear Friend"*
	Garrett, T., & Still, W. *Collaborators on the Underground Railroad*
Lowry, L. *Number the Stars*	Frank, A. *Diary of A Young Girl*
	Perl, L., & Lazan, M. *Four Perfect Pebbles*
Nixon, J. L. *A Family Apart*	Warren, A. *Orphan Train Rider*
Gregory, K. *The Great Railroad Race: The Diary of Libby West*	Blumberg, R. *Full Steam Ahead: The Race to Build a Transcontinental Railroad*

(continued)

FIGURE 3.4. Fiction and nonfiction book pairs.

Fiction/poetry title	Nonfiction title
Intermediate (continued)	
Rinaldi, A. *The Blue Door*	Freedman, R. *Kids at Work*
Bunting, E. *SOS* Titanic	Ballard, R. *Exploring the* Titanic
	Tanaka, S. *On Board the* Titanic: *What It Was Like When the Great Liner Sank*
Snyder, Z. *The Egypt Game*	Perl, L. *Mummies, Tombs and Treasures*
De Young, C. *A Letter to Mrs. Roosevelt*	Freedman, R. *Eleanor Roosevelt*
D'Aulaire, I. & E. *Greek Myths*	Fleischman, P. *Dateline: Troy*
Uchida, Y. *Journey to Topaz*	Stanley, J. *I Am An American*
	Houston, J. W., & J. D. *Farewell to Manzanar*
Upper grades	
Rylant, C. *Waiting to Waltz*	Rylant, C. *But I'll be Back Again*
London, J. *Call of the Wild*	Dyer, D. *Jack London: A Biography*
Cushman, K. *Catherine Called Birdy*	Hanawalt, B. *Growing Up in Medieval London: The Experience of Childhood in History*
Paulsen, G. *Hatchet*	Paulsen, G. *Puppies, Dogs and Blue Northers*
	Armstrong, J. *Shipwreck at the Bottom of the World: The Extraordinary True Story of Shackleton and the* Endurance
Avi. *The Fighting Ground*	Murphy, J. *A Young Patriot: The American Revolution as Experienced by One Boy*
Soto, G. *Baseball in April and Other Stories*	Bode, J. *New Kids in Town: Oral Histories of Immigrant Teens.*
Gunther, J. *Death Be Not Proud*	Krementz, J. *How It Feels to Fight for Your Life*
Hunt, I. *No Promises in the Wind*	Meltzer, M. *Brother Can You Spare a Dime?*
Salisbury, G. *Under the Blood Red Sun*	Sullivan, G. *The Day Pearl Harbor Was Bombed: A Photo History of World War II*
Fleischman, P. *Bull Run*	Murphy, J. *A Boy's War*
Paulsen, G. *Nightjohn*	Lester, J. *To Be a Slave*

FIGURE 3.4. (*continued*)

members targeted for arrest make the words of Anne's diary even more personal and meaningful. These powerful visuals lend authenticity to the diary and make the terrible events of the Holocaust vividly real.

Small-Groups/Multiple Books

A third model for using nonfiction is the small-groups/multiple-book model. With this model, students work in small groups to read different books related to a common theme. Alan Trent, for example, used multiple copies of several nonfiction titles to supplement textbook content and enrich his fifth-grade students' study of the Civil War. Students formed groups based on their selection of one of four different books: *The Long Road to Gettysburg* (Murphy, 1992); *A Separate Battle: Women and the Civil War* (Chang, 1991); *A Nation Torn* (Ray, 1990); and *A Boy's War: Confederate and Union Soldiers Talk about the Civil War* (Murphy, 1993). Students read and discussed each title in literature circles (see Chapter 5) over a 2-week period. They then shared the information obtained through creative extensions including projects, dramatic presentations, and debates.

Individual Inquiry

The fourth model for using nonfiction involves having each student select a different book. This might be for voluntary reading during sustained silent reading time or for out-of-school reading. Students also need their own books when doing individual inquiry (see Chapter 6). Individual inquiry is an increasingly popular way to involve students in research by letting them explore issues of personal interest. Through these research projects students investigate topics and collect, analyze, and organize information. They later present this information through a project or report. By using several sources about the same topic, students can examine multiple points of view and evaluate the accuracy of information.

Inquiry projects can combine fiction with nonfiction. In an inquiry project for older students, Joan Kaywell (1994) linked fiction and nonfiction trade books. Her class first generated a list of problems affecting adolescents such as anorexia nervosa, stress, suicide, pregnancy, and sexual abuse. The class narrowed the number of topics to five and formed inquiry groups based on each topic. At this point each student in a group selected and read a different young-adult novel related to the identified problem.

After reading their novels, students used nonfiction materials to conduct research about the problem posed in their novel. Each student located at least one nonfiction source and cited a minimum of 10 facts related to the topic. At this point, students reconvened in their small groups, where they pooled these facts.

They then selected the 25 most pertinent facts to be included in an information sheet about the problem. They discussed source credibility, recency, and relevancy of information as they narrowed down their lists. They then presented this information to the larger group.

SUMMARY

Bringing nonfiction into the classroom need not be difficult; it simply involves having teachers use nonfiction literature with students in many of the ways they already use fiction. Making nonfiction both acceptable and accessible though teacher read-alouds, uninterrupted sustained silent reading (USSR) time, classroom libraries, book displays, book talks, and technology can open up children to the possibilities that the nonfiction genre has to offer. Engaging students in literature study through the various models provides them with opportunities to examine particular nonfiction works in-depth, as well as in relationship to other works of fiction or nonfiction. All of these strategies can motivate children to read to explore topics of interest inside the classroom as well as beyond the classroom walls. They can help students realize that the worlds of the past, present, and future can be explored through nonfiction as well as fiction.

REFERENCES

Bauer, C. F. (1993). *New handbook for storytellers*. New York: American Library Association.

Beers, K. (1990). *Choosing not to read: An ethnographic study of seventh-grade alliterate students*. Doctoral dissertation, University of Houston, Houston, TX.

Bishop, N. (2000, October 26). Acceptance speech for *Boston Globe–Horn Book* Award Picture Book Award Winner [Online]. Available: *www.hbook.com/bghb_pb.shtml* [2000, October 26].

Campbell, J. (1996). *National assessment of educational progress 1994 reading report card for the nation and the states*. Washington, DC: National Center for Education Statistics.

Carr, J. (1987). Filling vases, lighting fires. *Horn Book Magazine, 63*, 710–713.

Chambers, A. (1995). *The reading environment: How adults help children enjoy books*. York, ME: Stenhouse.

Duke, N. (1999). *Print environments and experiences offered to first-grade students in very low- and very high-SES school districts*. Unpublished doctoral dissertation, Harvard University, Cambridge, MA.

Gale Research. (1986). *Something about the author*. Detroit, MI: Author.

Giblin, J. C. (2000). More than just the facts: A hundred years of children's nonfiction. *The Horn Book, 76*, 413–424.

Hancock, M. R. (2000). *A celebration of literature and response: Children, books and teachers in K–8 classrooms*. New York: Prentice Hall.

Hoffman, J., Roser, N., & Battle, J. (1993). Reading aloud in classrooms: From the modal to a "model." *Reading Teacher, 46*, 496–503.

Kamil, M., & Lane, D. (1997). *Using information text for first grade reading instruction: Theory and practice.* Presentation at the annual meeting of the National Reading Conference, Scottsdale, AZ.

Kaywell, J. (1994). Using young adult problem fiction and nonfiction to produce critical readers. *The ALAN Review, 21*, 29–32.

Kotch, L., & Zackman, L. (1999). *The author studies handbook: Helping students build powerful connections to literature.* New York: Scholastic.

Moss, B. (1995). Using children's nonfiction trade books as read-alouds. *Language Arts, 72*, 122–126.

Vardell, S., & Copeland, K. A. (1992). Reading aloud and responding to nonfiction: Let's talk about it. In E. B. Freeman & D. G. Person (Eds.), *Using nonfiction tradebooks in the elementary classroom: From ants to zeppelins* (pp. 76–85). Urbana, IL: National Council of Teachers of English.

CHILDREN'S BOOKS

FICTION AND POETRY

Adoff, A. (1977). *Tornado!: Poems.* New York: Delacorte. (2–5)
    These poems address the tornado that struck Xenia, OH, and its aftermath.

Barrett, J. (1982). *Cloudy with a chance of meatballs.* New York: Simon & Schuster. (3–5)
    A humorous story about weather in the land of Chewandswallow.

Conrad, P. (1991). *Pedro's journal: A voyage with Christopher Columbus August 3, 1492–February 14, 1493.* Boyds Mills, PA: Boyds Mills Press. (4–6)
    A fictionalized account of Columbus's voyage, told through the eyes of Pedro, a ship's boy on the *Santa Maria.*

Hesse, K. (1997). *Out of the dust.* New York: Scholastic. (5–6)
    Karen Hesse's lyrical description of the life of a young girl living in the Dust Bowl of the 1930s won the Newbery Medal.

King-Smith, D. (1983). *Babe: The gallant pig.* New York: Crown. (4–6)
    An about-to-be-butchered pig befriends a sheep dog and discovers the secret to success.

Livingston, M. C. (1993). *Abraham Lincoln: A man for all the people—A ballad.* Illustrated by S. Byrd. New York: Holiday House. (4–6)
    A poem detailing the life of the 16th President.

London, J. (1960). *The call of the wild, and other stories.* New York: Dodd, Mead. (6–8)
    This classic work, first published in 1906, focuses on Buck, a beloved pet that is transformed into the fierce leader of an Alaskan dog sled team during the gold rush of the 1890s.

Rylant, C. (1985). *A Blue-Eyed Daisy.* New York: Bradbury. (3–5)
    Describes everyday life for Ellie, an 11–year-old in a West Virginia coal-mining town.

White, E. B. (1952). *Charlotte's web.* Illustrated by G. Williams. New York: Harper. (3–5)
    A classic story of friendship between a spider and a pig.

NONFICTION

Aliki. (1987). *Mummies made in Egypt.* New York: Crowell. (K–3)
>   Detailed explanations of mummification and Egyptian religious beliefs.
Allen, J. (1993). *What is a wall, after all?* Cambridge, MA: Candlewick. (3–5)
>   Rhymed text describes walls, their construction, and their purposes.
Ames, L. J., & Budd, W. (1991). *Draw 50 buildings and other structures.* New York: Econo-Clad Books. (5–6)
>   Ames and Budd provide students with step-by-step instructions for drawing 50 man-made and natural structures from around the world.
Ancona, G. (1989). *The American family farm: A photoessay.* New York: Harcourt Brace. (2–4)
>   Describes farms and the families that own them in Iowa, Massachusetts, and Georgia.
Bartoletti, S. C. (1998). *Growing up in coal country.* Boston: Houghton Mifflin. (5–8)
>   Describes the lives and work of U.S. coal miners in the 19th and early 20th centuries.
Bash, B. (1989). *Desert giant: The world of the Saguaro Cactus.* New York: Little, Brown. (4–6)
>   Explains the life cycle and ecosystem of the giant Saguaro Cactus.
Berger, M. (1995). *Germs make me sick!* New York: HarperCollins. (1–3)
>   Introduces young children to germs in the form of bacteria and viruses.
Brandenburg, J. (1993). *To the top of the world: Adventures with Arctic wolves.* New York: Walker. (4–6)
>   A wildlife photographer describes wolves he filmed in Ellesmere Island in the Northwest Territories of Canada.
Burleigh, R. (1998). *Home run: The story of Babe Ruth.* San Diego, CA: Silver Whistle. (2–5)
>   A poetic description of Babe Ruth before he hits a home run.
Chang, I. (1991). *A separate battle: Women and the Civil War.* New York: Dutton. (5–8)
>   This book describes the contributions of women during the Civil War through personal stories of both the famous and the obscure.
Cherry, L. (1992). *A river ran wild.* San Diego: Harcourt Brace. (2–4)
>   A beautifully illustrated nonfiction picture book that traces the 7,000–year history of the Nashua River in north central Massachusetts and southern New Hampshire.
Cowley, J. (1999). *The Red-Eyed Tree Frog.* Photography by Nic Bishop. New York: Scholastic. (K–2)
>   This stunning photoessay uses close-ups to capture dramatic moments in the life of a Red-Eyed Tree Frog.
Dorros, A. (1987). *Ant cities.* New York: Crowell. (K–2)
>   Simple, basic information about ant behavior for young readers.
D'Aulaire, I., & D'Aulaire, E. (1939). *Abraham Lincoln.* New York: Doubleday. (2–4)
>   An adulatory picture-book biography of Abraham Lincoln.
Dyer, D. (1997). *Jack London: A biography.* New York: Scholastic. (5–6)
>   Dyer captures London's spirit in this biography of his amazing life.

Dyson, J. (1992). *Westward with Columbus: Set sail on the voyage that changed the world*. New York: Scholastic. (5–7)

   This book describes how, in 1990, the author retraced Columbus's 1492/93 voyage aboard a replica of the *Niña*.

Ehlert, L. (1987). *Growing vegetable soup*. San Diego, CA: Harcourt Brace. (K–2)

   Brilliantly colored illustrations depict a father and child's pleasure in watching seeds grow into vegetables that become a delicious soup.

Ehlert, L. (1996). *Under my nose*. Katonah, NY: Owen. (2–4)

   Ehlert gives insights into her childhood and her work as a children's author and illustrator.

Evans, M., & Caras, R. A. (1993). *ASPCA pet care guides for kids: Fish*. New York: DK Publishing. (4–6)

   In this colorful work, children demonstrate aspects of fish care like setting up and cleaning the aquarium.

Frank, A. (1967). *Anne Frank: The diary of a young girl*. New York: Doubleday. (5–6)

   The famous diary of a young Jewish girl living in hiding in Amsterdam during the Holocaust continues to speak to people of all ages.

French, V. (1996). *Spider watching*. Illustrated by A. Wisenfeld. New York: Candlewick. (1–3)

   Helen learns about the fascinating world of spiders.

George, J. C. (1995). *Everglades*. Illustrated by W. Minor. New York: HarperCollins. (3–5)

   Describes the impact of humans on the life forms of this famed watery region of southern Florida.

George, J. C. (2000). *How to talk to your dog*. Illustrated by S. Truesdale. New York: HarperCollins. (K–3)

   This celebration of the human–canine relationship helps children understand how to communicate with their four-legged friends.

Gibbons, G. (1985). *The milk makers*. New York: Atheneum. (1–3)

   Helps young readers understand how milk makes its way from cows to the store.

Gibbons, G. (1989). *Monarch Butterfly*. New York: Holiday House. (1–3)

   Using clear illustrations and engaging text, this book traces the life of the Monarch Butterfly.

Gibbons, G. (1991). *From seed to plant*. New York: Holiday House. (1–3)

   Takes young readers through the metamorphosis of seeds to plants.

Heller, R. (1994). *Chickens aren't the only ones*. New York: Putnam. (K–2)

   Bright illustrations and informative text teach children about animals that lay eggs.

Hirschi, R. (1991). *Summer*. Illustrated by T. D. Mangelsen. New York: Cobblehill. (K–3)

   Baby animals play, learn, and grow in the summer.

Hollander, P., & Hollander, Z. (1990). *Amazing but true sports stories*. New York: Demco. (4–6)

   Brief, exciting stories from every type of sport.

Irvine, J. (1992). *How to make super pop-ups*. New York: Morrow. (3–5)

   A guide to making different kinds of paper pop-ups.

Jenkins, S. (1998). *Hottest, coldest, highest, deepest*. Boston: Houghton Mifflin. (1–3)
    Describes a variety of unique geographical regions including the hottest, coldest, highest, and deepest places on earth.
Jiang, J. L. (1997). *Red scarf girl: A memoir of the Cultural Revolution*. New York: HarperCollins. (5–6)
    This powerful memoir portrays the suffering of a teenager and her family that results from the 1960s Chinese Cultural Revolution.
Kalergis, M. M. (1998). *Seen and heard: Teenagers talk about their lives*. New York: Stewart, Tabori & Chang. (5–6)
    This compilation of interviews with 51 teenagers provides insights into their hopes, dreams, and fears for the future.
King-Smith, D. (1995). *All pigs are beautiful*. Illustrated by A. Jeram. Cambridge, MA: Candlewick. (1–3)
    Information about pigs is presented in a light, entertaining style.
Krull, K. (1993). *Lives of the musicians: Good times, bad times (and what the neighbors thought)*. San Diego, CA: Harcourt Brace. (5–6)
    Short, breezy profiles of great musicians.
Kynaston, N. (2000). *Guinness world records 2000*. New York: Bantam. (4–6)
    The classic compendium of facts and figures about various worlds records.
Lankford, M. D. (1992). *Hopscotch around the world: Nineteen ways to play the game*. Illustrated by K. Milone. New York: Morrow. (3–5)
    Specific directions for playing each of 19 country-specific forms of hopscotch are provided, along with information about each country and culture.
Lasky, K. (1990). *Dinosaur dig*. Photography by C. Knight. New York: Morrow. (3–5)
    An east coast family follows a paleontologist to Montana where he digs for dinosaur bones.
Lauber, P. (1996). *Hurricanes: Earth's mightiest storms*. New York: Scholastic. (5–6)
    Lauber focuses upon the destruction caused by hurricanes and the use of scientific instruments to track their paths.
Lobel, A. (1998). *No pretty pictures: A child of war*. New York: Greenwillow Books. (5–6)
    Children's book illustrator Anita Lobel describes her childhood during the Holocaust.
Macaulay, D., & Ardley, N. (1998). *The new way things work*. New York: Houghton Mifflin. (3–6)
    The authors explain the intricacies of a plethora of machines, including those unique to the digital age.
McKissack, P. (1997). *Can you imagine?* Katonah, NY: Owen. (2–4)
    This noted author reflects upon her childhood memories of listening to stories and other experiences that contributed to her choice of profession.
Monjo, F. N. (1973). *Me and Willie and Pa: The story of Abraham Lincoln and his son Tad*. Illustrated by D. Gorsline. New York: Simon & Schuster. (3–5)
    Abraham Lincoln as seen through the eyes of his young son Tad.
Muhlberger, R. (1993). *What makes a Monet a Monet?* New York: Penguin Putnam. (3–5)
    This book, one in a series about great artists, gives an overview of Claude Monet's life and artistic style.
Murphy, J. (1992). *The long road to Gettysburg*. New York: Clarion. (5–6)

Murphy uses primary-source documents to portray the campaign that led to the horrific battle of Gettysburg, culminating on July 1–4, 1863.

Murphy, J. (1993). *A boy's war: Confederate and Union soldiers talk about the Civil War.* New York: Clarion. (5–6)

Interesting anecdotes and primary source documents tell the stories of the lives of boys who served in the Civil War.

Parker, N. W. (1987). *Bugs.* Illustrated by J. R. Wright. New York: Morrow. (5–6)

Describes characteristics and habits of 16 common insects through couplets, illustrations, and diagrams.

Perl, L., & Lazan, M. B. (1999). *Four perfect pebbles: A story.* New York: Morrow. (5–6)

The harrowing story of a family's courage and triumph during the Holocaust.

Pringle, L. P. (1997). *Nature!: Wild and wonderful.* Katonah, NY: Owen. (2–4)

Pringle shares with young readers his lifelong interest in nature and writing.

Ray, D. (1990). *A nation torn: The story of how the Civil War began.* New York: Lodestar. (5–6)

The author skillfully recounts the conflicts that led to the firing of the first shots at Fort Sumter.

Reeves, N. (1992). *Into the mummy's tomb: The real-life discovery of Tutankhamun's treasures.* Photograph by Nam Froman. New York: Scholastic/Madison. (5–6)

This account of Howard Carter's discovery of the tomb of Tutankhamun is written by the former curator of Egyptian antiquities at the British Museum.

Ride, S., & Okie, S. (1986). *To space and back.* New York: Lothrop, Lee & Shephard. (4–6)

This fascinating book combines interesting information about life in space with extraordinary color photographs.

Rylant, C. (1989). *But I'll be back again.* New York: Orchard. (4–6)

Rylant describes the influences on her life in this moving autobiography.

Scott, E. (1998). *Close encounters: Exploring the universe with the Hubble Space Telescope.* New York: Hyperion. (5–6)

This beautifully photographed work teaches what scientists have learned about the universe from the Hubble Space Telescope.

Simon, S. (1991). *Storms.* New York: Morrow. (3–5)

This renowned science writer for children explains how and why storms occur.

Simon, S. (1997). *Lightning.* New York: Morrow. (3–5)

Brilliant full-color photographs accompany this information on various forms of lightning.

Sohi, M. E. (1993). *Look what I did with a leaf.* New York: Walker. (2–6)

Provides directions and great visuals for using leaves to creating unique creatures.

Stanley, J. (1992). *Children of the Dust Bowl: The true story of the school at Weedpatch Camp.* New York: Crown. (5–6)

The book describes the plight of the Okie children and the determination of Leo Hart, the man who pursued his dream of building them a school.

St. George, J. (2000). *So you want to be president?* Illustrated by D. Small. New York: Penguin Putnam. (4–6)

A creative and witty examination of past and present-day presidents.

Tanaka, S. (1996a). *On board the* Titanic: *What it was like when the great liner sank.* Illustrated by K. Marschall. New York: Hyperion. (4–6)

  The story of the *H. M. S. Titanic* is told from the point of view of Jack Thayer, a wealthy passenger, and Harold McBride, the wireless operator.

Tanaka, S. (1996b). *The disaster of the* Hindenberg: *The last flight of the greatest airship ever built.* New York: Scholastic. (4–6)

  Describes the final voyage of the *Hindenberg* and possible causes for the disaster that doomed the hydrogen-filled dirigible.

van der Rol, R., & Verhoeven, R. (1993). *Anne Frank: Beyond the diary.* New York: Viking. (5–6)

  This visually appealing book extends the information in Anne's diary through the use of primary-source documents and photographs.

Warren, A. (2001). *Surviving Hitler: A boy in the Nazi death camps.* New York: HarperCollins. (5–6)

  Provides an effective introduction to the Holocaust by telling the story of Jack Mandelbaum, a teenage death camp survivor.

Waters, K. (1992). *The story of the White House.* New York: Scholastic. (4–6)

  Portrays rooms within the White House and surveys the history of the structure.

Wick, W. (1997). *A drop of water.* New York: Scholastic (4–6)

  A series of experiments teach youngsters about the properties of water.

Wick, W. (1998). *Walter Wick's optical tricks.* New York: Scholastic. (4–6)

  These optical illusions are designed to trick the eye and beguile the reader.

CHAPTER FOUR

Helping Students Read Nonfiction Strategically

The title of the chapter was confusing because it didn't make sense with what was in the chapter.

The author needs to explain some of the words a little more thoroughly.

Sometimes there are just too many facts.

The captions under the pictures mess me up from the story that is being told. It would help if there were less captions and just the pictures. It helps me when I read the whole book and then go back to the captions.

The author is always going back and forth; that gets confusing after a while.

The author doesn't stick to the topic.

I can read nonfiction, but not at the same speed as fiction.

—Sixth Graders' Comments about Reading Nonfiction

Nonfiction trade books give children the opportunity to read interesting, appealing books on a wide range of topics. As these sixth graders' comments reveal, however, students often find the process of getting meaning from nonfiction trade books challenging. Nonfiction literature often poses comprehension problems for students that fiction does not. Research confirms that students themselves identify nonfiction as more difficult than fiction.

Several factors make nonfiction trade books more difficult than fiction:

First, students may have little prior knowledge of the content found in some nonfiction books. Topics like how a cathedral is built (*Cathedral: The Story of Its Construction*; Macaulay, 1973) or how man learned to measure longitude (*The*

Longitude Prize; Dash, 2000), for example, are likely to be challenging simply because students have had little exposure to the information found in them.

Secondly, nonfiction books contain expository text structures, not the narrative structures more commonly found in fiction. These expository text structures are more varied and complex than narrative ones (as discussed in a later section of this chapter) and are generally unfamiliar to students. According to Englert and Hiebert (1984), few children of any age are aware of the organizational patterns of expository text.

Third, the expository text found in nonfiction trade books often contains unfamiliar technical vocabulary unique to a particular discipline. Terms like "embalmers," "statuary," and "papyrus," for example, found in Perl's (1987) *Mummies, Tombs, and Treasure: Secrets of Ancient Egypt,* pose challenges to readers that are unlike the vocabulary challenges they may face in narrative texts.

Finally, students lack exposure to exposition. Most primary graders seldom read or listen to nonfiction literature. Yet, by the time they reach the fourth grade, they are expected to effectively make the transition from learning to read to reading to learn. Experts often attribute the nationwide decline in fourth-grade standardized reading test scores, or the "fourth-grade slump," to students' inability to read the expository text that predominates on these tests.

Children must develop facility in reading and comprehending the expository text found in nonfiction trade books. Understanding exposition is necessary not only for reading to get new information but for developing multiple perspectives about issues. This type of reading becomes increasingly important as children advance through the grades; by sixth grade the vast majority of school reading demands are expository. This ability becomes even more crucial as children move into adulthood and the world of work, where expository reading associated with task completion predominates (Venezky, 1982).

Content literacy strategies can support students' use of reading and writing for the acquisition of new content in a given discipline (McKenna & Robinson, 1990). In some classrooms, teachers give instruction in these strategies to aid students in comprehending their content area textbooks. Content area strategies can be equally effective in helping students master content found in information trade books. While some strategies will work with biographies as well as information books, most are best suited to the non-narrative text found in information trade books.

What can teachers do to support students as they interact with information trade books? In order to help youngsters strategically approach expository text, teachers need to (1) help youngsters understand how narrative text and expository text differ, (2) help students strategically link their prior knowledge of a topic to new information, (3) help students understand common expository text structures, and (4) develop student understanding of visual displays.

At this point, however, a caution is in order. The purpose of using content literacy strategies with nonfiction literature is to help students read it more effectively. Such strategies should, however, be used judiciously. There is no need for students to complete a strategy lesson for every nonfiction book presented in the classroom. By the same token, there is no need for students to complete a strategy lesson related to every chapter in a longer book. Teachers would do well to heed the words of Carol Otis Hurst (personal communication, 2001) in this regard: "Don't go overboard with activities. Don't use so many that the book lies dead on the floor when you are finished. Sometimes in our zeal to use good literature in the classroom, we succeed only in making the good literature dull."

The first part of the chapter examines what it means to be a strategic reader of informational text. It explains the importance of prior knowledge, metacognition, and learning strategies. The second section of the chapter discusses the differences between fiction and factual literature and describes how shared reading and book previews can help children recognize these differences. The third section addresses the importance of prior knowledge and vocabulary to student understanding of exposition and describes two strategies, anticipation guides and "list–group–label," that can help youngsters link new knowledge to the known. The fourth section of this chapter explains commonly encountered expository text structures and describes strategies that can help children understand these structures. The final section discusses the forms of visual display found in nonfiction and illustrates one way teachers can help students understand these displays.

STRATEGIC READERS OF INFORMATIONAL TEXT

Reading involves constructing meaning through interaction with a text. As readers interact with text they use prior knowledge along with clues from the text to create their own meanings. Effective readers generally use a flexible strategy: they have purposes for reading, and they adjust their purposes depending on the text at hand and the type of reading task.

Strategic readers have a plan for approaching a text. They are active, not passive, readers. They are constantly predicting, anticipating, and reflecting as they read. Researchers have identified three critical components to being a strategic reader: (1) prior knowledge, (2) metacognition, and (3) learning strategies.

Prior knowledge refers to the knowledge that the reader brings to the text. Dozens of studies confirm that the more knowledge of the topic children bring to the text, the better they will understand the material. The more familiarity children have with the vocabulary of a discipline, the better they will comprehend the technical terms authors use to inform readers about that discipline.

Prior knowledge is critical to student understanding; it is more important to comprehension than either IQ or reading achievement level (Johnston & Pearson, 1982).

Secondly, strategic readers possess metacognition, or awareness and understanding of their own learning processes. Metacognitively aware readers know when they are encountering difficulty with a text and take steps to correct the problem. They monitor their own reading: they recognize when their comprehension falters and use "fix-up" strategies to compensate. For example, when effective readers experience comprehension failure they may go back and reread a particular section more carefully. Their experiences with texts have taught them that they can successfully fix up their problems and continue reading.

Finally, effective readers know strategies that enhance their understanding of what they read and employ these strategies before, during, and after reading. Before reading, for example, good readers predict what the text content will be; they have a purpose or goal for reading. During reading, good readers rehearse, infer, summarize, and question as they read. After reading, good readers evaluate, draw conclusions, reflect on their reading, and connect their new learning to their prior knowledge.

Because children have less prior knowledge about content area topics and less experience with texts than adults do, they will often need support as they interact with informational texts. Young readers develop the use of strategies by reading and writing and by being given the support they need to grow in these areas. The strategies described in this section can be used to support students' reading of nonfiction, whether in large groups, small groups, or individually (see Chapter 3).

Teacher modeling is vital to helping students read more strategically. Teachers should model only one strategy at a time using nonfiction literature students are actually reading. Modeling should occur at the point when it is most useful to students and should be followed by practice and application. This modeling, practice, and application should be both interactive and collaborative, occurring within the context of real reading and writing. As children gain greater control over a strategy, teachers should gradually decrease modeling and increase student monitoring of strategies. When students can select and use a strategy automatically, they have mastered it.

UNDERSTANDING FACTUAL TEXTS

The purpose of this section is to provide teachers with information that can help them teach their students about the unique features of expository text. The first part of this section will provide background information about the characteristics of informational text and the differences between expository and narrative texts. The second part will provide detailed information about how to help children understand these characteristics by using the shared reading strategy.

How do children's fiction and nonfiction trade books differ from one another? What characteristics make these two genres different from one another? How is reading a fiction book different from reading a nonfiction book? This section describes the features of the two different types of texts and consider factors that influence the ways students read these texts.

Authors use different "tools" as they construct stories and informational texts. Most of the time, stories are written in a narrative form whereas information books are written in an expository one. Narrative texts and expository texts have different purposes: the main purpose of narrative texts is to tell a story; the main purpose of expository texts is to inform, describe, or report. When authors write a story, they create people and events from their imaginations and craft these into stories using a narrative structure. When authors write information books, they conduct research to gain information on the topic at hand. They organize the information as logically and interestingly as they can using different expository text structures.

Certain literary conventions define each type of text. When creating narrative texts, for example, authors most frequently write in first or third person. They use devices like dialogue, specific settings, and a prose paragraph style. They often use the past tense, arranging the story sequentially, and use descriptive language to create a particular mood or tone.

Authors of factual texts, on the other hand, focus on a particular topic and present that topic at the beginning of the book. They may use various organizational patterns including description, time order, cause–effect, explanation, examples, or a combination of these. They often use present tense and employ technical vocabulary related to the topic.

Physically, storybooks look different from information books. Stories contain paragraphs of prose that continue one after another unless interrupted by illustrations. Longer works of fiction are usually divided into chapters. Illustrations may be used to extend the meaning of the text.

Informational texts, however, may contain boldface headings and italic or boldface vocabulary terms. Visuals including photographs, graphs, cross sections, and timelines help to clarify, explain, or extend text information. Maps not only help to pinpoint locations but can also provide a spatial picture of the progress of an event. Jim Murphy's (1995) *The Great Fire*, for example, contains a series of maps that demonstrate the progress of the Chicago fire at various points in time.

Readers experience different forms of involvement with each type of text.

When reading narrative, readers usually identify with the characters, gaining meaning from the events and interactions of the characters (Rosenblatt, 1985). As readers engage with narrative, the plot holds their attention, compelling them to read on. When reading informational text, readers draw meaning from the information itself. The information itself may hold their attention, but they must also attend to the organization of the information. Because of this, readers tend to read expository text more slowly than they read narrative. Figure 4.1 summarizes the differences between the two kinds of text.

Using Shared Reading with Expository Text

The shared reading strategy can help children of all ages understand how expository text works and how it differs from narrative text. Shared reading is a supportive reading strategy that "scaffolds" student reading of books they may not be ready to read by themselves. It can be particularly useful as a means to introduce non-narrative text. Shared reading can help students of all ages develop in-depth understanding of expository text. It provides a way for teachers to demon-

Narrative	Expository
Story containing characters, plot, theme, and setting	Explains or sets forth information; reports events, actions, and behaviors
Seeks to entertain	Seeks to inform
Uses illustrations to extend text meaning	Uses illustrations to clarify or explain
Written in past tense	Written in present tense
Written in first person	Written in third person
Organized in time sequence	Organized by description, sequence, comparison/contrast, cause–effect, and problem–solution
Uses dialogue	Uses information-giving words
Uses prose paragraph style	Uses headings and titles
Uses descriptions and repeats vocabulary	Uses technical vocabulary that is not repeated
Elaborate writing style	Terse writing style
Concrete concepts related to experiences	Abstract concepts
Reader gets meaning from events and characters	Reader gets meaning from information
Reader suspends disbelief	Reader assumes information is accurate
Plots holds reader's attention	Reader attends to organization of information
Reader may read material quickly	Reader uses flexible, slower reading rate

FIGURE 4.1. Comparisons of narrative text and expository text.

strate how this type of text works and how it differs from narrative. Demonstrations and discussions of the features found in these two types of text are essential for children of all ages. These demonstrations and discussions can develop children's metacognitive awareness of the characteristics of the two text types and add to their prior knowledge about the nature and purposes of informational text.

Bea Rebenack, for example, uses shared reading to teach her third graders the characteristics of informational text. She uses *The Big Book of Animal Records* (Drew, 1989), an information book, to increase student understanding of nonfiction. First she reads the book aloud to her students. Then she goes through it again, pointing out its organizational structure. After that she demonstrates and explains how children can use locational devices like tables of contents, indexes, glossaries, and headings to help them locate specific information. Finally, she points out visual information, including charts, graphs, maps, diagrams, and timelines. As children increase their level of comfort with this type of text, she uses the following questions (adapted from Green, 1992) before, during, and after reading, as a guide for instruction.

Predictions

What kind of book is this?
How do you know?
What kind of information do you expect to find?
What kind of illustrations do you expect to find?

Reading the text

What do the headings and subheadings tell me?
What parts of the book help me find information?
How is the information organized?
How do I read the diagrams (or maps, graphs, timelines)?

Locational devices

What is the table of contents for? When and how is it used?
What are the page numbers for?
Why are the pages numbered?
What is the index for? When and how do I use it?
Do all information books have contents and indexes? Why? Why not?

Eventually Bea brings in stacks of storybooks and informational titles and involves students in comparing fictional texts with factual ones, encouraging them to note the differences between the two using the following questions (Moss, Leone, & DiPillo, 1997):

Do we read information books the same way as we read stories? Why? Why
  not?
What are some of the differences in the way we read the two text types?
What do information books have that stories do not?
What do storybooks have that information books do not? Why are they dif-
  ferent?

These types of questions can help children of all ages develop the meta-
cognitive awareness so critical to creating strategic readers. By helping children reflect on their own reading processes and behaviors, teachers reinforce
children's understanding of the need to approach expository text differently
from narrative text.

Building on Shared Reading with Book Preview Guides

Book preview guides offer a means of building on shared reading experiences.
They can provide an excellent introduction to nonfiction trade books for students who have limited awareness of the layout and functions of this type of
text. Most appropriate for intermediate- and upper-grade students, book preview guides can orient students to a particular text while heightening student
understanding of expository content and text features in general.

Wanda Green, a sixth-grade teacher, created a book preview guide for *Hurricanes: Earth's Mightiest Storms* (Lauber, 1996), which contains many features
of nonfiction text. She distributed copies of the book to each student, and then
had students complete the book preview in Figure 4.2 in pairs. Not only does
this preview point out typical features like the table of contents and index, but it
also alerts students to visual displays like maps and sidebars.

ACTIVATING PRIOR KNOWLEDGE

As noted earlier, numerous studies have established the critical importance of
prior knowledge to student understanding of text. Nothing is of more importance to students' understanding of text than the knowledge they already have
about a topic. This knowledge serves as the foundation for all future learning
and provides the "hooks" on which students can hang their new learning about
a topic. This section describes three different strategies for activating prior
knowledge: K-W-L, anticipation guides, and list group label.

Schema is a word used to describe how people organize and store the information in their heads that constitutes their prior knowledge; schemata are complex networks of information that people use to make sense of new situations,
learning, or events. Children as well as adults possess these networks of infor-

1. How many chapters are in this book? *p. 5*

2. What chapter do you think will tell how a hurricane is formed? "The Making of a Hurricane"

3. What pages contain the index? *pp. 62–63*

4. Why are some page numbers italicized in the index? *They indicate pages with photos.*

5. Using the index answer the following question:
    What pages will tell you how to prepare for a hurricane? *pp. 7, 38, 59–60*
    What page will give you information about Hurricane Edna? *p. 50*
    What pages will tell you about a hurricane that hit Cape Hatteras? *pp. 8, 22–23*

6. Look at the two maps comparing South Florida around 1871 with South Florida today on p. 45. Using the map legend to help you, identify some of the changes in the plant life in the area that have occurred over the past 30 years.
    a. *Today the coastal marshes and mangrove swamps are found mainly in the southern end of Florida, whereas they used to extend up to Miami on the eastern coast.*
    b. *The Everglades region of sawgrass and tree islands has shrunk to only a fraction of its size today compared to what it was in 1871.*
    c. *There are more agricultural lands and urban areas in South Florida today there were than in 1871.*

7. What is the purpose of the blue sidebar on p. 59?
    To provide additional information on topics related to the text, like telling people what to do if a hurricane strikes.

8. Where can you find books for further reading on hurricanes? *p. 63*

FIGURE 4.2. Book preview guide for *Hurricanes: Earth's Mightiest Storms* (Lauber, 1996b).

mation. However, children may have less well-developed schemata for different topics because they have fewer experiences than adults.

All too often, too, children lack awareness of the knowledge that they already have about a topic. Without support from their teachers, some youngsters may not realize how much they know about a given subject. Through the use of prereading strategies, teachers can activate the knowledge children already have about a topic. These strategies can build prior knowledge, stimulate curiosity, help students anticipate text content, and allow time for text preview. They can also provide exposure to unfamiliar technical vocabulary that will be found in the text. Prereading strategies "prime the pump" for students; they help them anticipate and mentally prepare for what they will read. A number of prereading strategies can help to achieve these goals; as discussed in the next subsection.

Strategy Lessons for Activating Prior Knowledge

K-W-L (Ogle, 1986) is an excellent prereading strategy that not only helps students activate their prior knowledge about a topic but also helps them actively and purposefully search for information as they read. During the prereading phase, K-W-L helps students identify what they *know* about a topic and what they *want* to learn about it; after reading, students have the opportunity to determine what they have *learned* about the topic.

As part of a summer workshop on using nonfiction, first-grade teacher Kim Rawson created a lesson based on *This Is the Way We Go to School* (Baer, 1992). Before reading this book, she asked students how they usually get to school. She listed responses to this question on the board, and students then considered how children in other places might get to school. To enhance this discussion the teacher used maps and photographs illustrating different geographic and climatic regions. The children hypothesized about how children in these regions might get to school; names of countries and/or regions and possible modes of travel for each were charted on the board.

Children worked in cooperative learning teams to complete a K-W-L chart. They wrote or drew what they already knew about the ways people get to school, using original examples or those prompted through the class discussion. They recorded these in the K, or "know," column of the chart. Students then shared these responses with the entire group. The children then teamed once again to discuss what they "wanted to know" and listed these questions in the W portion of the chart. After they finished reading, the children worked in small groups once again to complete the L, or "what I learned," column of their charts (see Figure 4.3).

K-W-L charts can be used with older students as well. Figure 4.4 illustrates a K-W-L chart created by Judith Hendershot's sixth-grade class as part of their study of *Orphan Train Rider: One Boy's True Story* (Warren, 1998). This biography combines the history of the abandoned orphans who were sent to the West with the story of one orphan train rider, Lee Nailling. Judy's students had little knowledge of this time period or these children's experiences. They used the knowledge they gained from reading Russell Freedman's (1994) *Kids at Work: Lewis Hine and the Crusade Against Child Labor*, however, to help them complete the K portion of the chart. After reading the first two chapters of *Orphan Train Rider*, they completed the W column by identifying questions raised by their reading at that point. After completing their reading of the text they completed the L column of the chart.

K	W	L
Some kids walk to school.	How do kids in Alaska get to school?	They go by copter or skidoo.
Some kids ride their bikes.	Why do some kids ski to school?	They live in the mountains.
Some kids take the bus.	Why do some kids take a horse and buggy?	They are Amish, and their religion says they can't ride in cars.
Some kids' parents drive them to school.		Some kids in Australia go to school by radio.
		Some kids ride a ferry or other boats to school.

FIGURE 4.3. First graders' K-W-L chart for *This Is the Way We Go to School* (Baer, 1992).

K	W	L
Poor orphans had to ride the trains	Why didn't they tell the kids where they were going?	They were afraid the kids would try to go back to the place they came from.
Poor children had to work.	Why weren't kids allowed to have communication with their real parents?	They wanted them to forget about their real parents.
Kids could get hung for stealing back then.	Why did some people treat the kids like slaves?	Some people just took in the orphans so they would do farmwork for them.
	Why didn't some kids get enough food to eat?	Some people held back food as a punishment.

FIGURE 4.4. K-W-L chart for *Orphan Train Rider: One Boy's True Story* (Warren, 1998).

Anticipation guides (called prediction guides by Herber, 1978) are another effective prereading strategy for use with either biographies or informational texts at all levels. Anticipation guides activate students' knowledge about a topic before reading, and they also serve as guides for subsequent reading. They ask students to react to statements that focus their attention on the topic to be learned. In this way, students' activate their prior knowledge by considering carefully worded statements designed to arouse their curiosity.

Anticipation guides are especially useful with science-related content, as the example in Figure 4.5 illustrates. Many children have misconceptions about science-related information. Anticipation guides can help children confront and later reflect upon their misconceptions.

As part of a summer workshop on using nonfiction in the classroom, Wendy Pelfrey designed a lesson plan for her second graders studying a science unit on Healthy Living. As part of that unit, students read one of their first nonfiction titles, *Germs Make Me Sick!* (Berger, 1995), from the "Let's Read and Find Out" series. Through engaging text and cartoon-like illustrations, this simple book explains how bacteria and viruses cause infections and how the body fights back.

Wendy introduced the children to the book with a brief discussion of the meaning of the term *germs*. After this, she put students in pairs. They then worked together to complete an anticipation guide similar to that in Figure 4.5.

We are going to read a book called *Germs Make Me Sick!* about a boy who is not feeling well and has to go to bed. The book tells how the germs made him sick and how he got well.

Directions: With your partner, read the list below. If you think the sentence is true, circle *Yes*. If it is not true, circle *No*. Be ready to explain why you marked your answer the way you did.

Yes   No   1. Germs are only found on your hands.

Yes   No   2. There are millions of bacteria in your body.

Yes   No   3. You can get germs from a friend who coughs or sneezes.

Yes   No   4. Wash your hands with soap and warm water to get rid of germs.

Yes   No   5. Your body can't fight germs.

Yes   No   6. Bacteria in your body will make you feel better.

FIGURE 4.5. Anticipation guide for *Germs Make Me Sick!* (Berger, 1995a).

After students completed their guides, they reviewed their answers as a group. She asked children to explain why they made the choices they did. After reading the book, they could change their answers based on their new information. At this point, children explained why they changed their answers and identified the place in the book where they got their new information.

Anticipation guides require preparation on the part of the teacher. Here are suggested steps in creating and using anticipation guides:

1. Analyze the text to identify key ideas and information.
2. Anticipate ideas from the text that students may have misconceptions about.
3. Create four to seven written statements.
4. Develop directions for the activity.
5. Have students work on the guide in pairs or teams after the topic has been briefly introduced.
6. Allow time for small- and large-group discussion of the guide before and after reading.

When using anticipation guides with younger children, teachers often read the items aloud and let them do "thumbs up/thumbs down" as a group response to each statement. Older children can read the items themselves and complete the guides in small groups.

List–Group–Label (Taba, 1967) is a form of brainstorming that helps students make predictions about the vocabulary they will encounter in a particular content. This strategy goes beyond simple brainstorming, however, since students must not simply predict possible vocabulary they will encounter but must also categorize those terms. This strategy is useful for students of all ages and can involve students before, during, and after reading.

Before reading, students *list* words related to the topic addressed in the reading material. Next they can be invited to *group* the words into categories. This can form the basis for a small-group learning activity. After completing this step, the students identify words that can serve as *labels* for each category. At this point, students read the assigned material. During their reading, students can jot down new words that they have learned about the topic. After reading, they add these terms to those identified before their reading.

Shelley Jones, a fourth-grade teacher, involved her struggling readers in reading *Never Kiss an Alligator* (Bare, 1989), which uses a humorous format to describe the behaviors of alligators. She knew that many of her students knew very little about this animal and was concerned that many of the vocabulary terms found in this book would be unfamiliar to many of the students. She decided to use the list–group–label strategy to support her students' reading of this text. Shelley began the lesson by asking the group to brainstorm a list of things they knew about alligators. She said, "Think of any word or words that remind you of the topic 'alligator.' " She then recorded students' responses on the board. Their responses included the following:

strong	eat snakes	lay eggs
sharp teeth	rough skin	mean
long tail	short legs	eat people
live in Florida	can swim	live in swamps

At this point, Shelley wrote four categories on the board: "Where they live," "What they eat," "How they look," and "Behaviors." Students then formed small groups, and in these groups they classified each word from the list on the board into one of the four categories. Each group shared their responses with the larger group and explained their reasons for classifying each word the way they did. Here is a sample of one group's work:

Where they live	What they eat	How they look	Behaviors
live in Florida	people	sharp teeth	can swim
live in swamps	snakes	long tail	mean
		short legs	strong
		rough skin	lay eggs

Finally, students read the text silently. Shelley asked students to form small groups once again. She instructed them to reflect on the new information gained through their reading by adding new words to the categories they had already identified. Students explained their reasons for adding words to the particular categories, and Shelley recorded their answers on the board. The bold-face words and categories in the accompanying chart represent the additional information included by the previously mentioned group. Teachers might extend this activity by having students write summaries of the information they obtained, using each heading as the basis for a different section of the summary.

Where they live	What they eat	How they look	Behaviors	What people use them for	Baby alligators' enemies
live in Florida	people	sharp teeth	swim	**purses**	raccoons
live in swamps	snakes	long tail	mean	**shoes**	skunks
China	**insects**	short legs	strong	**belts**	bobcats
Louisiana	**turtles**	rough skin	lay eggs	**wallets**	snakes
ponds	**frogs**	**eyes on top of their heads**	**stay under-water**		river otters
swimming pools	**birds**	**males are 13 feet long**	**an hour**		

UNDERSTANDING EXPOSITORY TEXT STRUCTURES

Narrative texts have a specific structure that readers encounter over and over again. This structure, or story grammar, includes characters, a setting, a problem (or conflict), a climax, or high point of the action, and a resolution. Expository texts, like narrative, have their own structures. Authors arrange ideas according to particular structure, depending on their purpose. For example, if authors want to describe historical events over a period of time, they typically use a sequential pattern to outline the events in time order. The best children's informational texts typically use this pattern and others like description, comparison–contrast, cause–effect, and problem–solution to organize their writing.

Why point out these patterns to children? Developing understanding of these patterns can help students as they seek to make sense of the expository texts they will encounter as they progress through school. Not only will they encounter exposition in nonfiction trade books, but they will find it in textbooks, references books such as encyclopedias, almanacs, and how-to manuals, as well as in "real-life" materials and on standardized tests.

Research indicates that children and adults understand well-organized text better than poorly organized text (Thorndyke, 1977). As noted earlier, nonfiction trade books often contain more clearly organized text than that found in textbooks. Well-organized text is, however, not enough. Even with well-organized text, readers who lack awareness of text structures recall information less well than those who know about the various expository text structures (McGee, 1982).

First, understanding text patterns helps children recognize how expository text is constructed. It provides them with a map that guides them as they travel through a text. The greater children's awareness of the various expository text structures and organizational patterns, the better they can follow the thread of the author's message. Second, understanding these patterns help children see how ideas within texts are connected to each other. It heightens awareness of the ways authors choose to create links from one sentence or paragraph to the next. Third, research tells us that children who are aware of and understand these patterns comprehend and recall exposition better than those who don't. It tells us that the time it takes to teach students about these patterns is time well spent. The next subsection illustrates the various patterns found in expository texts using selected examples from children's nonfiction trade books.

These expository text structures work on two different levels. In expository books for young children, they may provide the macrostructure, or overall structure, for a particular book. Ruth Heller (1983) in *The Reason for a Flower*, for example, uses a cause–effect macrostructure to describe how flowers come to be. At the microstructure level, or paragraph level, however, authors will make use of many of these structures within a given book, or even within a given chapter.

Information is provided below on commonly encountered expository text structures, which include description, sequence, comparison–contrast, cause–effect and problem–solution (Meyer & Freedle, 1984; Niles, 1974). Following that discussion, examples are provided of teaching strategies designed to help students recognize and comprehend text reflective of these patterns.

Common Text Structures

The five most common expository text structures are described below. Figure 4.6 summarizes these structures, providing descriptions of each, examples of words that signal each one, and graphic organizers appropriate to each.

Description

Description presents a topic and provides details that help readers understand characteristics of a person, place, thing, or idea. No specific signal words are typically associated with description. In *The Perilous Journey of the Donner Party*,

Pattern	Description	Signal words	Graphic organizers
Description	Provides characteristics of a person, place, thing, or idea	None	Semantic map
Sequence	Puts facts, events, or concepts in their order of occurrence	First, second, third, then, next, last, before, after, finally	Series of events chain
Comparison–contrast	Identifies similarities and/or differences in facts, concepts, people, etc.	Different from, same as, alike, similar to, resembles, compared to, unlike, but, yet	Comparison–contrast matrix
Cause–effect	Describes events and their causes	If, so, so that, because of, as a result of, since, in order to, cause, effect	Cause–effect map
Problem–solution	Illustrates development of a problem and solution	Because, cause, since, as a result, so, so that	Problem–solution outline

FIGURE 4.6. Common expository text structures.

Calabro (1999), uses this pattern to describe the special wagon (later known as the Pioneer Palace Car) that James Reed built for his family in preparation for their trip West:

> The palace car probably wasn't bigger than most family wagons, but it was a luxurious home on wheels. Many wagons forced riders to enter in the front, right behind the oxen, or to jump aboard in back. Reed had his builders put doors at the side, with a neat little set of portable steps. There were extensions over the wheels, upon which decking was laid. That expanded the usable space. And there was heat, thanks to a little wood stove with a chimney that poked through the canvas roof. (p. 21)

Sequence

Sequence involves putting facts, events or concepts in their order of occurrence. It is most like time order in narrative, and for this reason it is the easiest expository structure to teach. Sequence is used to provide directions for making or doing something. Signal words like *first, second, third, then, next, last, before, after,* and *finally* indicate the order of events. In this excerpt from *Mummies, Tombs, and Treasure: Secrets of Ancient Egypt,* Lila Perl (1987) uses the signal words *after* and *then* to describe the order in which mummies and objects were buried within the pyramids:

> Starting with the First Dynasty, it became the custom for the kings of Egypt to be buried beneath a structure known as a mastaba. . . . After everything had been carefully placed in the burial chamber, the shaft was filled with closely packed broken stones. Then it was sealed up and the entrance to it from inside the mastaba was cleverly concealed. (pp. 47–48)

Comparison–Contrast

When authors point out similarities and/or differences among facts, concepts, people, and so on they use the comparison–contrast text pattern. Signal words include *same as, alike, similar to, resembles, compared to, different from, unlike, but,* and *yet.* In this paragraph from *Franklin Delano Roosevelt* Russell Freedman (1990) uses the signal words *yet* and *but* to contrast different examples of this contradictory man's behavior.

> Those who knew FDR were fascinated by the mysteries and contradictions of his personality. He could ask Congress to appropriate billions, yet he himself would work patiently on a knot in order to save the string. He delighted in new faces, new ideas, and new projects, but in his personal habits he resisted change, wearing favorite old sweaters with holes in them and living all his life in the house where he was born. (p. 113)

Cause–Effect

The cause–effect structure includes a description of events and their causes. Cause–effect is often signaled by words like *if, so, so that, because of, as a result of, since,* and *in order to,* as well as the words *cause* and *effect.* In *Girls Think of Everything: Stories of Ingenious Inventions by Women,* Caroline Thimmesh (2000) describes the relationship between women's roles in the community and their invention of various everyday items:

> Because of their responsibilities, it appears that women were the first to invent tools and utensils—including the mortar (a heavy bowl) and pestle (a clublike hammer) to prepare food, such as flour, and botanical medicines. They spun cotton together with flax, thereby inventing cloth. And they created the first shelters by designing and constructing huts and wigwams. (p. 5)

This example of a cause–effect relationship, signaled by the words *because of,* indicates the many inventions that resulted from women's societal roles that involved them in feeding, clothing, and even housing their families.

Problem–Solution

This structure shows the development of a problem and its solution. Typical signal words include *because, cause, since, as a result,* and *so that.* In the following excerpt from *Ospreys* (Patent, 1993), the author describes the problems that ospreys create by nesting on power poles. She then goes on to explain how some companies address the problem.

> In some areas ospreys have become pests by nesting on power poles. Their large nests can damage the wires. Or even worse, the birds can touch their wings to the two wires at once, killing themselves and shorting out the power. Some companies solve this problem by putting up spiked poles where the birds can't nest. (p. 53)

STRATEGY LESSONS FOR TEACHING TEXT STRUCTURES

Teaching text structure can be effective at virtually any grade level. It can heighten children's schemata for the different expository structures so that they can begin to anticipate their presence. Research suggests that formal teaching of these structures should occur beginning in third or fourth grade. Less formal instruction, however, can begin at lower grade levels.

Below are introduced text-previewing strategies and graphic organizers designed to sensitize students to the various expository text structures. The first subsection discusses text-previewing strategies that can help students develop awareness of the overall structure of a text, or its macrostructure. Then selected graphic organizers are described, including series-of-events chains, cause–effect maps, and others that can alert students to the structures found within the text.

Text-Previewing Strategies

Text-previewing strategies can often alert children to the overall structure of a book. By pointing out various features of a text, teachers can help students anticipate the structures that the author will use. Teachers can demonstrate to children that examining the table of contents, for example, can often help the reader recognize the path the author will take through the material. The table of contents of *Amazing Snakes* (Parsons, 1990) lists the following topics: the sunbeam snake, the egg eater, the deadly cobra, and the tree boa. These titles signal the readers that the text will use description to inform them about a variety of different snakes. The table of contents of Aliki's (2000) *William Shakespeare and the Globe,* conversely, is arranged in acts, beginning with Act One and ending with Act Five. Obviously, this author plans to relate her information about Shakespeare's life sequentially.

Another way to identify text organization within a short book or a given chapter is through careful examination of text headings. Gail Gibbons's (1988) *Sunken Treasure*, for example, provides large-print headings identifying the topic for each section of this picture book. These include "The Sinking," "The Search," "The Find," "The Recording," "The Salvage," and so on. The headings alert the reader to the information that will be described in each section.

Sometimes graphic aids provide a visual parallel for the various expository text structures. For example, in *Digging Up Dinosaurs* (Aliki, 1988), maps comparing the world of 200 million years ago to today's world visually represent the comparison–contrast structure. A pictorial timeline tracing the discovery of dinosaur bones from 1824 to 1914 illustrates the sequence of these events. *Exploring the* Titanic (Ballard, 1988) contains a labeled diagram illustrating the depth of the water in which the *Titanic* sank. It indicates the deepest a scuba diver has ever gone (437 feet), the depth at which naval submarines dive (1500 feet), and the depth at which the *Titanic* sank (12,460 feet). This diagram makes clear the cause–effect relationship between the sunken ship's location and the need for a manned submarine to recover the wreck.

Teaching Text Structures through Visual Organizers

Three factors are required if teachers are to successfully teach children about text structures. First, teachers must be knowledgeable about each structure.

They must analyze texts in order to develop questions that focus students' understanding of the structure. Second, they must select passages that clearly illustrate each text pattern. Third, they must teach students a strategy that they can actively use while they read, such as completing a visual organizer (McGee & Richgels, 1992).

Visual organizers can help learners understand and retain essential information found in a text. They sensitize students to the structure of a text by providing a visual representation of that structure. As students learn to use and construct visual organizers, they gain control of strategies that can help them identify important information as well as recognize interrelationships among ideas. This section introduces five different visual organizers: a semantic map, a series-of-events chain, a comparison–contrast matrix, a cause–effect map, and a problem–solution outline. Each of these organizers is associated with one of the expository text patterns described earlier. These organizational pattern guides (Herber, 1978) require students to reconstruct text in a visual way through identification of the overarching pattern of a text as well as the relationships among the ideas in the text.

1. Introduce the pattern and explain when authors might use it. Note cue words that signal the pattern. Point out, however, that authors sometimes hint at these patterns rather than using signal words to indicate them directly.
2. Share an example of a paragraph that demonstrates the pattern as well as a graphic organizer. Read the paragraph together. Ask students to identify signal words in the paragraph.
3. Distribute copies of an appropriate graphic organizer. Place a copy of the organizer on the overhead projector. Assist students in completing the organizer as a group.
4. Involve students in analyzing examples of the pattern in trade books (Tompkins, 2000). A list of information books illustrating the five expository structures can be found in Figure 4.7. Children can examine a variety of trade books to identify the structure being studied. Some of these books will clearly signal the pattern through headings or signal words, whereas others do not. Students can diagram the structure using a graphic organizer.
5. Engage students in writing texts reflective of each structure (see Chapter 5).

Semantic Map

Semantic maps provide visual representations of how text information is organized. They effectively illustrate the relationships between ideas. They are partic-

Description

Balestino, P. *The Skeleton Inside You*
Gibbons, G. *Bats*
Gibbons, G. *Nature's Green Umbrella*
Hansen, R., & Bell, R. A. *My First Book of Space*
Parish, P. *Dinosaur Time*
Parsons, A. *Amazing Snakes*
Dorros, A. *Ant Cities*

Sequence

Cole, J. *My Puppy Is Born*
Gibbons, G. *Pirate*
Hampton, W. *Kennedy Assassinated! The World Mourns*
Knowlton, J. *Geography A to Z*
Lasky, K. *Sugaring Time*
Provensen, A. *The Buck Stops Here*
Selsam, M. *How Kittens Grow*

Comparison–Contrast

Gibbons, G. *Fire! Fire!*
Knight, M. B. *Talking Walls*
Markle, S. *Outside and Inside You*
Rowan, J. P. *New True Book of Butterflies and Moths*
Rauzon, M. J. *Horns, Antlers, Fangs and Tusks*
McKissack, P., & McKissack, F. *Christmas in the Big House, Christmas in the Quarters*

Cause–effect

Branley, F. *Flash, Crash, Rumble and Roll*
Branley, F. *What Makes Day and Night?*
Showers, P. *What Happens to a Hamburger?*
Smith, R. *Sea Otter Rescue: The Aftermath of an Oil Spill*
Maestro, G. *How Do Apples Grow?*
Wick, W. *A Drop of Water: A Book of Science and Wonder*

Problem–solution

Cherry, L. A. *A River Ran Wild: An Environmental History*
Cole, J. *Cars and How They Go*
Levine, E. *If You Traveled on the Underground Railroad*
Ancona, G. *Man and Mustang*
Thimmesh, C. *Girls Think of Everything: Stories of Ingenious Inventions by Women*

Combination

Aliki *Digging Up Dinosaurs*
George, J. C. *Everglades*
Cesarani, G. P. Illustrated by Venutra, P. *In Search of Tutankhamen*
Fleischman, P. *Dateline: Troy*
King-Smith, D. *All Pigs are Beautiful*
Rylant, C. *Appalachia: The Voices of Sleeping Birds*

FIGURE 4.7. Trade books representing expository text structures. Adapted from Tompkins (2000).

ularly useful in helping children understand texts that are descriptive in nature. David Dias's third-grade students were about to read Gail Gibbons's (1993) *Spiders* as part of a science unit. He placed a semantic map on the overhead. The center circle of the map contained the word "spiders." He recorded the title of each of the topics found in the book on seven circles radiating from the center circle. These included "appearance," "their bodies," "how they reproduce," "spirderlings," "types of webs," "types of spiders," and "enemies." After reading the text, the class worked as a group to complete the web, filling in descriptive details about each section of the text. Their completed map is found in Figure 4.8.

Series-of-Events Chain

Sequencing is one of the easiest structures for children to grasp because it is found in narrative text as well as expository. Following a text's sequence is necessary to understanding simple trade books arranged in time order but is just as important when older students tackle more sophisticated texts like *The Heart and Blood (How Our Bodies Work)* (Burgess, 1988). Julianne Graffin used an excerpt from this book entitled "How the Heart Works" (p. 12) to create a lesson plan demonstrating sequential text structure for her fifth-grade science students. She began the lesson by asking students to speculate on how blood moves around the body. Students then read a passage explaining this process. She showed students an example of a sequentially organized paragraph using signal words like *first*, *second*, *then*, and *after*. She encouraged students to look for

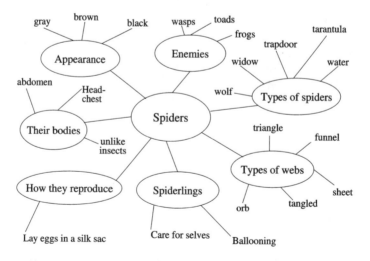

FIGURE 4.8. Semantic map of *Spiders* (Gibbons, 1993).

these signal words to guide them through the passage detailing the progress of the blood through the heart.

At this point Julianne distributed copies of a series of events chain. A series-of-events chain is a visual organizer designed to help students recognize the progression of events in a process. Students read the passage silently and recorded key events in order on the chart (see Figure 4.9 for an example). They then formed teams to compare answers. Each team shared their answers with the entire group. Following this, Julianne divided the class into two large groups. One group carried red sheets of construction paper (to represent oxygenated blood) and the other would carry blue (to represent deoxygenated blood). Eight students formed pairs and acted as the gatekeepers in the valves. Student desks were arranged into the shape of the heart, and stations represented the lungs and other body parts. Students then moved around the room, simulating the flow of blood through the heart and other organs. Finally, students wrote about what they learned in their learning logs.

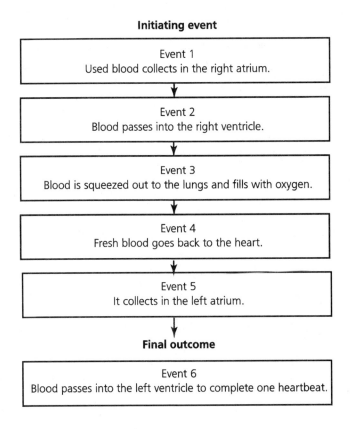

FIGURE 4.9. Series-of-events chain for *The Heart and Blood: How Our Bodies Work* (Burgess, 1988).

Compare–Contrast Matrix

Comparison–contrast is a commonly encountered text structure. A comparison–contrast matrix provides a visual roadmap for helping students organize information to be compared or contrasted. With this type of organizer, students can consider particular attributes that are being compared and consider how they are similar and different.

Janet James's students were studying whales as part of a study of mammals. To clarify student understanding of the differences between whales and fish and introduce her students to the comparison–contrast structure, Janet James's read aloud a section from *A Whale Is Not a Fish—and Other Animal Mixups* (Berger, 1995b). Following this, her students completed a compare–contrast matrix as a large group. Janet recorded student answers on a chart in front of the classroom. Figure 4.10 provides an example of the matrix her students developed based on the various attributes of whales and fish discussed in this section of the book.

Cause–Effect Map

Another text structure that children encounter frequently in science and social studies is cause and effect. Alan Jacobs used the book *Oil Spill!* (Berger, 1994) to provide a simple introduction to the concept of cause and effect to his

Attribute	Whales	Fish
Habitat	Water	Water
Size	Immense	Range from small to large
Fins	Swing up and down	Swing from side to side
Speed	35 mph	45 mph (tuna)
Skin	Smooth	Smooth or scaly
What they breathe	Oxygen from air	Oxygen from water
How they breathe	Blowholes act like nostrils	Take water in through mouth and out through gills
Reproduction	Have babies born live one at a time	Lay many eggs in water that hatch into fish
Body temperature	Warm-blooded body temperature never changes	Cold-blooded body temperature changes with the water temperature

FIGURE 4.10. Comparison–contrast matrix for *A Whale Is Not a Fish—and Other Animal Mix-Ups* (Berger, 1995).

third graders. This easy-to-read title describes the *Exxon Valdez* disaster off of Alaska and explains the causes of oil spills and their effect on the environment.

Alan began the lesson by asking students to write about their favorite use for water. He then asked students to predict what would happen if that water was mixed with oil. He also asked the question "How would it affect the way you use that water?" He then created a "mini oil spill" in a tub in the classroom. Students discussed what happened to the water and why.

At this point Alan read students some easy examples of cause–effect structures. He introduced the idea of signal words and listed them on chart paper. He explained that authors do not always use signal words. He then asked students to listen for signal words as he read a passage aloud. He then used the think-aloud strategy to help children understand the thinking involved in identifying cause and effect.

Next, students read the book to themselves. They worked in groups to complete cause–effect maps (see the sample in Figure 4.11). When they finished they shared and explained their answers using the overhead projector. Students were encouraged to go back to the text to defend their answers. As a follow-up activity, students wrote letters to elected officials expressing their concern about the effect of oil spills on the environment.

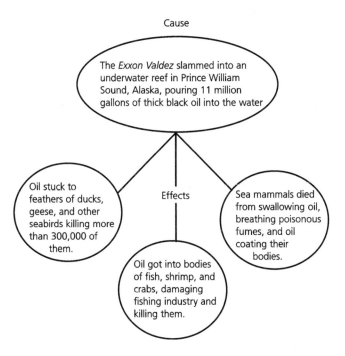

FIGURE 4.11. Cause–effect map for *Oil Spill!* (Berger, 1994).

Problem–Solution Outline

The problem–solution outline focuses attention on passages that present a particular problem and a potential solution or solutions. The problem–solution outline helps students understand who has the problem, what the problem is, and why it was a problem. It then requires them to consider attempted solutions to the problem, outcomes, and the end result.

Sixth-grade science teacher Ed Allen was involved his students in a unit of study on inventors and inventions. As part of that study, his students read *The Wright Brothers: How They Invented the Airplane* (Freedman, 1991). During the reading of Chapter 5, "Back to the Drawing Board," he focused their attention on the problem the brothers encountered when, every so often, their glider would spin out of control when the pilot tried to level off after a turn. After reading the chapter, students worked in small groups to complete the problem–solution outline illustrated in Figure 4.12. The students then discussed the problem and its solution as a large group.

Problem

Who had the problem? *The Wright brothers*
What was the problem? *During one flight in fifty, their glider would spin out of control as the pilot tried to level off after a turn.*
Why was it a problem? *The malfunction could result in a crash.*

Solutions

Attempted Solutions	Outcomes
1. They altered the wingtips.	1. The glider spun out of control on a turn.
2. They made the tail movable like a ship's rudder and connected it to the wings.	2. The glider would make a smooth turn.

End Result
The system of aircraft control the Wright brothers developed is the basis of the system used in the present day. Once this was mastered, they were able to move on to the use of a motor to propel their glider.

FIGURE 4.12. Problem–solution outline for *The Wright Brothers: How They Invented the Airplane* (Freedman, 1991).

Teaching Visual Displays

To fully understand the content of nonfiction trade books, learners need familiarity with the many forms of visual display appearing in today's nonfiction trade books. Made possible through the use of the computer, these visuals explain information in ways that words cannot. They do this with precision and conciseness, condensing large amounts of information into a single pictorial representation.

The ability to understand visual displays is an important skill for today's young readers. With the increasing use of such displays in magazines, newspapers, and other everyday reading material, it is imperative that students develop skill in "reading" these forms of text. Visual displays range from the very simple to the highly abstract. Photographs, diagrams, and maps are generally fairly concrete forms of visual display. Graphs, tables, and charts are usually more complex, providing a higher degree of abstraction.

Diagrams, like most visuals, take a number of forms. *Labeled diagrams* are among the simplest forms of display, and ones that children can readily understand. These types of diagram often identify parts of something, such as the parts of a plant or the parts of an airplane. *Scale diagrams* help children judge the size of an object. By juxtaposing objects, learners can develop perspective about the size of a particular object or natural phenomenon. *Cross sections* allow children to analyze what is beneath the surface of an object. The cross section of the *Titanic* in *On Board the* Titanic: *What It Was Like When the Great Liner Sank* (Tanaka, 1996), for example, allows the viewer to clearly see the different decks on which people in each class stayed. *Flow diagrams* are often used to explain processes or illustrate cause–effect; *timelines* represent a particular type of flow diagram.

Maps help to clarify spatial relationships in nonfiction books. Maps can be simple or complex. They can be used to pinpoint a location or show change over time. Maps can give students the "big picture" about topics of interest. For example, in Shelley Tanaka's (1998) *Graveyards of the Dinosaurs*, a large world map at the back of the book identifies "New Dinosaur Finds Around the World." The map legend identifies recent dinosaur discoveries at 19 locations around the world.

Graphs differ from diagrams in that they are typically more abstract and seek to measure or quantify information. Bar, line, and column graphs are typically taught in mathematics classes, but they are also increasingly common features of nonfiction trade books. *Tables* often show relationships between ideas in a visual way. Tables are usually constructed of columns and rows. Each component of a table is referred to as a cell. The I-chart in Figure 6.3 (see Chapter 6) is an example of a table.

Because they will need to access information from these visuals, teachers should orient students to these forms of display. Students need to recognize the different elements in these graphic aids and understand the relationships between them. They also need to be taught to make inferences and draw conclusions from these visuals. In addition, these maps, graphs, diagrams, and so on can provide models for students to use in displaying information in their own work.

During their reading of Shelley Tanaka's (1996) *On Board the* Titanic: *What It Was Like When the Great Liner Sank*, teacher Jennifer Lewis used a diagram entitled "Who Died and Who Was Saved?" to help her students understand how visual displays complement and extend text information. She constructed a series of statements to which students responded as they analyzed the diagram on p. 44 of the text (see Figure 4.13). Through careful examination of this diagram, students clarified their understanding of the information it contained.

SUMMARY

If students are to successfully read nonfiction literature, they need to become strategic readers. The uses of prior knowledge, metacognition, and learning strategies all contribute to the develop of strategic reading. If students are to be strategic, they need to know some of the basic differences between narrative text and expository text. In addition, teachers need to scaffold their efforts to read

---

Circle the statements about the diagram on p. 44 that you think are true:

1. More first-class passengers died on the *Titanic* than were saved.
2. Almost as many second-class passengers died as were saved.
3. Almost three times as many third-class passengers died as were saved.
4. The majority of people on the *Titanic* who died were crewmembers or in third class.

Answer the following questions. Consider your reading of the text as you do so. You might also wish to refer to the cross section of the ship on pp. 8–9.

1. Why do you think so many third-class passengers and crewmembers died?
2. How do you explain why relatively few first- and second-class passengers died?
3. What might have been done to save larger numbers of third-class passengers and crewmembers?

FIGURE 4.13. Studying a diagram from *On Board the* Titanic (Tanaka, 1996).

strategically by teaching students strategies designed to activate their prior knowledge before reading. Teachers also need to familiarize students with commonly encountered expository text patterns, since this has been shown to improve student understanding of expository text. By teaching strategies that sensitize students to these structures, which include description, sequence, comparison–contrast, cause–effect, and problem–solution, teachers can help youngsters increase their comprehension of nonfiction text. Finally, teachers need to teach students ways to approach the many forms of visual display found in today's nonfiction. In this way students will have deeper understanding of the dense amount of information that is often condensed into a visual display.

REFERENCES

Englert, C. S., & Hiebert, E. (1984). Children's developing awareness of text structures in expository materials. *Journal of Educational Psychology, 76,* 65–74.

Green, P. (1992). *A matter of fact: Using factual texts in the classroom.* Armadale, Victoria, Australia: Curtain.

Herber, H. (1978). Prediction as motivation and an aid to comprehension. In *Teaching reading in content areas* (2nd ed., pp. 173–189). Englewood Cliffs, NJ: Prentice-Hall.

Johnson, P., & Pearson, P. D. (1982). *Prior knowledge, connectivity and the assessment of reading comprehension* (Tech. Rep. No. 245). Champaign: University of Illinois, Center for the Study of Reading.

McGee, L. M. (1982). Awareness of text structure: Effects on children's recall of expository text. *Reading Research Quarterly, 17,* 581–590.

McGee, L. M., & Richgels, D. J. (1992). Text structure strategies. In E. K. Dishner, T. W. Bean, J. E Readence, & D. W. Moore (Eds.), *Reading in the content areas: Improving classroom instruction* (3rd ed., pp. 234–247). Dubuque, IA: Kendall/Hunt.

McKenna, M. C., & Robinson, R. D. (1990). Content literacy: A definition and implications. *Journal of Reading, 34,* 184–186.

Meyer, B. J., & Freedle, R. O. (1984). Effects of discourse type on recall. *American Educational Research Journal, 21,* 121–43.

Moss, B., Leone, S., & DiPillo, M. L. (1997). Exploring the literature of fact: Linking reading and writing through information trade books. *Language Arts, 74,* 418–429.

Niles, O. S. (1974). Organization perceived. In H. L. Herber (Ed.), *Perspectives in reading: Developing study skills in secondary schools* (pp. 57–76). Newark, DE: International Reading Association.

Ogle, D. (1986). K-W-L: A teaching model that develops active reading of expository text. *Reading Teacher, 39,* 563–570.

Piccolo, J. (1987). Expository text structure: Teaching and learning strategies. *Reading Teacher, 40,* 838–847.

Rosenblatt, L. (1985). The transaction theory of the literary work: Implications for research. In C. R. Cooper (Ed.), *Researching response to literature and the teaching of literature: Points of departure* (pp. 33–53). Norwood, NJ: Ablex.

Taba, H. (1967). *Teacher's handbook for elementary social studies*. Reading, MA: Addison-Wesley.

Thorndyke, P. W. (1977). Cognitive structures in comprehension and memory of narrative discourse. *Cognitive Psychology, 9*, 77–110.

Tompkins, G. E. (2000). *Teaching writing: Balancing process and product*. Columbus, OH: Merrill.

Venezky, R. (1982). The origins of the present-day chasm between adult literacy needs and school literacy instruction. *Visible Language, 16*, 113–126.

CHILDREN'S BOOKS

Aliki. (1988). *Digging up dinosaurs*. New York: Crowell. (1–3)

> Simple, clear text explains how dinosaur bones are extracted from the earth and reassembled.

Aliki. (2000). *William Shakespeare and the Globe*. New York: Scholastic. (4–6)

> Aliki's award-winning biography of Shakespeare and description of the Globe Theater feature extraordinary drawings and captions.

Baer, E. (1992). *This is the way we go to school: A book about children around the world*. Illustrated by Steve Bjorkman. New York: Scholastic. (1–3)

> Children around the world use different forms of transportation to get to school.

Ballard, R. (1988). *Exploring the* Titanic. New York: Scholastic. (5–6)

> This is the story of Robert Ballard's amazing discovery of the *Titanic* in the depths of the Atlantic Ocean.

Bare, C. S. (1989). *Never kiss an alligator*. New York: Penguin. (2–4)

> This title provides simple but accurate information about the habits of alligators.

Berger, M. (1994). *Oil spill!* ("Let's read and find out" series). Photography by Paul Mirocha. New York: Harper Trophy. (1–3)

> Berger explains the causes of oil spills, their effect on the environment, and the technologies created to address the damage they cause.

Berger, M. (1995a). *Germs make me sick!* ("Let's read and find out" series). Illustrated by Marilyn Hafner. New York: HarperCollins. (1–3)

> This simple introduction to bacteria and viruses combines informative charts and diagrams with a humorous text and interesting illustrations.

Berger, M. (1995b). *A whale is not a fish—and other animal mix-ups*. Illustrated by Marshall Peck III.New York: Scholastic. (4–6)

> Using two-page spreads, Berger compares frequently confused animals.

Blumberg, R. (1989). *The great American gold rush*. New York: Atheneum. (5–6)

> Blumberg traces the causes and effects of the gold rush in America.

Burgess, J. (1988). *The heart and blood (how our bodies work)*. Englewood Cliffs, NJ: Silver Burdett. (5–6)

> This information book discusses how the heart and circulatory system work, the functions of blood, how doctors help those with blood and heart problems, and ways to keep the cardiovascular system healthy.

Calabro, M. (1999). *The perilous journey of the Donner party*. Boston: Houghton Mifflin. (5–6)

  Details the disastrous journey of the Donner party through the deep snow of the Sierra Nevada.

Dash, J. (2000). *The Longitude Prize*. New York: Frances Foster. (5–6)

  This biography of John Harrison describes his lifelong efforts to develop instruments that could accurately measure longitude at sea.

Drew, D. (1989). *The book of animal records*. Crystal Lake, IL: Rigby. (K–3)

  This big book provides information on animal record holders such as the most deadly snake and the most dangerous fish.

Freedman, R. (1990). *Franklin Delano Roosevelt*. New York: Clarion. (5–6)

  Details the tragedies and triumphs of the life of this wartime President.

Freedman, R. (1991). *The Wright brothers: How they invented the airplane*. New York: Holiday House. (5–6)

  The compelling story of how the Wright brothers' tenacity led to the invention of the airplane.

Freedman, R. (1994). *Kids at work: Lewis Hine and the crusade against child labor*. New York: Clarion. (5–6)

  Freedman uses photographs by Lewis Hines to tell the story of child labor and the efforts of Hine to bring it to an end.

Gibbons, G. (1988). *Sunken treasure*. New York: Crowell. (3–6)

  This picture book describes Mel Fisher's search for the Spanish galleon *Atocha*.

Gibbons, G. (1993). *Spiders*. New York: Holiday House. (1–3)

  Gibbons's picture-book introduction to spiders provides information about spiders and their habits.

Heller, R. (1983). *The reason for a flower*. New York: Stern Sloan. (1–3)

  Uses poetry and vivid illustrations to describe flowers and their parts.

Lauber, P. (1996). *Hurricanes: Earth's mightiest storms*. (5–6)

  Explains hurricanes through clear, relevant text and photographs, diagrams, and maps.

Macaulay, D. (1973). *Cathedral: The story of its construction*. Boston: Houghton Mifflin. (5–6)

  Traces the building of a Gothic cathedral in the year 1252.

Murphy, J. (1995). *The great fire*. New York: Scholastic. (5–6)

  Through photographs, illustrations, and eyewitness accounts, Murphy details the progress of the great Chicago fire in this Newbery Honor Book.

Parsons, A. (1990). *Amazing snakes*. Photography by Jerry Young. New York: Knopf. (2–4)

  Stunning photographs and minimal text introduce several varieties of snakes.

Patent, D. H. (1993). *Ospreys*. New York: Clarion. (4–6)

  The author, a zoologist, describes these unique marine birds and explains how conservation efforts have returned them to their original habitats.

Perl, L. (1987). *Mummies, tombs, and treasure: Secrets of ancient Egypt*. Boston: Houghton Mifflin. (5–6)

  This account of the early Egyptians' way of death is clearly explained and thoroughly researched.

Tanaka, S. (1996). *On board the* Titanic: *What it was like when the great liner sank.* Illustrated by K. Marschall. New York: Hyperion. (4–6)

     Describes the fate of the *Titanic* through story as well as fact.

Tanaka, S. (1998). *Graveyards of the dinosaurs.* New York: Hyperion. (5–6)

     Details the work of those who discover prehistoric creatures around the world.

Thimmesh, C. (2000). *Girls think of everything: Stories of ingenious inventions by women.* Boston: Houghton Mifflin. (4–6)

     Intriguing vignettes of ingenious women and their varied inventions.

Warren, A. (1998). *Orphan train rider: One boy's true story.* Boston: Houghton Mifflin. (5–6)

     The compelling story of the orphan trains and a boy who rode them in the 1920s.

CHAPTER FIVE

Guiding Student Response to Nonfiction

Chapter 5 was a really heart-filling experience. I know if I had gone down with the *Titanic* I would cry. Even today it makes me feel so bad that over 1,000 people died just because some people told them it was an unsinkable ship. I wish someone could have stopped this tragic accident.

I'm reading *Children of the Dust Bowl* and I think it is very sad. The hospitals wouldn't take in a sick child only because he is an Okie.

I have just finished reading *Buried in Ice*. I thought it was awful just awful how all those crewmen and sailors died. Without their families, alone in the freezing Arctic.

What is keeping me interested in this book is that it is based on kids' actual lives. To think that parents don't want their kids. Kids are actually killed because they are hungry [*Orphan Train Rider*; Warren, 1998].

It is terrible reading about how they lived in a place that had a bedroom, small living room, and parents and five kids lived there. I think everyone should have running water and their own toilet, and those immigrants didn't even have that. I saw a picture of a girl in a tub of nasty water. I thought it was sad. They should have what they need [*Immigrant Kids*; Freedman, 1980].

During the past decade, more and more teachers have begun to involve their students in activities designed to encourage response to literature. The increased use of literature in classrooms has heightened teacher interest in helping students engage more deeply with literature through response. Response ac-

117

tivities can take both oral and written forms, and may include discussion, creative dramatics, literature circles, or writing.

Many teachers involve their students in responding to fiction. In recent years, however, children's literature advocates have drawn attention to the possibilities and potential of having students engage in response to nonfiction literature. As Hancock (2000) notes, "Teachers and media specialists are challenged to create a new vision for the informational book by exploring afresh, moving it beyond a traditional research tool, and considering its potential as a valid option for reading and responding" (p. 274.).

As the above examples of sixth graders' journal responses to nonfiction trade books suggest, books from this genre, both biography and information, can elicit meaningful and even profound responses from youngsters. Through engagement with nonfiction books that address their preferences and passions, students build connections between texts and their own lives and often respond emotionally to the content of these books. A necessary prerequisite to response, however, is immersion in nonfiction through the use of strategies like those described in Chapters 3 and 4.

This chapter investigates the many ways teachers can prompt student response to nonfiction. The first section gives an overview of response theory and provides a rationale for using nonfiction response activities in the classroom. The next section discusses oral response activities, including various forms of discussion and drama. The third section continues with classroom-based suggestions for encouraging various forms of written response to nonfiction.

UNDERSTANDING RESPONSE TO LITERATURE

Reader response refers to the way a person reacts to hearing or reading a piece of literature. It describes the unique interaction that occurs between a reader's mind and heart and a particular literary text (Hancock, 2000). Three components define response to literature: the reader, the text, and the context. Reader response is based on the view that reading is not a passive act but a process of continuous interactions between the reader, the text, and the context. Readers seek to construct meaning from the text, and these responses are dynamic, fluid, and varied. Different readers construct different meanings from texts; no two readers are inclined to interpret the same work in the same way.

A student's reaction to a particular literary work involves a complex interplay of factors influenced by (1) who he or she is—his or her life experiences, beliefs, and family background; (2) the particular type of text he or she is reading, whether a poem, a recipe, a romance novel, or a biography; and (3) the particular setting in which the reading event occurs. This can refer to the broad setting, or the sociocultural context, or the specific setting, such as a particular classroom.

Readers, whether they are first graders tackling *Trucks* (Barton, 1998) or adults immersed in the best-selling biography *John Adams* (McCullough, 2001), engage with texts in different ways. For first graders, response may be physical (Hickman, 1983); it may involve pointing at the various types of trucks in the illustrations. For adults, it may involve an emotional response to the passionate love letters of John and Abigail Adams.

Both children's and adults' responses to texts are shaped by many factors: family and cultural background; ages and stages of development; background knowledge; facility with text; and previous experiences with books and reading. In Figure 5.1 sixth graders describe their reasons for selecting particular nonfiction books. The influences on their selections are telling; most are influenced by experiences of other family members, prior knowledge about particular topics, previous exposure to a topic, previous experiences with literature, or a "need to know."

Young readers are likely to have simpler, less analytical responses to literature than older readers do. As indicated earlier, young children often respond physically to text. They may move toward a text to see the pictures or imitate the movement of animals they hear about during a class read-aloud. Their responses are more likely to be literal than interpretive. Older children, conversely, are able to respond to text in more complex ways, using literary terminology and exhibiting the ability to analyze, draw conclusions, and evaluate texts (Hickman, 1983).

Facility with reading also influences response. Unfortunately, struggling readers sometimes produce more limited responses to literature than do more facile readers, simply because the act of reading itself places such great demands on them. Limited understanding of a text may result in responses that are less

---

- I wanted to learn more stuff about our planet.
- I chose this title because my dad was in the war and I wanted to learn more about it.
- I like to learn about sharks and I know a lot about them.
- I watched the movie *Apollo 13* and wanted to find out more about it.
- I chose *Lost Star* because I have heard part of the story of Amelia Earhart in my fifth-grade class.
- I chose *Women of the Old West* because I would like to find out how my ancestors might have lived.
- I chose *Hiding to Survive* because it looks like it is a lot like *Number the Stars*.

FIGURE 5.1. Sixth graders' reasons for selecting nonfiction trade books: Voices of students.

imaginative and more predictable than teachers would like. Capable readers, however, will be more likely to provide deeper, more insightful responses reflective of their more sophisticated understanding of text content. Interestingly, simply *participating* in response activities can help students *at all levels of ability* comprehend text more effectively and develop deeper understanding of it (Hickman, 1983).

Text genre also impacts responses. Readers may have preferences for particular genres that influence their attitudes towards reading. If readers lack interest in particular text genres or topics, their lack of motivation may color their reactions to a text. Their responses are more likely to be halfhearted or abbreviated. Student self-selection of literature may increase the probability that responses are meaningful and genuine.

Literary aspects of a text can also affect response. Use of first person, for example, may heighten learner identification with a character or subject of an autobiography and increase emotional involvement with that person's fate. When the author uses the third person to tell the story, the reader may feel more distanced from events and not as emotionally connected to them.

Finally, the context of the reading event influences response. The sociocultural context, which includes family socioeconomic status, culture, and beliefs, influences student responses in myriad ways. For example, young Mexican Americans may particularly enjoy *Day of the Dead: A Mexican-American Celebration* (Hoyt-Goldsmith, 1994) because it depicts uniquely Mexican foods, customs, and experiences. Their prior knowledge of and interest in the activities described in the story may improve the depth and quality of their responses.

The classroom context also has a critical impact on student response. Students in classrooms where literature and literature-related events abound will be more accustomed to responding to literature. Access to books and literature study are essential to creating a context that supports response. Assigning appropriate tasks for students and helping them identify purposes for reading also contribute to a classroom context that supports response.

The work of Louise Rosenblatt (1978, 1994) has had an enormous influence on teachers' uses of literature during the 1980s and 1990s. Rosenblatt's transactional theory of response maintains that individuals construct their own meanings from text through interactions with it. The meaning of a text does not reside in the text but in the reader. The transaction between a reader and a text occurs as the reader brings his or her experiences to the text and begins to respond to it. This response reaches its highest point when the reader focuses awareness on the personal meanings he or she is shaping. Only then will the reader create his or her unique perspective on the text. As this process occurs, the reader considers a constant stream of thoughts, feelings, connections, and so on (Hancock, 2000).

Aesthetic and Efferent Responses to Literature

Readers assume two roles, or stances, as they read, and a reader's emphasis shifts from one to the other depending on a variety of factors, including the material read and the purposes for reading (Rosenblatt, 1976, 1978) In the efferent stance, the reader is concerned with taking information from the text. If, for example, a sixth-grade girl were reading the fictionalized biography *Mary, Bloody Mary* (Meyer, 1999) in preparation for a quiz over the book, she would read efferently. Her attention would be focused on remembering facts about Mary Tudor's life, including her date of birth, lineage, and changing status as the daughter of Henry VIII. As Spiegel (1998) notes, "When individuals read literature efferently, they are reading to study it, not to experience it" (p. 41).

At the same time, the student might focus attention on the "lived-through" experience and the feelings and images that come and go as she reads. If her parents have recently divorced, for example, she might read this book aesthetically, identifying emotionally with Mary Tudor's suffering as she struggled to come to terms with her father's affair with Anne Boleyn and her parents' subsequent divorce.

Rosenblatt does not view efferent and aesthetic responses as mutually exclusive, but rather envisions a continuum of response with the efferent stance at one end and the aesthetic stance at the other. Nor does she suggest that stance is static; it changes as the reader interacts with the text. We can, in effect, read using both stances: we may read for information at the same time that we feel emotions about what we are reading (Rosenblatt, 1994). This certainly could be the case in the example of the sixth-grade girl described above.

BRINGING RESPONSE INTO THE CLASSROOM

Teachers are critical catalysts in creating classroom contexts where effective literacy learning and response occurs. Effective literacy teachers provide child-centered instruction based on student interests and integrate all areas of the language arts, including reading, writing, speaking, and listening. They create active learning environments that encourage both efferent and affective responses to literature. They act as facilitators of learning, and they encourage student-led activities whenever possible.

Authentic children's literature is the centerpiece of response-centered classrooms. Students read and self-select literature every day. Students and teachers in these classrooms often form a "community of readers." In this community students and teachers support each other in selecting, reflecting on, and responding to literature. Teachers value students' thoughts and feelings about the literature students read, write, and talk about. Multiple viewpoints and interpretations of literature are not only accepted but encouraged. Through this type of scaffolding, teachers help students become aware of the possibilities and power of literature.

In fact, research has found that students grow in several different areas when engaged in response-based activities (Spiegel, 1998):

- They develop ownership of their reading and their responses.
- They make personal connections with literature.
- They gain appreciation for multiple interpretations and tolerance for ambiguity.
- They become more critical readers and attain higher levels of thinking and richer understandings of literature.
- They increase their repertoire of responses to literature.
- They begin to view themselves as successful readers.
- They develop greater awareness of the literary quality of a work.

Many teachers involve students in response to narrative literature. Shared reading experiences (see Chapter 4) and other approaches involve students in reading and responding to literature through writing or discussions. Literature circles are another well-known strategy for promoting response (discussed later in this chapter). Any and all of these strategies can be used to promote response to nonfiction.

Response-centered classrooms can help students grow in their understanding and appreciation of nonfiction just as surely as of fiction. Teachers often assume that nonfiction literature will elicit only efferent responses, but studies have found that readers do respond aesthetically to nonfiction (Vardell & Copeland, 1992). Effective teachers guide students' responses to both biography and information books in ways that encourage both efferent and aesthetic responses. By providing a supportive context and engaging activities that promote both oral and written responses, teachers can extend and deepen students' literary experiences with both nonfiction and fiction.

The rest of this chapter is devoted to examples of instructional strategies that teachers can use to promote responses to nonfiction literature. Strategies for promoting oral responses range from discussion to drama, while written response strategies include journaling, text innovations, and retellings. All of the strategies described are designed to help teachers encourage meaningful student responses, both aesthetic and efferent, to the excellent nonfiction literature available today. Through these experiences, students can make personal connections between these texts and their lives and reflect on what these texts have to teach them. In this way students deepen their involvement with this genre and become more aware of its possibilities.

ORAL RESPONSES TO NONFICTION LITERATURE

Oral language activities provide an important way for learners to express their responses to nonfiction literature. Through both discussion and dramatic response activities students develop speaking and listening skills. These experiences can lay the foundation for a variety of written activities as well.

Responding to Nonfiction through Discussion

Literacy learning is socially constructed. Students do not learn to be literate in isolation but through social interaction with others. By talking about the texts they read, students collaboratively construct meanings around texts. Discussion implies conversation. Conversations about books should include both students and teachers, but no one, including the teacher, should dominate the talk that ensues. Discussion should not involve student recitation of answers to teacher questions; rather, it should actively engage learners in reflecting on texts and revealing their personal interpretations of the author's message.

Discussion also implies sharing; students share their views, refine them, and reflect on them in view of their peers' responses to literary works. In other words, discussions involve an open exchange of ideas, where students respond not just to the teacher but also to one another. Discussion can help students "work out" their questions about a text by comparing their thoughts with one another. It can help them become more effective at social interaction and contribute to their enjoyment of literature. Students who participate in discussions of literature increase the amount and complexity of dialogue about text compared to students who simply recite answers to teacher-led questions (Almasi, 1995). They make discoveries about themselves as learners and grow cognitively, socially, and emotionally. Perhaps most importantly, students who talk about what they read are more likely to engage in reading. Discussion can prompt students to read more widely, expanding both their curiosity and their interests.

Vacca and Vacca (2001) offer suggestions to teachers for creating classroom environments conducive to discussion. These include the following ideas:

- Arranging the classroom so that students can see each other and move easily into small groups
- Encouraging and modeling good listening
- Starting with small discussion groups of two or three students
- Establishing purposes and goals for the discussion
- Keeping discussion focused on the topic at hand

- Showing sensitivity to the needs of second-language learners by simplifying and clarifying language
- Avoiding the squelching of discussion by repeating questions, allowing insufficient "wait time," or interrupting students

Questioning Strategies

As teachers first implement nonfiction literature discussions, whether in large or small groups, they will discover that many of their "tried-and-true" questions about character, plot, and setting will have little relevance to nonfiction. They will need to use different types of questions to engage students in discussions of nonfiction literature. Three different question types can be useful for promoting response to nonfiction: process-centered questions, content-centered questions, or aesthetic questions. These questions can be adapted for use with children of any age. Depending on their goals for a lesson, teachers might focus student attention on one of these three types of questions. Most of the time, however, teachers will want to include questions of all three types. Selected examples of these questions can form the basis for large- or small-group discussions.

Process-centered questions engage students in thinking about *how* they read nonfiction literature. These questions (adapted from Chambers, 1996) can give teachers important insights into students' reading behaviors and meta-cognitive awareness:

1. Why did you select this book?
2. How did you read this book? At one sitting? A little at a time?
3. Was it a fast read for you? A slow one? Why?
4. Which parts of the book were most intriguing to you and why?
5. Which parts of the book failed to hold your interest? Why?
6. What made this text easy or hard to read?
7. Did this book remind you of any other books you have read?
8. How did reading this book compare to reading a fiction book on the same subject? Which would you rather read and why?

Content-centered questions focus student attention on the information found in the text, or *what* students read. These questions will elicit efferent responses and can help teachers assess whether or not students understand text information. Many of these questions go beyond asking for simple factual responses; they require students to think critically about the content of the literature. Examples (adapted from Smith, Hammond, Ogle, & Kutiper, 1995, and Carter & Abrahamson, 1990) include the following questions:

1. What is one interesting fact you learned from this text?
2. Where does this information fit into what we are studying?
3. Develop three questions you could use to evaluate someone's understanding of this text?
4. What organizational pattern did the author use to organize the information?
5. Analyze the title and cover. Do they accurately reflect the content? Why or why not?
6. Think of another title you could give to this text?
7. How useful or important was the information in this text?
8. What else would you like to know about this topic? How could you find out more information about it?
9. How would this book be different if written for an older child? A younger one?
10. How is this book different from an encyclopedia article on the same topic?
11. What kind of research do you think the author had to do to create this book?

Aesthetic questions encourage learners to reflect on their feelings about the nonfiction titles they read. They can help teachers understand students' thoughts, reactions, and preferences regarding the information they have read about in these books. Examples of aesthetic questions (adapted from Grolier Classroom Publishing, 1995) include these:

1. What did you think or feel about what you read in this book?
2. Describe three facts, theories, or incidents you read about that you found interesting.
3. Where do you think the author got the information for writing this book?
4. What fact did you enjoy learning about most?
5. What pictures or illustrations did you find most interesting?
6. What does the information in this book mean to you?
7. Would you like to read more books about this topic? What else would you like to find out about?
8. Compare this book with another you have read on the same topic: How do they differ? How are they alike? Which do you like best?
9. What would you like to tell this author about this book?
10. What would you like to ask the author about this book?

Discussion Webs

Discussion webs (Alvermann, 1991) are a postreading graphic aid that, like the questions presented in the previous section, helps promote critical thinking. Discussion webs encourage students to consider different points of view about an issue. They give learners the opportunity to consider different sides of an issue as part of a discussion. They can help to focus discussions and ensure that students support assertions with relevant information. This organizer presents students with a key question to consider, along with spaces where readers can fill in evidence in support of differing points of view (see Figure 5.2).

The following procedures can guide teachers as they use discussion webs (Alvermann, 1991):

1. Engage students in prereading activities.
2. After students have read, introduce the central question and the discussion web. Students can work in pairs to discuss the points of view defined by the web. They should jot down reasons in the two support columns (see Figure 5.2), listing the same number of reasons in each.
3. At this point, combine partners to create groups of four. Ask each of the four students to present at least one reason to the rest of the group. This ensures that each student participates. Have the new group of four compare their discussion webs and reach a group conclusion. Dissenters may develop a minority report. Each group should get 3 or 4 minutes to present its single best conclusion and any dissenting opinions. Finally, open the discussion up to the entire class.
4. As a follow-up, ask students to use their webs and the ideas presented to write individual answers to the central question.

Julianne Graffin created a lesson for her sixth graders involved in the study of floods and other natural disasters. As a group the class read Patricia Lauber's (1996) *Flood: Wrestling with the Mississippi,* a highly acclaimed photoessay focusing on the 1993 flood of the Mississippi and its aftermath. The section entitled "As the Waters Fell" explores the perennial conflict between the river's propensity to flood and the need to keep it away from where people live and work.

After reading this section, students completed a discussion web that posed the following question: "Should the people whose homes and property were affected by the flood of 1993 relocate to another area?" In planning the lesson, Julianne followed the four-step procedure described earlier, which provided the opportunity for all students to engage in discussion of a topic that evolved logically from the assigned reading. A sample of such a discussion web appears in Figure 5.2.

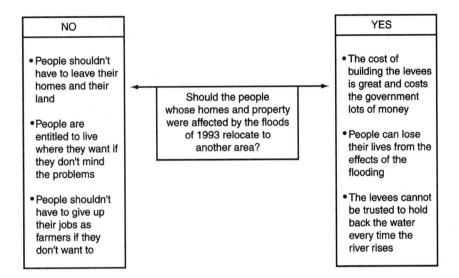

FIGURE 5.2. Discussion web based upon *Flood: Wrestling with the Mississippi* (Lauber, 1996).

Small-Group Literature Study

Grouping five to eight students for the discussion of particular nonfiction books allows students to share their responses to nonfiction. Groups can be formed on the basis of interest in a particular title, student reading abilities, or previous reading experiences (Fountas & Pinnell, 2001). Regardless of the basis on which the group is formed, children should be permitted to choose the books they want to discuss. Prior to engaging in small-group literature study, students need to develop understanding of routines for participation in these groups. Teachers should discuss and model appropriate group behaviors, emphasizing the need for students to allow each student the opportunity to talk, treat each other with consideration, and support their responses with evidence from the text. As groups meet, the teacher acts as a facilitator, observing and sometimes guiding the groups (Fountas & Pinnell, 2001).

Literature circles represent one form of small-group literature study that can prompt student discussion of nonfiction. Literature circles are student-led discussions where students form groups based on common book selection. Literature circles empower students to make decisions about what they will read, how much they will read before the next group meeting, and what aspects of a text they will choose to explore in their group. Literature circles are most effective with students in fourth grade or higher, but they can be adapted for use with younger children (see Hill, Johnson, & Noe, 1995).

Experts describe a variety of formats for literature circles. With some formats, students record responses to their reading in journals and share those responses with a group. These can include responses to specific questions or lists of questions provided by the teacher. Sometimes journal responses are more creative in nature, requiring students to draw, create mind maps, or write poetry in response to their text. Another popular means for sharing involves asking students to select favorite passages from the book and discuss those during the literature circle.

Literature circle discussions of nonfiction books might involve asking students in the group to respond to several of the process-centered, content-centered, or aesthetic questions suggested earlier. Or, the teacher might select two process-centered questions, two content-centered questions, and two aesthetic questions for discussion. For example, small groups of students might discuss the following questions during nonfiction literature circle time:

1. Why did you select this book?
2. Which parts of the book were most intriguing to you and why?
3. Do the title and cover accurately reflect the text content? Why or why not?
4. What else would you like to know about this content?
5. Where do you think the author got the information for writing this book?
6. What does the information in this book mean to you?

Harvey Daniels's (1994) *Literature Circles: Voice and Choice in the Student-Centered Classroom* provides one model for using literature circles. With this model students assume specific roles for discussion sessions and rotate those roles as they work their way through a text. Nonfiction discussion roles, which differ slightly from those used with fiction, include Discussion Director, Passage Master, Vocabulary Enricher, Illustrator, and Connector. The Discussion Director identifies discussion questions based on the literature the group will discuss. The Passage Master identifies sections of the text to be shared with the group in some way, most often through reading aloud. The Vocabulary Enricher identifies words to be discussed and explored, while the Illustrator draws something reflective of the text meaning. This drawing can take the form of a flow chart, sketch, cartoon, or graphic. The Connector draws connections between the text and other literary works or people, places, or events.

Teaching students to conduct their own literature circle discussions is a process that evolves over time. The teacher introduces each discussion role, modeling the responsibilities for each. Students learn, for example, to create effective discussion questions and select interesting and meaningful excerpts for read alouds.

After introducing each role, Judith Hendershot involved her sixth-grade students in forming literature circles around six nonfiction books: *I Am an Ameri-*

can (Stanley, 1996), *Four Perfect Pebbles* (Perl & Lazen, 1996), *Lost Wreck of the Isis* (Ballard, 1990), *Buried in Ice* (Beattie, Geiger, & Tanaka, 1993), *Kids at Work: Lewis Hine and the Crusade Against Child Labor* (Freedman, 1998), and *On Board the* Titanic (Tanaka, 1996). They assumed their assigned roles and rotated roles over time as they completed the books.

One Discussion Director's questions based on *I Am an American* (Stanley, 1996), which describes the internment of a Japanese American family in a concentration camp, reveal his understanding of the ways effective questions can promote personal response to literature:

1. How did you feel when they said the Japanese were refused admittance to movies and cafés?
2. Do you think the Okies *(Children of the Dust Bowl*; Stanley, 1992) were like the Japanese? Why? Why not?
3. Did anything surprise you while reading this chapter?
4. What do you think of this book so far?

Betsy, a Connector, listed the following connections between *I Am an American* (Stanley, 1996) and other people, places, events, and books. Through these responses, she reveals other books she has read, as well as tragic events that she has read about or learned about in school.

1. The persecution of the Jews, like in *I Have Lived a Thousand Years: Growing Up in the Holocaust* (Bitton-Jackson, 1997)
2. The killing of people in Tiananmen Square in China
3. The bombing of Pearl Harbor

After her students had used literature circles for about 6 months, Judith asked them to think about how literature circles had helped them as readers. Here are some of their responses:

"Literature circles give me a chance to hear other people's ideas about a book. Sometimes they say things I'd never think about."
"Listening to the other people gives me more ideas. I pay more attention to the things they think are important."
"I like to compare my thinking with theirs. Sometimes by listening, I get the answers to some of my questions about the book."
"When someone says something interesting, I go back and reread that part. It shines another light on it."
"It lets me find out what others like and don't like about a book."
"I like it because we get to talk more in a small group than in a whole-class discussion."

Creative Dramatics

Through creative dramatics, learners can reshape learning obtained through print into a dramatic form. Dramatic activities encourage changes in student thinking and promote positive experiences with literature. By combining reading with dramatic experiences, students enhance listening and speaking skill as well as language acquisition, vocabulary, and fluency. Dramatic activities encourage learners to listen for cues and learn to use their voices to convey emotion. In addition, they help children develop self-confidence and cooperative learning skills. These activities also offer a natural entry point into the world of writing; students can move from simply dramatizing the words of others to creating their own scripts that can be performed.

For many children, drama can heighten understanding of the often dense and complex expository material found in today's nonfiction. It can enhance student understanding of both technical vocabulary and specific content-related concepts. It can motivate children to explore the content of these books more deeply. Most of all, it can bring abstract information to life, making it concrete and therefore comprehensible, which can be particularly helpful for struggling readers or second-language learners.

Dramatic responses to literature have other benefits as well. Responses of this type require in-depth familiarity with the text to be dramatized. Generally learners need repeated exposure to a text before they can formulate a response to it. This repeated exposure can be particularly beneficial for struggling readers.

Spontaneous drama involves children in active response to literature and allows them to invoke their imaginations. It can be very beneficial for young children, who often find dramatic play extremely motivating. Spontaneous responses to nonfiction can help primary graders mediate nonstory-type texts in ways that make them interesting, memorable, and comprehensible. Putnam (1991) described how kindergartners dramatized a variety of scenes in response to nonfiction read-alouds. They portrayed bears hibernating in their dens, dinosaurs moving through swamps, thunderstorms brewing, volcanoes erupting, and the earth rotating on its axis around the sun. Children not only enjoyed these activities but appeared to retain much of the information presented as a result of the dramatizations.

Students in this classroom engaged in spontaneous dramatics after hearing a read-aloud about honeybees. They simulated the nectar-collecting process, the life cycle of the honeybee, and life inside a beehive. The teacher integrated "bee-related" terms like *petal, nectar, pollen,* and *honeycomb* into these dramatic experiences. On other occasions, the teacher stopped reading at critical points so that students might dramatize particular words or scenes. These experiences helped children connect physical actions with particular words.

Additional forms of dramatic response can sensitize children to expository text organization. For example, students can dramatize the steps in the process of getting milk to the table outlined in Gail Gibbons's (1985) *The Milk Makers*. Students might begin by creating a chain of events chart (see Chapter 4). They could then assume different roles such as the truck driver, the grocery story employee, and the stock clerk, to dramatize the process (Stewig & Buege, 1994).

Older students might enjoy creating pantomimes in response to Aliki's (1983) *A Medieval Feast*. Pantomime requires learners to communicate through movement of their bodies without relying on verbal communication. This particular book contains many scenes that students could pantomime, including depictions of turning boars on the spit, fencing the fields, and sounding the trumpets (Stewig & Burge, 1994). Nicholas Reeves's (1992) *Into the Mummy's Tomb*, for example, could stimulate dramatizations including the building of the pyramids, the burial of Tutankhamen (also called Tutankhamun), the process of mummification, or the purposes of the artifacts found in the tomb.

Tableau is another motivating dramatic play activity. This activity works extremely well with biographies, but could certainly be adapted to other forms of nonfiction. Small groups of students select and read a biography. After they have read the book, teachers distribute a three- or four-sentence scene from the story. The biography *El Chino* (Say, 1990), which describes the life of Billy Wong, the first Chinese matador, includes scenes that could be dramatized in this way. These could include Billy's years as a basketball player, his efforts to become a matador, or his first bullfight. Each person in the group would assume a role, which could involve characters, props, or animals. After practicing, students could create their "frozen moments." The other students in the class could then attempt to identify the scene portrayed.

Readers' theatre involves oral presentation of a text by two or more readers. No props, costumes, or memorization of lines is required. Students must, however, read their parts fluently, with appropriate dramatic flair. Readers' theatre is often used with folktales or narrative text but can be easily adapted to nonfiction.

Information books and biographies with dialogue are easily adapted to this format, but picture books or excerpts from longer books can also be most effective. Informational titles like the Magic School Bus books (e.g., Cole, 1989) or biographies like Jean Fritz's (1974) *Why Don't You Get a Horse, Sam Adams?* are ideal for this purpose. The following guidelines can help teachers adapt nonfiction texts to a readers' theatre script:

1. Choose an interesting section of text containing the desired content.
2. Reproduce the text.
3. Delete lines not critical to the content being emphasized, including those that indicate that a character is speaking.

4. Decide how to divide the parts for the readers. Dialogue can be assigned to appropriate characters. With some texts, it will be necessary to rewrite text as dialogue or with multiple narrators. Changing a third-person point of view to a first-person (I or we) point of view can create effective narration.

5. Add a prologue to introduce the script in storylike fashion. If needed, a postscript can be added to bring closure to the script.

6. Label the readers' parts by placing the speaker's name in the left-hand margin, followed by a colon.

7. When the script is finished, ask others to read it aloud. Listening to the script may make it easier to make appropriate revisions.

8. Give students time to read and rehearse their parts (Young & Vardell, 1993). A sample adaptation of an excerpt from Joan Anderson's (1984) *The First Thanksgiving Feast* appears in Figure 5.3 (Young & Vardell, 1993).

An obvious next step for using readers' theatre is to involve students in selecting books from which they can develop their own readers' theatre scripts. Through this activity, learners develop critical thinking skills, make decisions, work cooperatively, and engage in the process of revision.

Discussion activities that involve questioning, discussion webs, and literature circles can ensure that students engage in meaningful reflection in response to nonfiction trade books. These experiences can heighten student engagement with nonfiction, at the same time they empower students to weigh their own reactions to a text against those of their peers. Dramatic activities like spontaneous drama, tableaux, pantomime, and readers' theatre engage students in transforming the often abstract concepts found in nonfiction literature into concrete experiences. These oral activities, which involve students in speaking and listening in response to nonfiction, provide powerful means to enhance their understanding and appreciation of this genre.

WRITTEN RESPONSES TO NONFICTION

Writing involves thinking on paper. Reading and writing are intertwined processes; they both involve purpose, commitment, working with ideas, rethinking, and so on. Reading and writing can be thought of as two sides of the same coin. A reader works to make sense of text content; a writer works to create a text that makes sense (Vacca & Vacca, 2001). Both reading and writing involve construction of meaning (Tierney & Pearson, 1983).

The value of linking classroom reading and writing experiences has been well established. Combining reading and writing improves achievement. When

SUSANNAH WINSLOW: 'Twas not so pleasant spending sixty-six days aboard that tiny ship, the *Mayflower*. We never knew if we would reach our destination. 'Twas most comforting that God gave us once again the sight of land. How grateful we were when we set foot on solid ground.

ISAAC ALLERTON: I had hoped that the *Mayflower* would take us farther south. But due to tides and currents and the lateness of the year, we found ourselves here. I was most fearful because of tales about the ill feelings the Indians did have for the white man. This "thievish harbor" was said to be heavily populated with Indians. But I and the other members of our search party found no one to fear.

JOHN ALDEN: I was in the search party that stumbled upon a hill of sand under which was a great basket. It was full to the brim with fair kernels of Indian corn. After giving the matter prayerful consideration, we filled a kettle with the kernels and took it aboard the *Mayflower*. We thought we would pay the Indians for their corn when at last we met up with them.

PETER BROWNE: Thanks be to God that we found fields already cleared for planting. Imagine the hours of labor it would have taken to cut down trees, pull out stumps, and carry away rocks. We would not have been able to plant a single seed until late summer, and that would have done us hardly any good. Cleared fields assured us of a goodly harvest.

MYLES STANDISH: I will never forget that cold March day when the Indian named Samoset suddenly appeared in our street. We were taken by surprise, and I had not time to even grab my musket. But he greeted us with, "Welcome, welcome, Englishmen." We invited him to stay the night, and we finally learned why there were cleared fields. The Indians who did live here had died in a plague, which left our Plymouth area empty. Our fear of Indians did diminish that night.

FIGURE 5.3. Excerpt from a readers' theatre adaptation of *The First Thanksgiving Feast* (Anderson, 1984), appearing in Young and Vardell (1993).

learners write about what they have read, engagement with text is enhanced, recall of key ideas improves, and thinking about text deepens (Tierney & Shanahan, 1996). This construction process is more obvious in writing than in reading, since the writer must create a text from scratch.

The Writing Process

The writing process involves five stages: prewriting, drafting, revising, editing, and publication.

The *prewriting stage* involves deciding on a topic, brainstorming ideas, and developing an organizational plan for the writing. Sometimes referred to as the rehearsal stage, this is the point at which the writer thinks out or rehearses what will be written.

The *drafting stage* involves getting thoughts down on paper. At this point the writer creates a rough draft, giving little attention to punctuation, spelling, and other conventions. A paper may go through many drafts before it reaches final form.

The *revision stage* involves rearranging words, sentences, or paragraphs, and adding or deleting text to best convey the author's message. During this stage writers try to clarify their meaning by "reseeing" what they have written. The editing stage involves attention to the conventions of print: spelling, punctuation, and grammatical elements. During the revision stage the emphasis is on meaning; the editing stage emphasizes form.

The *publication stage* involves sharing one's writing, either through actual publication or by reading aloud, sharing with peers, and so on. When students publish their work, in a school newspaper, for example, they go through all the stages in the writing process. For many classroom assignments, however, students will not engage in all of the stages of the process. For example, when doing in-class journal writing or other activities designed to promote reflection, students might only use the prewriting and drafting stages.

The writing process is recursive, not linear. This means that writers do not always move sequentially through the stages; they move back and forth among the stages as they work. Even during the final editing stage, a writer might recognize the need to add information on a topic. At this point, he or she might find it necessary to return to the prewriting stage to brainstorm additional ideas.

The process writing movement has led to an unprecedented increase in emphasis on classroom writing. Unfortunately, however, opportunities for learners to write non-narrative texts or in response to non-narrative materials are often limited. Teachers persist in the perennial story writing assignment, rather than encouraging students to write in other genre. As Daniels (1990) states:

> The writing curriculum experienced by many American students as they go through the grades is essentially: story, story, story, story, story, story, story, story, story, story, story, term paper. This collision with the dreaded term paper assignment is the most dramatic, most worried over, and perhaps most emblematic demonstration of the "expository gap" in the curriculum. A predictable outcome of this unbalanced curriculum is that today's students write much better stories than they write reports, arguments, or essays. The average American school child, from the primary grades upward, can churn out remarkably fluent, elaborated, and engaging chronological narratives of fiction or personal experience. When it comes to task of persuasion, information, explanation, description, or analysis, however, the same child is far less fluent and experienced. (p. 107)

In many classrooms narrative literacy continues to eclipse information literacy at just the time when the ability to read and write exposition is becoming more critical in our society. The rest of this chapter suggests ways teachers can involve learners in writing in response to expository text. From these experiences, students gain deeper understandings of the forms and functions of exposition, a critical component in comprehending non-narrative material.

Extended exposure to nonfiction texts is an important precursor to writing in response to this type of text. Through the forms of engagement described in earlier chapters, students learn how expository texts are created and why and when to use them. Eventually, students develop the ability to read these texts as writers and begin to search for ideas to use in their own writing. In this way, learners become empowered to create their own texts based on their understanding of these models. As children become immersed in nonfiction texts and begin to understand their structures, writing becomes a natural means for extending their experiences with this genre.

Writing in response to literature, whether fiction or nonfiction, allows learners to share their thoughts and feelings about a text. It can help students construct meanings of texts at the same time it improves their writing fluency. Writing in response to nonfiction literature can both involve the evocation of feelings and enhance learning of text content. This "writing to learn" can help students think about what they will be reading or reflect on what has been read. It can improve understanding of difficult concepts, increase retention of information, prompt learners to elaborate on and manipulate ideas, and gain insight into the author's craft (Moss & Leal, 1994; Farest, Miller, & Fewin, 1995).

A variety of written response activities encourage students to think in different ways. Some response activities described in this section focus on helping students respond emotionally to nonfiction; others help them process information or record what they have learned. Some of the activities are formal, whereas others are informal in nature.

Journaling

Many elementary teachers involve students in writing journal responses to fiction; journals can be used for recording responses to information texts as well. While children may focus on their feelings about particular characters or events when journaling about a fictional work, they may respond to the people, places, or things that form the topics of information trade books. Teachers may use prompts including questions, visual stimuli, or situations to focus children's responses to information trade books, or they may invite children to respond to their reading in a more open-ended way.

Response journals allow students to create a written record of their reactions to texts. These responses can be prompted or unprompted. A prompted response might ask a student to respond to questions like these: What did you learn from this text? What would you tell a friend about this book? An un-prompted response might involve asking students to write whatever they want about the book. After hearing the book *Flight* read aloud, Amy, a first grader, wrote about how she thought Lindbergh felt during his flight across the Atlantic. She made the following response: "My hrt is biting. I was skad. I'm happy now. I'm going to sleep now." Her response deftly illustrates her understanding of the book, which discusses Lindbergh's trepidation during the trip and ends with a wonderful illustration of him falling asleep in Paris after his arrival.

Older students might maintain response journals while reading a longer in-formation book. For example, Julia Simmerer's class read *Shh! We're Writing the Constitution* (Fritz, 1987) as part of a fifth-grade thematic study of the American Revolution. At strategic points, students recorded open-ended responses to the book; on other occasions they responded to specific questions posed by the teacher. At one point, the teacher asked students to compare reading this trade book with learning the same information from a textbook. One young critic ex-pressed his preference for the trade book and noted the author's knack for in-cluding fascinating facts that make history human. He stated: "I would rather read the book over a social studies book, because it gives you true facts you wouldn't find in a social studies book. Like the man who ate the mummy finger" (Moss, Leone, & DiPillo, 1997).

Two-column journals let older children not only record but respond to ex-pository information. This type of journal promotes both aesthetic and efferent responses to literature. In two-column journals, children record text-based in-formation on the left side of the page. They can record notes or phrases directly from the text or reword text information in their own words. On the right side they record personal feelings about the information. The example in Figure 5.4

What it said	What I thought
Wilma got polio when she was four. They said she would never walk again.	I didn't know that polio made you crippled.
Wilma couldn't go to school because she couldn't walk.	Today lots of kids who can't walk go to school.
Wilma was going to run in the 1960s Olympics, even though people thought women couldn't run very well.	Lots of women are great runners, like Flo Jo Joyner.
Wilma won three gold medals at the Olympics.	I wondered if other women have won that many medals in one Olympics.

FIGURE 5.4. Two-column journal based on *Wilma Unlimited: How Wilma Rudolph Became the World's Fastest Woman* (Krull, 1996).

illustrates a sample of a two-column journal created in response to *Wilma Unlimited: How Wilma Rudolph Became the World's Fastest Woman* (Krull, 1996).

Creating Text Innovations Using Exposition

A second way to link reading and writing through information trade books is by creating innovations on such texts. This strategy involves reading a pattern book to the class, helping children identify the pattern within the text structure, and having them imitate this pattern in their own writing. By patterning their own work after that of a known book, children's early written efforts at exposition are scaffolded. This allows them to explore new structures for their writing in a secure, nonthreatening way.

The Important Book (Brown, 1949), while not strictly a nonfiction title, can model information writing in many content areas. Each paragraph of this book states an important characteristic, or main idea, about a common object. This trait is followed by supporting details that further enhance the description of the object and concludes with a restatement of the main idea. The teacher read the model to the class, instructing them to listen carefully for the pattern. After identifying the textual frame, "the important thing about _____ is _____," students identified the main idea of pages in their science text and inserted them into the textual frame. Supporting details followed, and the writing concluded with a restatement of the main idea. Two examples follow:

> The important thing about the intertidal zone is that it is a zone of great change. The conditions of the intertidal zone change because of high and low tides. Many different organisms live in the intertidal zone. You can find tide pools there. But the important thing about the intertidal zone is that it is a zone of great change.

> The important thing about animals of the rocky shores is that the animals must withstand the force of strong waves. Barnacles give off glue that cements them to the rocks. The limpet stays down with its strong foot. Mussels attach themselves to rocks by a group of threads. Other animals hide in seaweed that clings to the rocks. But the important thing about animals of the rocky shores is that the animals must withstand the force of strong waves.

The children added illustrations to complement their writing and compiled a class book as a culminating unit activity.

Information ABC books provide another excellent model for text innovations. This text structure is comfortable and easily understood. Such books are easy to compile and offer a format children of all ability levels can easily adapt. Jerry Pallotta's information alphabet books *The Ocean Alphabet Book* (1986) and *The Yucky Reptile Book* (Pallotta, 1989) illustrate the possibilities of this format. After perusing these books, learners can discuss the details included in the books and the research necessary to write them. The teacher can then assign groups of children specific letters of the alphabet. Students can peruse textbooks and other nonfiction resources for key vocabulary and concepts. They can then use the information collected to write pages for a class alphabet book. Samples of their work included the following:

> A is for adaptation. Adaptation is a trait that helps an organism survive in its environment. Animals in the ocean need their adaptations to fight the conditions where they live. For example, the limpet adapts to living on the rocky shore by clamping on to a rock with its strong foot.

> C is for camouflage, an adaptation that helps an animal blend in with its environment. A flounder blends in with the ocean bottom so it cannot be seen by sharks and other dangerous fish. (Moss, Leone, & DiPillo, 1997)

Writing frames provide another form of text innovation. They help learners create texts that reflect the expository text structures described in Chapter 4. These structures include description, sequence, comparison–contrast, cause–effect and problem–solution. Learning the various patterns of expository writing can help students construct meaning from this type of text. Equally important, it can help students learn to write in these forms, which are so common in everyday life. Directions for completing income tax forms, newspaper articles, and many other common forms of print use these patterns.

Writing frames can help scaffold both young and older students' writing reflective of each of these structures. An easy way to help students learn to write using these structures is to first have them read books reflecting the structure to be taught. Chapter 4 provides examples of books that can be used for this purpose.

How a Book Is Made (Aliki, 1986) and *How Is a Crayon Made?* (Charles, 1988), for example, provide powerful models for text that is organized in a sequential pattern. The latter book details the step-by-step process of making crayons. It includes wonderfully vivid facts about a common school supply.

Linda Miller used this text with her fourth graders as a step-by-step model for writing directions. She read it to her class and facilitated a discussion on the important signal words the author used to indicate sequence: *first, next, then, now, finally*, and *so on*. Sally then helped students brainstorm a list of tasks they could write directions for such as making a sandwich, setting a table, folding a paper crane, making a crayon rubbing, or growing a garden. Sally had students work as a group to list the steps in the process of making a sandwich.

She then introduced a blank writing frame that illustrated a sequential pattern (see below). To create this frame she simply used a "fill in the blank" format to help structure students' responses. The group worked together to complete the frame. Students then selected a task they could write directions for. At this point, students jotted down the steps in completing the task. Finally, they completed their own sequence frames. The following example illustrates one fourth grader's directions on how to make a snowman:

Step 1. First *make 3 snowballs and roll them in snow. Make one big, one medium, and one small.*

Step 2. Then *put the biggest snowball on the bottom, the medium in the middle, and the small at the top.*

Step 3. Next *put 2 rocks at the top of the smallest snowball.* Then *put rocks down the middle and put a carrot under the two rocks. Put the hat on top of the smallest snowball.*

Step 4. After that, *put the scarf in between the middle and the top snowball.*

Step 5. Last *put the 2 sticks in the middle of the medium snowball and put the gloves on the sticks.*

Figure 5.5 provides an example of a blank writing frame that illustrates a variety of patterns. The comparison–contrast frame, for example, can scaffold student writing that compares and contrasts people, ideas, objects, or events. Students could, for example, use this writing frame to compare two people described in a collective biography like *Girls Who Rocked the World: Heroines from Sacajawea to Sheryl Swoopes* (Welden, 1999). Teachers can create additional writing frames depicting other text structures such as cause–effect and problem–solution.

Still another type of frame, the response frame, can scaffold students' reactions to nonfiction trade books. Response frames let students reflect on a particular title and record what they have learned from it. These response frames can be used in connection with response journals and might be particularly useful for students who have difficulty in recording journal responses from scratch. An example of a blank response frame appears in Figure 5.6.

Oral and Written Retellings

Written retellings let children play an active role in reconstructing expository text. Students can recast materials they have read into their own form, a process requiring clear understanding of text content. Written retellings provide evidence of *how* as well as *how much* information children retain after reading or listening to a text. They also illustrate children's sensitivity to genre and their ability to organize information. Moreover, they allow children to record their thoughts about the connections between their own lives and the information trade books they are reading (Moss & Leal, 1994).

Description
_____ have many interesting features. First, they have _____,
which allow them to _____. Second, they have _____, which are
_____. Last they have _____, which _____.

Sequence
The first step in making a _____ is to _____. After that you must
_____. Third, you need to _____. Finally, you
_____.

Comparison–Contrast Frame
Both _____ and _____ are similar in many ways. They are similar
because _____. They are also similar because _____. In some
ways, though, _____ and _____ are different. They are different
because _____ is _____. So, _____ and _____
have both similarities and differences.

Cause–Effect Frame
Because of _____, _____ happened. Therefore, _____.
This explains why _____.

Problem–Solution Frame
The problem was that _____. This problem happened because
_____. The problem was finally solved when _____
_____.

FIGURE 5.5. Paragraph writing frames. Adapted from Anderson, T. H., Armbruster, B., and Ostertag, J. (1989).

I learned new things about _____ from reading about them. For
example, I learned that _____. Another fascinating thing I found out was
that _____. I'd still like to know _____. The most interesting
thing I learned was that _____.

FIGURE 5.6. Sample response frame.

Prior to involving children in written retellings, students should have ample experience in oral retellings of nonfiction. These oral retelling experiences can occur after teacher read-alouds of nonfiction or following silent reading. Children can do oral retelling in pairs or even in small groups. Since nonfiction is more difficult to retell than fiction, the use of props may aid children as they retell nonfiction orally. Mary Marvin, for example, involved her second graders in retelling *The Magic School Bus Inside the Human Body* (Cole, 1989). She created cardboard paper doll outlines of a body. As children retold the book, they glued down pieces of felt representing the various organs through which the magic school bus passed.

Written retellings of expository text are best used with children in grades 3 and up, although some younger children may have success with this strategy as well. Brown and Cambourne (1987) recommend these steps for involving children in written retellings:

1. For several days prior to retelling, students should be immersed in study of the topic of the text that will be retold. This can involve shared book experiences, sustained silent reading, and/or brainstorming of information learned.
2. The teacher distributes the expository text to be retold, folded so that only the title shows.
3. Students write a sentence or two indicating what they think the text will be about, predict words that might be found in the selection, and then share their predictions with one another.
4. At this point, the teacher reads the text aloud as students follow along. Students reread the text as many times as they wish, jotting notes or creating visual organizers. Many of the organizers described in Chapter 4 could be used at this point. They then write their retellings.
5. After writing their retellings, students share with one another. They compare their work with one another, discussing similarities and differences in their work. They may also evaluate their retellings using a checklist or rubric.

Using the steps outlined above, Karen McCune, a third grade teacher, involved her children in written retellings of *How Do Plants Get Food?* (Goldish, 1989). Samples of two different students' retellings of this text provide "windows" that illustrate how each child processes the same information differently.

Plants have three parts. They are roots, leaves, and a stem.
   Plants need water and light and air. The water gos to the rorts then it carrese the water to the leaves. On the botum of a leave is a hole so they can breathe. Green plants help make food. If there is not light the plant will die. If

the plants have no water they will die. If the plants have no air they will die. Plants need three things or else they will die. We need plants and plants need us.

This child has clearly integrated the information provided in the text, relating the concepts of light, air, and water to the three parts of the plant: roots, leaves, and stems. In the final sentence, she goes beyond the text to makes the important observation that we need plants and plants need us, but she does not elaborate on this information.

Another child completed the following retelling of the same book:

Roots are like steralls they driek up food and deliver it to the leaves. Seeds make butaful flowers. The only way your gonna get a nice flower is by taking care of it by doing these plant steps: fristh you hafto water it. Then put it by widow and let the air in. Leaes have holes in them to bring in the air and thats all.

This child's retelling is much less sophisticated than that of the first child, but still captures the essence of the text. This child is less aware of the parts of the plant and has not integrated information about these parts and the plant's needs. Even so, this learner clearly recognizes the need of plants for air and water, but does not directly indicate the need for light. He does, however, personalize the information about the plants' need for air and water, noting that "the only way you gonna get a nice flower is by taking care of it by doing these plant steps."

Written retellings can also give teachers valuable information about children's development in understanding expository text. As part of a dissertation study, Leone (1994) examined third and fifth graders' ability to complete written retellings of Gail Gibbons's (1993) *Pirates* after hearing it read aloud. Though children were not given the opportunity to reread the text, one-third of the third graders and two-thirds of the fifth graders studied were able to adequately complete a written retelling of this information text. Consider, for example, this fifth grader's effort:

The pirates are known as the robbers of the high seas because they would get on the ship and rob it and then make the captains and crew walk the plank and then set the ship on fire. They've been roaming the seas as soon as people set sail to travel new worlds and oceans. Stories about pirates came from letters diaries and logs. Once pirates captured Julius Caesar until a ransom was paid. These pirates were so powerful that they banded together to steal goods and cargo. They were very greedy. The pirates ships were smaller and faster than galleons. The ships were also well armed. When pirates attached they fired large cannonballs. They are two types of pirates—buccaneers and privateers. (in Leone, 1994)

This written retelling reveals much about this student's understanding of the text. He clearly comprehends the text organization and sequence, and capably recalls main ideas and details. In addition, he reveals his feelings about the subjects of the text, noting that they were "very greedy."

Analysis of a third-grade retelling of the same text reveals a much less sophisticated understanding of it. The third grader clearly grasps many of the facts included in the book, especially those relating to particular examples of individual pirates. However, he has far less comprehension of the main concepts of the text than does the fifth grader. He exhibits little understanding of the structure of the text and is able only to string a series of facts together. This example illustrates the need for teachers to scaffold children's understanding of the relationships between ideas in such text, whether through discussion, visual organizers, or other strategies.

> I remembered some pretes: Black Beard, Kaptin Kid, Bloody Sword and Captin Hook. I remember that they made there maps relly fancy so people couldn't find there treaser. I remember they saied over lots of seas and that the King and Queen had a guy who helped them, then he went and became a prate and took the king and queens juls. Then the king found him and killed. I remember that a treasur is bared by North Carolina. And I remember if they got cot they would be hung. And that some treasus are still not found yet. (Moss, Leone, & DiPillo, 1997)

SUMMARY

Inviting children to respond to nonfiction books can help develop the problem-solving and critical thinking skills essential to their survival in the Information Age. By involving children in both verbal and written responses to nonfiction trade books, teachers can help children experience richer understanding of this type of text. Through response experiences that require learners' engagement in in-depth examination of this genre, teachers can increase students' familiarity and level of comfort with nonfiction and develop their facility in responding to these text forms. Through these types of response experiences, teachers ensure that today's children are prepared for the literacy demands of the world of tomorrow.

REFERENCES

Almasi, J. F. (1995). The nature of fourth graders' sociocognitive conflicts in peer-led and teacher-led discussion of literature. *Reading Research Quarterly, 30*(3), 314–351.

Alvermann, D. (1991). The discussion web: A graphic aid for learning across the curriculum. *The Reading Teacher, 45*, 92–99.

Brown, H., & Cambourne, B. (1987). *Read and retell*. Portsmouth, NH: Heinemann.

Carter, B., & Abrahamson, R. (1990). *Nonfiction for young adults: From delight to wisdom*. Phoenix, AZ: Oryx Press.

Chambers, A. (1996). *Tell me: Children reading and talking*. York, ME: Stenhouse.

Daniels, H. A. (1990). Developing a sense of audience. In T. Shanahan (Ed.), *Reading and writing together: New perspectives for the classroom* (pp. 99–125). Norwood, MA: Christopher-Gordon.

Daniels, H. (1994). *Literature circles: Voice and choice in the student-centered classroom*. York, ME: Stenhouse.

Farest, C., Miller, C., & Fewin, S. (1995). Lewis and Clark: An incredible journey into the world of information books. *New Advocate, 8*, 271–288.

Fountas, I., & Pinnell, G. S. (2001). *Guiding readers and writers grades 3–6*. Portsmouth, NH: Heinemann.

Grolier Classroom Publishing. (1995). *Using nonfiction effectively in your classroom*. New York: Author.

Hancock, M. (2000). *A celebration of literature and response: Children, books, and teachers in the K-8 classroom*. Upper Saddle River, NJ: Prentice-Hall.

Hickman, J. (1983). Everything considered: Response to literature in an elementary school setting. *Journal of Research and Development in Education, 16*, 8–13.

Hill, B. C., Johnson, N. J., & Noe, K. L. S. (Eds.) (1995). *Literature circles and response*. Norwood, MA: Christopher-Gordon.

Leone, S. (1994). *Using children's written retellings to assess comprehension of three types of text*. Unpublished doctoral dissertation, University of Akron, Akron, OH.

McCullough, D. (2001). *John Adams*. New York: Simon & Schuster.

Moss, B., & Leal, D. (1994, November). *A comparison of children's written responses to science-related information trade books and information storybooks*. Paper presented at the National Reading Conference, San Diego, CA.

Moss, B., Leone, S., & DiPillo, M. L. (1997). Exploring the literature of fact: Linking reading and writing through information trade books. *Language Arts, 74*, 418–429.

Putnam, L. (1991). Dramatizing nonfiction with emerging readers. *Language Arts, 68*, 463–469.

Rosenblatt, L. M. (1976). *Literature as exploration* (3rd ed.). New York: Noble & Noble.

Rosenblatt, L. M. (1978). *The reader, the text, the poem: The transactional theory of the literary work*. Carbondale: Southern Illinois University Press.

Rosenblatt, L. M. (1994). The transactional theory of reading and writing. In R. B. Ruddell, M. R. Ruddell, & H. Singer (Eds.), *Theoretical models and processes of reading* (4th ed., pp..1057–1092). Newark, DE: International Reading Association.

Smith, P., Hammond, D., Ogle, D., & Kutiper, K. (1995, May). *Beyond narration: Developing content literacy*. Paper presented at the International Reading Association, Anaheim, CA.

Spiegel, D. L. (1998). Reader response approaches and the growth of readers. *Language Arts, 76*, 41–48.

Stewig, J. W., & Buege, C. (1994). *Dramatizing literature in whole language classrooms*. New York: Teachers College Press.

Tierney, R., & Pearson, P. D. (1983). Toward a composing model of reading. *Language Arts, 60*, 568–580.

Tierney, R., & Shanahan, T. (1996). Research on the reading–writing relationship. In R. Barr, M. Kamil, P. Mosenthal, & P. D. Pearson (Eds.), *Handbook of reading research* (Vol. 2, pp. 246–274). Mahwah, NJ: Erlbaum.

Vacca, R., & Vacca, J. L. (2001). *Content area reading* (7th ed.) New York: Allyn & Bacon.

Vardell, S. M., & Copeland, K. A. (1992). Reading aloud and responding to nonfiction: Let's talk about it. In E. B. Freeman & D. G. Person (Eds.), *Using nonfiction trade book in the elementary classroom: From ants to zeppelins* (pp. 76–85). Urbana, IL: National Council of Teachers of English.

Young, T. A., & Vardell, S. M. (1993). Weaving reader's theatre and nonfiction into the curriculum. *The Reading Teacher, 46,* 396–406.

CHILDREN'S BOOKS

Aliki. (1983). *A medieval feast*. New York: HarperCollins. (3–6)
>   Describes the celebration of a medieval feast in an English manor house.

Aliki. (1986). *How a book is made*. New York: Harper & Row. (3–6)
>   Details the steps in creating and publishing a book.

Anderson, J. (1984). *The first Thanksgiving feast*. New York: Clarion. (3–5)
>   Depicts the trials of the passengers on the *Mayflower*, and describes their first Thanksgiving.

Ballard, R. (1990). *Lost wreck of the* Isis. New York: Scholastic. (5–6)
>   Ballard explores a Roman shipwreck site in the Mediterranean.

Barton, B. (1998). *Trucks*. New York: HarperCollins. (K–1)
>   Barton looks at delivery trucks, dump trucks, and other varieties of trucks in this simple book with bold illustrations.

Beattie, O., Geiger, J., & Tanaka, S. (1993). *Buried in ice*. New York: Scholastic. (5–6)
>   This book examines the fate of the lost Franklin Expedition of 1845 which sought the Northwest Passage from the Atlantic to the Pacific via Canadian Arctic waterways.

Bitton-Jackson, L. (1997). *I have lived a thousand years: Growing up in the Holocaust*. New York: Simon & Schuster. (5–6)
>   This powerful autobiography describes the chilling details of survival in a concentration camp but maintains a tone of hope.

Brown, M. W. (1949). *The important book*. New York: Harper & Row.
>   The author states an important characteristics and supporting details about common objects in a style that can model information writing in many content areas.

Charles, O. (1988). *How is a crayon made?*. New York: Simon & Schuster. (4–6)
>   Charles traces the making of a crayon from start to finish.

Cole, J. (1989). *The magic school bus inside the human body*. Illustrated by Bruce Degen. New York: Scholastic. (2–4)
>   The author blends fantasy and fact to take children on a journey through the human body.

Freedman, R. (1980). *Immigrant kids*. New York: Dutton. (5–6)
>   Freedman describes the lives of immigrant children at the start of the 20th century.

Freedman, R. (1988). *Indian chiefs*. New York: Holiday House. (5–6)
Details the crises faced by six Indian chiefs in the West as they struggle to maintain their lands and their way of life.

Freedman, R. (1998). *Kids at work: Lewis Hine and the crusade against child labor.* New York: Clarion. (5–6)
Freedman tells the story of child labor in early-20th century America, and Lewis Hine, whose photographs helped lead to its demise.

Fritz, J. (1974). *Why don't you get a horse, Sam Adams?*. New York: Putnam. (3–5)
Fritz employs her breezy style to inform learners about plainspoken rebellion-minded Sam Adams.

Fritz, J. (1987). *Shh! We're writing the Constitution*. New York: Putnam. (4–6)
Fritz provides unexpected details about the men who wrote the U.S. Constitution.

Gibbons, G. (1985). *The Milk Makers*. New York: Macmillan. (1–3)
Illustrates the sequence of events from the cow's production of milk to its processing and delivery to stores.

Gibbons, G. (1993). *Pirates*. Boston: Little, Brown. (3–5)
The author combines facts with fun in this informative look at pirates.

Goldish, M. (1989). *How do plants get food?* Milwaukee, WI: Raintree. (1–3)
Through texts and photographs, explains the ways that plants get food.

Hoyt-Goldsmith, D. (1994). *Day of the Dead: A Mexican-American celebration*. (3–5)
Provides a culturally authentic portrayal of this holiday through a photoessay format.

Krull, K. (1996). *Wilma unlimited: How Wilma Rudolph became the world's fastest woman*. Illustrated by D. Diaz. San Diego, CA: Harcourt Brace. (2–4)
This biography details the life of Wilma Rudolph, who overcame polio to win three gold medals in the 1960 Olympics.

Lauber, P. (1996). *Flood: Wrestling with the Mississippi*. Washington, DC: National Geographic Society. (5–6)
Effectively describes the natural and social history of the Mississippi River through full-color photographs.

Meyer, C. (1999). *Mary, bloody Mary*. San Diego, CA: Harcourt Brace. (5–6)
This fictionalized biography describes the childhood and youth of Mary Tudor, who later reigned as Queen Mary I of England.

Miller, B. M. (1995). *Buffalo gals: Women of the old West*. New York: Lerner. (4–6)
Describes the everyday lives of women on the Western frontier.

Pallotta, J. (1986). *The ocean alphabet book*. Illustrated by F. Mazzolla, Jr. Watertown, MA: Charlesbridge. (2–4)
Describes animals of the North Atlantic from A to Z.

Pallotta, J. (1989). *The yucky reptile book*. Illustrated by R. Masiello. Watertown, MA: Charlesbridge. (2–4)
Describes selected reptiles from A to Z.

Perl, L., & Lazan, M. B. (1996). *Four perfect pebbles: A Holocaust story*. New York: Morrow. (5–6)
Recounts the struggles of the Blumenthal family during the Holocaust.

Reeves, N. (1992). *Into the mummy's tomb: The real-life discovery of Tutankhamun's treasures*. New York: Scholastic/Madison. (5–6)

The author, an Egyptologist with the British museum, details Howard Carter's search for Tutankhamen's tomb through text and photographs, charts, and diagrams.

Say, A. (1990). *El Chino*. Boston: Houghton Mifflin. (2–4)

Tells the amazing life story of the first Chinese American matador.

Selsam, M. E. (1975). *How kittens grow*. New York: Four Winds Press. (1–3)

The birth and development of kittens is described through stunning illustrations.

Stanley, J. (1992). *Children of the Dust Bowl: The true story of the school at Weedpatch Camp*. New York: Crown. (5–6)

Describes the efforts of Leo Hart to build a school for the Okie children.

Stanley, J. (1996). *I am an American: A true story of Japanese internment*. New York: Crown. (5–6)

Recounts the experiences of Shi Nomura as his Japanese American family is interned during World War II.

Tanaka, S. (1996). *On board the* Titanic: *What it was like when the great liner sank*. Illustrated by K. Marschall. New York: Hyperion. (4–6)

The story of the sinking of the *Titanic* is told from the points of view of Jack Thayer, a wealthy 17–year-old passenger, and Harold Bride, a crewmember.

Warren, A. (1998). *Orphan train rider: One boy's true story*. Boston: Houghton Mifflin. (5–6)

The compelling story of the orphan trains and a boy who rode on them in the 1920s.

Welden, A. (1999). *Girls who rocked the world: Heroines from Sacajawea to Sheryl Swoopes*. Illustrated by J. McCann. New York: Stevens. (5–6)

Profiles 35 girls who were younger than 20 years of age when they changed history through their accomplishments.

CHAPTER SIX

Content Area Learning through Nonfiction

The world is filled with so many interesting things, isn't it? Flags of many nations, and the stories behind the designs of those flags; different breeds of dogs and what they were originally bred for; the compound eye of a fly; experiments you can do with ammonia and baking soda; how many stones there are in the Great Pyramid; how a radio works; what parakeets eat; microscopes and the stuff you can see with them; customs of ancient people; why it's faster to get to Japan from New York by going over the Arctic when it looks a lot shorter to go straight across; cameras; evolution. Nonfiction is a true cabinet of wonders.

—JENNIFER ARMSTRONG

In her 1999 acceptance speech for the Orbis Pictus Award for Excellence in Nonfiction, Jennifer Armstrong (2000), author of *Shipwreck at the Bottom of the World,* described how, as a child, nonfiction texts fueled her fascination with facts. As she noted in the quotation above, nonfiction is truly a "cabinet of wonders" containing a treasure trove of answers to the questions that pique the curiosity of today's students. These questions relate to virtually every curricular area and remind us of the powerful presence that nonfiction trade books can assume in the content area classroom.

Nonfiction trade books can teach students the knowledge, values, and skills necessary to understanding every content area. The proliferation of excellent nonfiction for elementary-grade readers makes it more possible than ever for students to pursue topics of personal interest through inquiry. As Sebesta (1989) notes, "Trade books serendipitous to a curricular topic can make the difference between a passive reader who quits when the bells rings and an active, life-long, self motivated reader/learner" (p. 114).

Inquiry is, or should be, an important part of every content area classroom. The pursuit of knowledge and understanding beyond information provided by the textbook is essential if students are to develop the critical thinking skills necessary to academic success in the 21st century. But, today's literacy experts advocate inquiry-based learning experiences for students that are somewhat different from those of the past, when teachers assigned students topics for research. Today's inquiry projects involve students in exploring, finding, and researching the answers to their own questions (Short, Schroder, et al., 1996). In addition, teachers scaffold student efforts by engaging students in minilessons designed to help them before, during, and after conducting their research. In others words, today's teachers emphasize the process of research as well as the product.

Two recent investigations of inquiry learning, both involving intermediate-grade learners, identify some of the difficulties associated with teaching the process. Tower (2000), in an article in *The Reading Teacher*, describes her students' confusion when asked to research information on a particular topic, in spite of her modeling and use of minilessons. Her students' frustration, lack of time on the task, and less than satisfactory products led her to identify ways to make the process more meaningful to her students. Palmer and Stewart (1997) examined middle-grade social studies students' uses of nonfiction trade books to locate information on theme-related research topics. They found that students had trouble reading and identifying important information from these sources, used nonfiction titles like encyclopedias rather than making full use of their contents, and viewed research as a "search-and-destroy" mission in finding facts rather than truly engaging in the process.

Both articles drew two important conclusions about the relationship between successful inquiry learning projects and nonfiction trade books: first, greater teacher awareness of the nonfiction genre and its uses in the classroom could lead to greater student success in conducting research projects; secondly, to effectively engage in inquiry, learners need lots of experience with nonfiction books. The authors recommended a variety of activities designed to increase student exposure to and understanding of nonfiction, many of which were explored in earlier chapters of this text.

The first five chapters of this volume have offered suggestions for using nonfiction trade books that can readily be implemented in content area classrooms. The recommendations for selecting nonfiction books found in Chapter 2 can help content area teachers decide which books will be most effective in their classrooms. The ideas for introducing nonfiction in the classroom, which include using read-alouds, book talks, displays, nonfiction author studies, and so on, can help content area teachers heighten student interest in nonfiction relevant to their content area. The reading strategies proposed in Chapter 4 and the response activities described in Chapter 5 can enrich content area study in myriad ways.

The present chapter specifically examines the role that nonfiction can play in the content area classroom. The first section familiarizes teachers with nonfiction titles that can help teach the content and processes associated with five specific content areas: science, mathematics, social studies, art, and music. The second section more closely examines the critical role that nonfiction plays in student inquiry. It outlines the steps in the inquiry process and recommends ways that teachers can use nonfiction to enhance the process at each step along the way.

NONFICTION TRADE BOOKS FOR CONTENT AREA TEACHING

A key theme of this volume is that nonfiction trade books can support instruction in virtually every subject. Subject area standards in every content area emphasize problem solving over rote memorization of facts and the essential role that higher level thinking abilities play in science, social studies, mathematics, art and music. All too often, content area textbooks fail to promote the achievement of these important goals. They often emphasize facts in isolation, without providing a context for the information presented. As Freeman and Person (1998) note:

> Textbooks do not create a sense of the time they are depicting but seem to teach facts in isolation. Science and mathematics texts do not portray the excitement of great discoveries and the impetus such discoveries give to other scientists, encouraging them to continue their labors. Social studies textbooks do not transmit the flavor of an era or demonstrate the impact of literature, art, science, and architecture upon political ideologies of an era. Nor is the impact of philosophical movements and major events on people and governments adequately presented. (p. 29)

The following subsections briefly discuss recent perspectives on instruction in five content areas and examine ways that nonfiction can support instruction in each of these areas. When pertinent, resources for lists of books related to particular content areas are described. In addition, selected books related to each of the five content areas are listed. Books designated "P" are for the primary grades, roughly grades 1–3; those designated "I" are for intermediate-grade students, approximately grades 3 and 4; those designated "U," or upper, are intended for fifth and sixth graders.

Teaching Science through Nonfiction Trade Books

Recent trends in science instruction advocate helping children learn the sciences in the same ways that scientists do—through observation, inquiry, and investigation. Nonfiction trade books can enhance children's opportunities to engage in all of these scientific behaviors, offering them multiple opportunities to learn about the sciences in the ways scientists do.

Titles like *Surtsey: The Newest Place on Earth* (Lasky, 1992), for example, illustrate the actual work of geologists and volcanologists, as they observe, measure, and classify information concerning a new island being formed by a volcanic eruption off of Iceland. This title provides a model for children to use as they engage in scientific inquiry in their own classrooms. In addition, titles like this one encourage students to think like scientists as they also observe, weigh evidence, and draw conclusions (Freeman & Person, 1998).

Nonfiction trade books related to science have several other advantages that make them an excellent complement to science textbooks. First, they provide multiple points of view surrounding scientific phenomena. In this way they can deepen student understanding of textbook content typically presented from a single point of view. Second, they provide up-to-date information that may not be available in other formats. Nonfiction trade books may address topics not even mentioned in dated textbooks. Laurence Pringle's (1990) *Global Warming*, for example, uses color illustrations, maps, graphs, and compelling text not only to explain the processes surrounding global warming, but also to increase student awareness of its ramifications for the world at large. Finally, science-related nonfiction trade books can promote student inquiry and provide models for student writing. They can help learners understand scientific processes at the same time that they suggest ways for students to share their own scientific learning in writing. The second section of this chapter will provide more information on this area.

A list of "Outstanding Science Trade Books for Children" appears annually in the March issue of *Science and Children*. A book review panel appointed by the National Science Teachers Association in collaboration with the Children's Book Council selects these titles. The major criteria for selection include the following: (1) the presence of substantial science content; (2) clear, accurate, and up-to-date information; (3) careful distinction between facts and theories; (4) no oversimplification or omission of significant facts; and (5) freedom from gender, ethnic, and socioeconomic biases.

The following nonfiction titles have appeared on the "Outstanding Science Trade Books for Children" list. Books are arranged by topic and include science-related biographies and books addressing both life science and physical science. Authors and titles are listed, as are suggested levels (P, primary; I, intermediate; U, upper grades):

BIOGRAPHIES

Snowflake Bentley by Jacqueline Briggs Martin (P)

Liftoff!: An Astronaut's Dream by R. Mike Mullane (I)

Marie Curie: Discoverer of Radium by Margaret Poynter (I)

Elephant Woman: Cynthia Moss Explores the World of Elephants by Laurence
  Pringle (U)

PHYSICAL SCIENCE

What Makes a Shadow? by Clyde Robert Bulla (P)

Comets, Meteors, and Asteroids by Seymour Simon (I)

Lightning by Seymour Simon (I)

Hurricanes: Earth's Mightiest Storms by Patricia Lauber (U)

Zero Gravity by Gloria Skurzynski (I)

Big Bang: The Story of the Universe by Heather Couper and Nigel Henbest
  (U)

LIFE SCIENCE

A Swim through the Sea by Kristen Joy Pratt (P)

Blood by Anna Sandeman (P)

Outside and Inside Birds by Sandra Markle (P, I)

Ancient Ones: The World of the Old-Growth Douglas Fir by Barbara Bash (I)

The Iceman by Don Lessem (I)

The Golden Lion Tamarin Comes Home by George Ancona (I)

Back to the Wild by Dorothy Hinshaw Patent (U)

The Most Beautiful Roof in the World: Exploring the Rainforest Canopy by
  Kathryn Lasky (U)

Teaching Social Studies through Nonfiction Trade Books

The social studies are not a single discipline but combine a number of different
areas including economics, geography, history, sociology, and political science.
The social studies are intended to prepare students for the decision-making
skills they need to function in a democratic society. This means not only preparing students with information about the democratic process but also empower-
ing them to effect social change.

   Through nonfiction literature, learners acquire knowledge of the social
studies—they learn about economics, psychology, etc. However, this content
cannot be presented as discrete subjects; each discipline must be integrated into
a meaningful whole. To truly understand social studies content, students must
understand how the various aspects of this discipline work in concert and develop multiple perspectives about a variety of issues.

Nonfiction titles can promote children's understanding of all categories of social studies knowledge, present multiple perspectives, promote understanding of the past, and (where appropriate) present primary source materials. Today's nonfiction also emphasizes a global perspective, helping students develop greater appreciation for the other cultures represented on our planet. Anno's (1999) *All in a Day*, for example, simultaneously depicts children's activities in eight different parts of the world over a 24-hour period. It effectively illustrates differences in time zones, climates, and other aspects of everyday life across the globe.

A list of "Notable Children's Trade Books in the Field of Social Studies" appears annually in *Social Education* and includes books from all genres. This list is selected by a committee appointed by the National Council for the Social Studies in cooperation with the Children's Book Council. The committee looks for books that (1) emphasize human relations; (2) represent diverse groups; (3) present an original theme; (4) are easily readable and of high literary quality; (5) have a pleasing format; and where appropriate, (6) have illustrations that enrich the text. The following books represent a sampling of the nonfiction titles that have appeared on that social studies list.

BIOGRAPHIES

Uncommon Traveler: Mary Kingsley in Africa by Don Brown (P, I)
Black Whiteness: Admiral Byrd Alone in the Antarctic by Robert Burleigh (I)
Annie Oakley: Legendary Sharpshooter by Jean Flynn (I, U)
Gandhi: Great Soul by John B. Severance (U)

CONTEMPORARY CONCERNS

Mommy Far, Mommy Near: An Adoption Story by Carol A. Peacock (P)
Iqbal Masih and the Crusade Against Child Slavery by Susan Kuklin (I)
Neale S. Godfrey's Ultimate Kids' Money Book by Neale S. Godfrey (U)
The Safe Zone: A Kid's Guide to Personal Safety by Donna Chalet & Francine Russell (U)

GEOGRAPHY, PEOPLE, AND PLACES

A is for the Americas by Cynthia Chin-Lee & Terri de al Pena (P)
Celebrations by Barnabas Kindersley and Anabel Kindersley (P, I)
Easter Island: Giant Stone Statues Tell of a Rich and Tragic Past by Caroline Arnold (I)
The Century that Was: Reflections on the Last 100 Years by James Cross Giblin (Ed.) (U)

HISTORY, LIFE, AND CULTURE IN THE AMERICAS

Barrio: Jose's Neighborhood by George Ancona (P)

Daily Life on a Southern Plantation 1853 by Paul Erickson (I)

The Lost Temple of the Aztecs by Shelley Tanaka (I, U)

Breaking Ground, Breaking Silence: The Story of New York's African Burial Ground by Joyce Hansen & Gary McGowan (U)

WORLD HISTORY AND CULTURE

A Street through Time: A 12,000-Year Walk through History by Anne Millard (I)

In Search of the Spirit: The Living National Treasures of Japan by Sheila Hamanaka & Ayano Ohmi (I, U)

Ten Queens: Portraits of Women of Power by Milton Meltzer (U)

No More Strangers Now: Young Voices from a New South Africa edited by Tim McKee (U)

Teaching Mathematics through Nonfiction Trade Books

Recent approaches to mathematics instruction emphasize mathematics in relationship to other subject areas, including literacy learning. The recent emphasis on using mathematics as a tool to develop mathematical understanding is also consistent with the idea that mathematical learning can and should occur in concert with language learning.

New views of mathematics place less emphasis on computation and greater emphasis on mathematical literacy. This shift in emphasis is reflected in the key goals that the National Council of Teachers of Mathematics has identified for children: (1) learning to value mathematics, (2) becoming confident in the ability to do mathematics, (3) becoming mathematical problem solvers, (4) learning to communicate mathematically, and (5) learning to reason mathematically.

Nonfiction trade books that address mathematical topics can help achieve all of these goals. Titles like Kathryn Lasky's (1994) *The Librarian Who Measured the Earth* describes how Eratosthenes devised a means of measuring the earth's circumference in the third century B.C. Describing the problem-solving processes he used as well as the underlying mathematical principles, this title represents an interesting melding of biography and mathematical content.

Mathematics-related nonfiction titles suitable for young children are fairly plentiful, whereas those for older students are in shorter supply. The following list contains general books about mathematics as well as specific topics like counting, computation, and geometry, plus puzzles, games, and other such mathematical activities:

GENERAL

Celebrating Women in Mathematics and Science edited by Miriam Cooney (U)

G is for Googol: A Math Alphabet Book by David Schwartz (U)

COUNTING

Fish Eyes: A Book You Can Count On by Lois Ehlert (P)

Underwater Counting: Even Numbers by Jerry Palotta (P)

Anno's Counting Book by Mitsumasa Anno (I)

The History of Counting by Denise Schmandt-Besserat (U)

Roman Numerals I to MM: Numerabilia Romana Uno ad Duo Mila by Arthur Geisert (U)

COMPUTATION

Twenty-Six Letters and Ninety-Nine Cents by Tana Hoban (P)

Sea Squares by Joy N. Hulme (P)

How Much Is a Million by David Schwartz (P)

Eating Fractions by Bruce McMillan (P)

Anno's Mysterious Multiplying Jar by Mitsumasa Anno (I)

Number Families by Jane Jonas Srivastava (I)

GEOMETRY

Color Zoo by Lois Ehlert (P)

Shape Up by David Adler (P)

So Many Circles, So Many Squares by Tana Hoban (P)

The Amazing Book of Shapes by Lydia Sharman (I)

MATH, PUZZLES, GAMES, AND THE LIKE

Anno's Math Games by Mitsumasa Anno (P)

Anno's Math Games II by Mitsumasa Anno (P)

Math-a-Magic: Number Tricks for Magicians by Laurence White & Ray Boekel (U)

The Great Book of Math Teasers by Robert Muller (U)

Teaching Art through Nonfiction Trade Books

Today's experts in art instruction emphasize the need for students to do art, rather than simply study the art of others. They recommend using art as a tool for doing, learning, and thinking, and focus on art as a talent to be developed in

all children, not just a few. They identify the need for children to explore an array of art forms from a variety of sources, time periods, cultures, and ethnic
groups.

Nonfiction trade books can provide support for this vision of art instruction.
They can provide opportunities for children to take on the role of artist and become active viewers of art by studying books about the old masters as well as
more contemporary artists. With this approach, children can create art imitative
of that found in the various books they encounter.

They may explore art through additional hands-on experiences suggested
by books such as *Playing with Plasticine* (Reid, 1988) or *Crayons* (Pluckrose,
1987). The former title directs children to paint a picture with this clay-like material by molding three-dimensional figures. *Crayons* moves children beyond
coloring with crayons to creating magical artworks by combining crayons with
glue, ink, and other common materials.

Many recent nonfiction titles can acquaint children with famous artists and
their paintings, the artistic process, and the study of architecture. The books
listed below represent but a sampling of the many books available and can help
classroom teachers involve children in art appreciation, creating art, examining
art history, examining the lives of famous artists, and developing understanding
of architecture:

ART APPRECIATION

Art Fraud Detective by Andrea Bassil & Anna Nilsen (I, U)

A Short Walk around the Pyramids and through the World of Art by Phillip
  M. Isaacson (U)

The Painter's Eye: Learning to Look at Contemporary Art by Jan Greenberg
  & Sandra Jordan (U)

The Key to Renaissance Art by J. F. Arenas (U)

CREATING ART

Playing with Plasticine by Barbara Reid (P, I)

Crayons by Henry Pluckrose (I)

Drawing from Nature by Jim Arnosky (I)

Ed Emberly's Drawing Book of Animals by Ed Emberley (I)

The Art of Eric Carle by Eric Carle (P, I, U)

EXAMINING ART HISTORY

The Yellow House: Vincent van Gogh and Paul Gauguin Side by Side by
  Susan Goldman Rubin (P)

History of American Art for Young People by H. W. Janson & A. F. Janson (U)

A History of the United States through Art by Eleanor Van Zandt (U)

Bibles and Bestiaries: A Guide to Illuminated Manuscripts by Elizabeth Watson (U)

ARTISTS

Angela Weaves a Dream: The Story of a Young Maya Artist by Michele Sola (I)

Michelangelo by Diane Stanley (I)

What Makes a Bruegel a Bruegel? by Richard Muhlberger (I)

Chuck Close: Up Close by Jan Greenberg & Sandra Jordan (I, U)

A Young Painter: The Life and Paintings of Wang Yani—China's Extraordinary Young Artist by Z. Zhensun & A. Low (U)

Lives of the Artists: Masterpieces, Messes (and What the Neighbors Thought) by Kathleen Krull (U)

ARCHITECTURE

The Inside–Outside Book of Washington, DC by R. Munro (P)

Liberty by Lynn Curlee (I, M)

Cathedral: The Story of Its Construction by David Macaulay (U)

Frank O. Gehry: Outside In by Sandra Jordan & Jan Greenberg (U)

Round Buildings, Square Buildings, and Buildings That Wiggle Like a Fish by Phillip Isaacson (U)

Teaching Music through Nonfiction Trade Books

Music is an integral part of children's lives. From their earliest years, children naturally sing and chant, play pretend musical instruments, and enjoy performing. While nonfiction trade books cannot replicate the musical experience, they can inform and enrich it. Recent trends in music instruction emphasize the development of musical listening skills, singing songs from this country and others, and creating and playing music.

Nonfiction books related to music can broaden children's exposure, heightening their awareness of its many and varied forms. For example, they can bring children into the world of jazz with titles like *Marsalis on Music* (Marsalis, 1995)

Recent nonfiction books can support teachers as they involve their students in the study of music and musicians. Audiotapes or CD-ROMs accompany many titles, providing the opportunity to listen to the music described. These titles can include students in learning about different types of music, studying the lives of composers, participating in singing or dancing, constructing instruments, and even composing their own music. The books listed below address a broad range of topics, including various types of music, musicians, songbooks, and instruments:

TYPES OF MUSIC

I See the Rhythm by Toyomi Igus (P, I)

Amazing Grace: The Story of the Hymn by Linda Granfield (P, I)

This Land Was Made for You and Me: The Life and Songs of Woody Guthrie by Elizabeth Partridge (I, U)

One Nation under a Groove: Rap Music and Its Roots by James Haskins (U)

Slave Spirituals and the Jubilee Singers by Michael L. Cooper (U)

MUSICIANS

Handel, Who Knew What He Liked by M. T. Anderson (P, I)

Mysterious Thelonius by Chris Raschka (P)

Letters to Horseface: Being the Story of Wolfgang Amadeus Mozart by F. N. Monjo (I)

Great Composers by Piero Ventura (U)

Scott Joplin and the Ragtime Years by Mark Evans (U)

Clara Schumann: Piano Virtuoso by Susanna Reich (U)

INSTRUMENTS

My First Music Book by Helen Drew (P)

Musical Instruments from A to Z by Bobbie Kalman (P)

Meet the Orchestra by Ann Hayes (P)

The Philharmonic Gets Dressed by Karla Kuskin (I)

The Story of the Incredible Orchestra: An Introduction to Musical Instruments and the Symphony Orchestra by Bruce Koscielniak (I, U)

Nonfiction trade books can effectively enhance instruction in every content area. They can enrich the study of every subject, providing both a depth not possible through use of the textbook alone. In addition, nonfiction trade books can be a valuable means of promoting inquiry learning, which is the subject of the next section.

INQUIRY IN THE CONTENT AREA CLASSROOM

Inquiry can take many forms. It can involve an activity within a particular content area class such as science, social studies, health, or music, or it can be part of an integrated thematic unit of study. It can engage students in short-term examination of a fairly narrow topic of interest or long-term investigation of a complex, multifaceted issue.

Children need to understand the inquiry process before seeking the answers to their own questions. They need to realize that inquiry is more than "writing a report"—it involves pursuing a topic with passion, ferreting out information, considering conflicting facts, and collaborating with others. It involves making many decisions about how to present the product of the research—whether through a book, a newspaper, a jackdaw, a slide show, a project, a web page, or another format. Teachers and learners need to reflect on the process and understand how authors of nonfiction engage in the process. In addition, teachers need to demonstrate for children their own process of inquiry.

When used across the curriculum, nonfiction books can help further the goals of inquiry learning. They can promote critical thinking, encourage lifelong reading, and provide models for student reporting of information. Nonfiction trade books can develop student understanding of the thinking processes associated with the disciplines of science, mathematics, social studies, art, and music.

Both teachers and children need experiences specifically geared toward viewing and using nonfiction as sources for inquiry. They need explicit instruction designed to illustrate the myriad ways this genre can be used to further student inquiry. They also need to develop awareness of the many ways nonfiction can serve as models for inquiry-based learning. In this section the many roles that nonfiction can play in furthering student understanding of the inquiry process are illustrated. Ways are suggested to use and increase student understanding at every point in the process. A variety of strategies designed to aid the inquiry process are described at strategic points in the discussion. The subsections below explore the following phases of inquiry: modeling the process, posing the questions, considering information sources, locating information, recording information, and reporting information.

Modeling the Process

An inquiry project can involve an entire class, a small team, or an individual. For learners engaging in inquiry for the first time, a whole-class project where each learner contributes part of the final product can acquaint students with the process and provide them with peer support. This approach lets learners work together on a common goal, allowing them to pool their resources and plan strategies as a team. As students gain experience with the process, they can move into individual projects based on topics for which they have a real passion.

Two excellent nonfiction books model the inquiry process through classroom-based accounts of important topics. *Come Back Salmon: How a Group of Dedicated Kids Adopted Pigeon Creek and Brought It Back to Life* (Cone, 1992) illustrates how an entire school in Everett, WA, engaged in an inquiry project designed to clean up a polluted creek, making it possible for salmon to spawn there. It demonstrates the steps in the process, as well as the difficulties that researchers often encounter.

Oh Freedom!: Kids Talk about the Civil Rights Movement with the People Who Made It Happen (King & Osborne, 1997) describes how a teacher in Washington, DC trained her students in interviewing techniques. She sent her students out with tape recorders to talk to their parents and other adults about their experiences during the civil rights movement. Youngsters can analyze the steps in the research process described in each title. They might even create a chart illustrating the sequence of events described in each text (see Chapter 4).

Nonfiction authors engage in varied forms of inquiry to create their books. They often provide "snapshots" of the research processes they use to locate information for a book. They give readers clues about the places they have been, the books and documents they have studied, or the experts they have consulted. Sharing these descriptions can make the research process real to students. This information often appears in the back matter of a nonfiction book in the form of general notes, authors' notes, or acknowledgments. James Cross Giblin's (1994) *Thomas Jefferson,* for example, contains acknowledgments that list books used in his research and mention his visit to Monticello, Jefferson's home. The back matter of the book includes a two-page description of "A Visit to Monticello."

In the "Acknowledgments and Picture Credits" section at the back of *Lincoln: A Photobiography*, Russell Freedman (1987b) acknowledges the help of experts at various Lincoln-related sites, including Lincoln's birthplace and boyhood homes, the Abraham Lincoln Book Shop in Chicago, and the Illinois State Historical Library. In an interview, Freedman made the following remarks about his research for this Newbery-winning book:

> For my Lincoln biography, I followed the Lincoln train from his log cabin birthplace in Kentucky to Ford's Theater in Washington, DC and the rooming house across the street where the President died. There is something magical about being able to lay your eyes on the real thing, something you can't get from reading alone. When I wrote about Lincoln, I could picture the scenes in my mind's eye. Some of my research is devoted to finding archival photographs. It is a real thrill! There is something about seeing an old photograph that evokes a sense of history in a way that nothing else can. (2000, pp. 8–9)

Posing the Questions

Once students develop a basic understanding of the inquiry process, they are ready to begin their own inquiry projects. The first step in student inquiry involves helping students find a focus for their research. Whether using group or individual inquiry, teachers will need to devote large amounts of time to helping students identify appropriate research questions. This subsection provides suggestions for that process.

Students often find it very difficult to identify a question that effectively frames their inquiry topic. Many teachers use K-W-L charts (see Chapter 4) to help children define the focus of their study. In this way, children can reflect on their prior knowledge (K) about a topic and pose their own questions (W—what I want to know) about it. However, oftentimes these K-W-L charts result in narrow, factual types of questions that can be easily answered with a single trip to the encyclopedia.

Experts suggest that before they can pose meaningful questions about a topic, children need to read and write widely in the area of interest. Learners need time to "muck around" in their topics (Short, Harste, & Burke, 1996). At the beginning of an inquiry study, children might examine books related to the topic, jotting down notes, perusing diagrams, charts, or photographs, discussing their findings with peers, and so on. Through this "mucking around," students eventually begin to identify broader questions that can be answered in more than one way.

While reading nonfiction titles during sustained silent reading, for example, learners might jot down on sticky notes any questions that come to mind as they read. While reading *Kids at Work* (Freedman, 1994), for example, Diana Dean's sixth graders recorded the following questions, many of which would be suitable for research projects related to Lewis Hine and/or the times in which he lived:

What if Louis Hine hadn't taken the pictures of the kids?
How could parents put their kids' lives at risk like this?
Why did Lewis Hine care so much about these children?
How was life for kids different then compared to now?

Nonfiction books themselves can provide models for young authors to use as they focus their research questions. By considering book titles and carefully reflecting on the author's focus, students can identify the questions authors pose as they gather information for their books.

Sometimes a nonfiction book title reveals the question the book answers, as in *What Is a Wall, After All?* (Allen, 1993) or *Where Does the Butterfly Go When It Rains?* (Garelick, 1997). Before reading, young children might predict the questions books with titles like *Cars and How They Go* (Cole, 1983) might answer. This type of prereading experience lets them not only anticipate text content but also understand how authors focus the information they share in a book. Through their predictions, children can also begin to speculate on how the author will answer the question.

Second-grade teacher Elaine Elias used Gail Gibbons's (1996) *The Reasons for Seasons* to help children reflect on the question the author answers in this book. After discussing the title with her students, she did a book "walk-through" with the class, pointing out the headings that define each section: summer, winter, spring, and fall. She then asked these young students to identify the major question the book answers, which is "Why do we have the different seasons?" Through discussion of the author's question and the way the author answers it, students can begin to sense how they can pose and answer their own research questions. Analysis of text features, content, illustrations, and visuals bring children into the process and can help them see how these features can be incorporated into their own writing.

Books for older children can demonstrate the different foci an author may take in regard to a topic. In some cases, authors ask broad questions; in other cases, more focused ones. Comparisons of texts can help learners distinguish among the different types of questions authors might ask about a single topic. Four different books about the Middle Ages illustrate this point. The following examples range from books that answer broad questions to those that answer narrow, more discrete ones.

Eyewitness: Medieval Life (Langley & Dann, 2000) broadly surveys the medieval period, answering the question, "What was life like in the Middle Ages?" *Castles* (Baines, 1995) provides a narrower focus, addressing the question, "What are the parts of a castle, and who lived and worked there?" David Macaulay's (1977) *Castle* narrows the focus further, answering the question, "How was a castle built?" and describing the steps in this process. *A Medieval Feast* (Aliki, 1983) provides an even more telescopic view. With detailed illustrations, the author answers the question, "What went on at a medieval feast?" From these and many other examples, older children can learn how authors pose questions and answer them through research. Students can also begin to reflect on how each of the authors researched their topic (see the next subsection).

Longer, more sophisticated titles obviously answer more than a single question. By examining chapter titles listed in the table of contents, it is often possible to identify additional questions the text will answer. For example, Ina Chang's (1991) *A Separate Battle: Women and the Civil War* will certainly answer the broad question, "What were women's experiences in the Civil War?" Chapter titles including "Supplying the Army," "Hospital Duty," and "Soldiers and Spies" suggest that more specific questions—like "How did women supply the army?"; "What duties did women assume in the hospitals?"; and "What did women combatants and spies do during the Civil War?"—will be answered within the covers of this book.

After children have considered the way authors pose and answer research questions, they need to practice posing their own questions. Topics for investigation should be of passionate personal interest to students, representing questions that truly matter to them. Regardless of the type of topic, research questions should meet the following criteria:

- They should be based on student knowledge of the topic.
- They should not be focused too broadly or narrowly.
- They should be personally meaningful to the researcher.
- They should be potentially interesting to others.
- They should be possible to answer with available resources.
- They should lead to other questions.
- They should promote learner thought and reflection

The question stems below can aid students as they identify author's questions or pose their own research questions. These stems can help students pose meaningful or "big" questions rather than trivial research questions that can be answered with a single trip to a reference work. They include the following (from Rankin, 1999, p. 39):

- How do/does/did . . . ?
- What procedures or actions . . . ?
- What problems . . . ?
- What happens when . . . ?
- What is/was the role of . . . in . . . ?
- What is/was the difference between . . . and . . . ?
- What causes/caused . . . ?
- What are/were the effects/results of . . . ?
- How/why did . . . decide to . . . ?
- Who/what influenced . . . to . . . ?
- What is/was the relationship between . . . and . . . ?
- What are the competing sides . . . ?
- How does/did . . . change . . . ?

Considering Information Sources

Once students have determined their research questions, they will need teacher scaffolding to identify useful sources of information. Looking at nonfiction authors' information sources can provide children with powerful models for their own work. Duthie (1996) suggests a focus on three information sources: personal knowledge and experience, interviews, and written sources and other media. She encourages teachers to get students thinking about authors' sources of information as they interact with nonfiction. After hearing *Whales* by Gail Gibbons (1993), for example, Duthie invited students to speculate on where the author got her information. Here are her first graders' responses (Duthie, 1996, p. 65):

"She probably went to Florida to watch whales."

"She must have gone to the ocean on a big ship and saw a whale real close up, or maybe she went to a circus."

"She probably read about whales in books."

"Maybe she asked a sea captain."

"She could ask a watermatician!"

This example illustrates that even very young children are well aware of information sources like personal experience, interviews, and other sources. The same question can be asked of older children as they engage with nonfiction titles that reflect works crafted from a wide range of sources. This section will describe several of those sources and examples of nonfiction titles based on them.

Personal Experiences

Children's experiences are particularly useful as an information source because they allow learners to draw on their background knowledge about a topic. Authors, too, draw on their personal experiences in their writing. In *Dive!: My Adventures in the Deep Frontier*, marine biologist Sylvia Earle (1999) describes her firsthand experiences as a diver studying undersea plants and animals. In *My Season with Penguins: An Antarctic Journal* biologist Sophie Webb's journal (2000) describes her trip to a penguin colony in the Antarctic. Using a field journal format, she documents the questions guiding scientists' work and their efforts to answer those questions. Webb's book also provides an excellent model of how the research process works.

Interviews

Interviews are excellent sources of information for students conducting research. They can be conducted face to face, over the phone, via e-mail, and so on. Interviews provide personal up-to-date information that can be invaluable to the researcher. Even young children can create interview questions and use them to collect information from others. As Graves (1989) states, "The interview is one of the cornerstones of information gathering throughout the child's career as a learner" (p. 20).

Nonfiction works for young and older children portray interviews as a rich information source. *Author Talk* (Marcus, 2000) is a series of interviews with 15 authors of books for young people. The question-and-answer format brings the childhood of each author into sharp focus and includes each author's own reflections on the art and craft of writing. *Darkness over Denmark: The Danish Resistance and the Rescue of the Jews* (Levine, 2000) is based on personal interviews with 20 Danish survivors, rescuers, and resistance fighters who provide eyewitness accounts of their experiences during World War II. The back matter of the book contains photographs and brief explanations of what happened to each individual after the war.

Written Sources and Other Media

Documents including original letters, photographs, cartoons, maps, and so on provide authenticity to books describing people and events of the past. They involve readers through the depiction of the actual words, thoughts, and appearances of those who lived through the events described. Authors locate these documents in libraries, on the Internet, and in museums. The inclusion of information from these primary-source documents is increasingly popular in children's nonfiction and particularly common in books relating events from history. Louise Peacock's (1998) *Crossing the Delaware: A History in Many Voices*, for example, combines fact with fiction to describe the stirring events of the stormy night of December 25, 1776, when Washington's troops captured Trenton in a surprise counterattack. She uses actual quotations from primary sources including memoirs, journals, letters, diaries, and a cartoon by Paul Revere.

The visuals found in nonfiction trade books are very important to readers of all ages. Historical photographs enhance student understanding of text content by providing arresting glimpses of people and events of the past. Through careful examination of historical photographs, children can "read" pictures and develop visual literacy skills as they collect data, draw inferences, and arrive at conclusions about their content. Through discussion or writing, students can share insights and interpretations about the content of these photographs. They can also develop greater awareness of how to select historical photos for inclusion in their own research projects. Titles like *Prairie Visions: The Life and Times of Solomon Butcher* (Conrad, 1991), *Anastasia's Album* (Brewster, 1996), *Buffalo Gals: Women of the Old West* (Miller, 1995), and *Indian Chiefs* (Freedman, 1987a) contain excellent historical photographs ideally suited for discussion activities.

Figure 6.1 contains a questioning model for studying historical photographs. Through this model, students examine photographs and hypothesize about the people and objects in them. They then identify or label people, groups, or objects. Students describe what they observe and draw inferences about this information, and then draw conclusions about the contents of the photograph.

As an introduction to reading *Immigrant Kids* (Freedman, 1980), sixth-grade teacher Judith Hendershot involved her students in studying the poignant cover photograph of two immigrant children. Using the questions listed in Figure 6.1, she involved her students in analysis of that photograph. During the description step, one student commented:

Step 1. Introduce the photograph.
Present the photograph, providing students with background information on it.

Step 2. Ask questions about the photograph.
Ask students to make predictions about the people, places, and objects shown.

Sample question: What are the people doing in this picture?
Record student hunches on the board.

Step 3. Identification
Ask students to list everything they can see in the picture. They should identify the people and objects in the photograph and compare these observations with their peers.

Step 4. Description
Ask questions that will elicit descriptions and identify relationships among people, animals, and/or objects.

Sample questions: How are the people dressed? What do you think they are doing? How would you describe the way they feel? What are they carrying in their hands?

Step 5. Inferences
Ask questions to guide students in making inferences.
Help students make educated guesses about what they see based on their observations and provide opportunities to modify, abandon, or confirm earlier predictions.

Sample questions: What clues are there to suggest that these children are from another country? What may be happening to them now? Where do you think their parents are?

Step 6. Conclusions
Return to student predictions about the photograph. Students can discard or change their predictions at this point. Students can share their conclusions, as well as their evidence, with the class.

FIGURE 6.1. Questioning model for historical photographs. Adapted from Felton, R. G., & Allen, R. F. (1990). Using visual materials as historical sources: A model for studying state and local history. *Social Studies, 81* March–April, 84–87.

As soon as I saw this photograph, I felt like I just could have been there to help them. It looked cold outside and the little girl had no jacket on. . . . I felt so sorry for them because the little girl was crying. Their shoes looked as hard as rocks and uncomfortable. If I had one wish I would help those children.

This aesthetic response to a photograph demonstrates the power that visuals can have in connecting today's children to people of the past. It reminds us that combining powerful visual content with effective verbal information can help today's children understand the lives of children of yesterday.

Reference books and periodicals represent a decidedly different form of information book from those discussed so far. Reference books help learners locate specific items of information and include glossaries, encyclopedias, bibliographies, dictionaries, atlases, almanacs, and periodicals. They can support student inquiry projects related to any content area. *Exploring Your World: The Adventure of Geography* (National Geographic Society, 1994), for example, is recommended for all age groups and provides 334 encyclopedia entries on a variety of geographical topics. It contains more than 1,000 photographs, diagrams, and charts. Specialized encyclopedias like *Plants and Plant Life* (Grolier, 2001) introduce principles of botany through a highly effective visual approach. The sophisticated *Eyewitness Visual Dictionary of Flight* (Dorling Kindersley, 1992) or the simple *Geography from A to Z: A Picture Glossary* (Knowlton, 1988) define and illustrate terms related to flight and geography respectively. The *Rand McNally Children's Millennium Atlas of the World* (Rand McNally, 2001) provides information on using maps and atlases, including use of bar scales, map keys, map symbols and legends, and longitude and latitude.

Numerous children's periodicals can contribute information to inquiry projects. *Chickadee*, for example, explores the world of science in a format appealing to children in kindergarten through fourth grade. *Cobblestone: The History Magazine for Young People* features themed issues on various topics or people from American history. *Sports Illustrated for Kids* introduces upper-grade students to professional and amateur sports figures.

Locating Information

The array of resources available to today's young researcher is overwhelming. Learners often need help in understanding these resources, their similarities and differences, and when to use each. This subsection describes ways to familiarize students with different reference resources and illustrate strategies designed to aid in the process.

When students begin locating information relevant to inquiry projects, it is imperative that teachers consider the availability of resources related to their research questions. When students are unable to locate information about their topics, their frustration increases, making a difficult task even harder.

The first step in the information location process is to plan the search. At this point students need to record their research questions and brainstorm key words to be used during the search process. Students should also, at this point, browse the library collection and list possible sources of information, whether nonfiction titles, reference books, on-line sources, CD-ROMs, and the like. They need practice in making "dry-run" searches designed to streamline the process and identify problems before the actual search begins.

As students begin to use nonfiction trade books to complete inquiry projects, teachers should prepare them for the task. Shared reading experiences (see Chapter 4) can heighten learner awareness of the various features of nonfiction text. Book "walk-throughs" in which teachers point out various nonfiction features like tables of contents, indexes, glossaries, and headings, alert students to these features. Most important of all, these features can be most effective in helping students locate information. Book preview guides (see Chapter 4) can provide another way to reinforce this information.

Activities requiring students to locate information in reference works can develop as extensions of experiences with nonfiction literature. Teacher Mary Malcolm's fourth graders were studying transportation. After her students read *Flight: The Journey of Charles Lindbergh* (Burleigh, 1991) she engaged her fourth graders in a library scavenger hunt, which required using an atlas, an encyclopedia, an almanac, a dictionary, and the Internet to locate information about Charles Lindbergh and his flight. This activity reinforced student understanding of these resources, which students had learned about during their library periods earlier in the year. Figure 6.2 illustrates the questions students researched as part of this activity.

Recording Information

As students move into the process of actually using the materials needed for their inquiry projects, they should consider the following questions:

> What information do I need?
> Does this resource help answer my question?
> Do I need all the information or just some parts?
> How is the information organized?
> How should I approach this material?
> Does the information make sense to me?

Once students have determined the information they are interested in, they need a procedure for recording that content. Information can be recorded on note cards,

Directions: Using the specified reference work, locate the answer to the question and record it on your sheet.

- Use an *atlas* to answer the following questions:
  1. Lindbergh flew over Nova Scotia at 12:08 and reached Newfoundland at 4:00. How many hours and minutes between the two? What was the distance between the two in miles? *3 hours, 52 minutes; approximately 130 miles*
  2. When Lindbergh reached England he still had another body of water to cross before he reached France. What is the name of that body of water between England and France? *The English Channel*

- Use an *encyclopedia* to locate the following information:
  1. What books did Lindbergh write? *We; The Spirit of St. Louis*
  2. Name the main parts of an airplane. *Fuselage, wings, tail assembly, landing gear*

- Use a *dictionary* to answer this question.
  1. Lindbergh spent his entire flight in a "boxlike cockpit." What is a cockpit? *The space where the pilot works*

- Use the *Internet* to answer the next question:
  1. When Lindbergh took his historic journey in 1927 there were fewer airports than there are today. How many airports are listed for our local area?

Name two of them. *Lindbergh Field; Brown Field* [*Note*: This will, of course, vary with the locality.]

FIGURE 6.2. Using reference resources to answer questions about *Flight: The Journey of Charles Lindbergh* (Burleigh, 1991).

on graphic organizers, on legal pads, or large sticky notes. Regardless of the strategy used, note taking should involve students in recording information in the briefest possible way, using the following ideas (adapted from Rankin, 1999):

- Condense information by using phrases and keywords, not sentences.
- Don't copy word for word but paraphrase.
- Don't include unnecessary words like *a, an, the*.
- Use math symbols like = + −.
- Make lists.
- Use bullets or arrows to identify each important idea.
- Record the source where the information was found.

Note-taking practice prior to inquiry study can increase student comfort levels with the process. Teachers need to model note-taking strategies on the overhead projector, demonstrating how to condense information most effectively. In addition, students can practice note taking. After listening to a few pages of a nonfiction read aloud, for example, learners can form small groups and discuss the most important points they hear. One person in the group can act as a secretary, recording notes for the group during the discussion. By rotating the secretary and providing multiple opportunities for practice, teachers can help students increase their proficiency in note taking (Harvey, 1998).

Another way to scaffold note taking involves summarizing sentences. With this strategy, teachers give students individual sentences that students turn into summarized notes. The best examples appear on a transparency and are discussed. Students continue this practice over time, then move on to summarizing paragraphs and longer amounts of text.

For young children or beginners involved in fairly simple inquiry projects, notes can be recorded directly on graphic organizers. When the note-taking process is modeled with older children engaged in large-group inquiry projects, note taking can become a key part of thr group project. Students can form groups, each of which is assigned one research question to answer. The title of the inquiry topic can be recorded on butcher paper, and the subquestions can also be recorded on different sections of the paper. Students in each group can then record notes related to their question on long sticky notes (3×5). These can be stuck on the butcher paper under the proper section. The sticky notes can then be moved around so that related pieces of information can be grouped together.

The ability to analyze information is critical during this phase of the research process. Skills like the ability to sequence, classify, compare and contrast, and problem solve are essential to the process. The strategy lessons described in Chapter 4 contribute to the development of these skills. Other visual organizers can also help children develop the critical thinking skills necessary to successful inquiry experiences. The I-chart is an example of one of these organizers.

The purpose of an I-chart (Hoffman, 1992) is to promote critical thinking by involving children in locating answers to guiding questions from multiple information sources. It lets children examine a topic from different points of view and helps them to view information more critically. It also provides practice in recording notes from multiple sources.

Fourth-grade teacher Sandy Minor involved her students in a miniunit on life during the time of the Pilgrims. To introduce inquiry research, she engaged her students in reading Kate Waters's trilogy of books about children's lives during Pilgrim times. Using the small-group/multiple-books model (see Chapter 3), students selected one of three different books: *Sarah Morton's Day: A Day in the Life of a Pilgrim Girl* (Waters, 1993), *Samuel Eaton's Day: A Day in the Life of a Pilgrim Boy* (Waters, 1996a), and *Tapenum's Day: A Wampanoag Indian Boy in Pilgrim Times* (Waters, 1996b).

These companion titles provide historically accurate visual glimpses of life in colonial New England in the early 1600s. All three are illustrated with photographs taken at the Massachusetts Plimouth Plantation historic site and contain language reflecting the vernacular of the time. The first title portrays a day in the life of a young Pilgrim girl as she completes her chores, learns her letters, and adjusts to her new stepfather. The second title follows 7-year-old Samuel Eaton's day as he shares a meal with his family, helps with the harvest, and plays with his younger sister. The third dramatizes a day in the life of a young Wampanoag boy who yearns to be chosen as a warrior. He hunts for food, goes fishing with a friend, and befriends a wise man who teaches him to make arrows.

After each group completed its reading, Sandy presented the entire class with an I-chart (see Figure 6.3). The chart listed four guiding questions on the far left side pertaining to chores, clothing, food, and free time. The top of the chart listed the three book titles, along with the heading "Children Today." Students who read *Sarah Morton's Day* worked in pairs to complete the first and fourth columns; those who read *Samuel Eaton's Day* completed the second and fourth columns; and those who read *Tapenum's Day* completed the last two columns. After this, the teacher completed a composite chart on the overhead as students from each group reported on their findings. This completed chart is illustrated in Figure 6.3.

After the chart was complete, all of the students engaged in a lively discussion about the similarities and differences in the lives of the children living at the same time in the past, as well as the similarities and differences between children's lives then and now. This led to an interesting discussion of gender stereotyping as it existed in the 1600s and today. Children identified questions for further research including these: What kinds of activities did Native American girls in the 1600s engage in? Why did Pilgrims and Indians eat different foods? How did the food preparation of Pilgrims and Native Americans differ?

Reporting Information

Inquiry projects can take myriad forms, from the simple to the highly sophisticated. Pamphlets, PowerPoint slides, reports, panel discussions, and debates all represent ways that students might choose to share their learning about a topic. Space limitations do not allow discussion of all the possible formats for sharing research. Therefore, this section focuses on ways teachers can involve learners in creating their own nonfiction books as a means of sharing their research.

Questions	Sarah Morton's day	Samuel Eaton's day	Tapenum's day	Children today
What chores do children do?	Tend the fire Make pudding and bread Set the table Serve food Feed chickens Milk cows Muck the garden Pound spices Polish brass Milk goats	Fetch water Catch game Gather wood Help with harvest	Carry water Gather wood	Feed pets Help set the table Put dishes in the dishwasher Babysit
What do children wear?	Petticoat Stockings Garters Waistcoat Coif Apron Pocket Shoes	Stockings Garters Breeches Doublet Shoes Points Hat	Breechclout	Jeans Tennis shoes Sweatshirts
What food do children eat?	Indian corn bread Pottage	Samp Corn Bread Cheese Mussels Coney Curds	Ground corn (*noohkik*) Rabbit stew Turkey Fish	Pizza Ice cream Soda pop Hamburger French fries
What do children do in their free time?	Play with knicker box Play with poppet Meet with friend	Rest by the brook Sing Meet with a friend	Fishing with a friend	Play video games Surf the Internet Watch TV Go to movies Rollerblade

FIGURE 6.3. I-chart comparing information about the lives of children in Pilgrim times and today.

By creating their own nonfiction books, learners of all ages can become involved in organizing information in interesting and meaningful ways. Today's nonfiction literature, both information and biography, can provide powerful and varied models for this effort. Simply folding and stapling paper together can create student-made nonfiction books, or students can get more elaborate—sewing and binding the pages as is done in real books.

By introducing learners to the unique formats nonfiction authors employ in their work, students not only get ideas for organizing their own information but develop appreciation for the creative processes involved in writing nonfiction books.

For young children, or students with little experience in writing in the expository mode, following particular book patterns can provide a structure for reporting expository information. A question-and-answer format is a simple way for students to organize the data they collect through their inquiry efforts. Seymour Simon's (1990) *New Questions and Answers about Dinosaurs* models this type of format, providing up-to-date information about the prehistoric creatures. For students wishing to compare and contrast information, Marilyn Singer's (1995) *A Wasp Is Not a Bee* uses a comparison contrast pattern to provide information.

"All about" books provide another easy format for young children to report factual information. These books usually focus on a single topic and include one fact and one related illustration per page. Models for "All about" books include Jim Arnosky's (1994) *All About Alligators,* which provides clearly written text and detailed illustrations. Ruth Oswald's second graders created "Facts about Crickets" books that detailed what they had learned as part of a 2-week study of crickets and grasshoppers. Figure 6.4 illustrates the cover of one student's book.

An alternate format for reporting the results of personal observations is the nature journal. *Salamander Rain: A Lake and Pond Journal* (Pratt, 2001) encourages older children to look more closely at local lakes and ponds. It features a journal and scrapbook of a young boy who became fascinated by the turtles, dragonflies, and water skimmers that populated a local pond. Teachers Jan Himmelbauer and Val Kortze at Green Intermediate School in Summit County, OH, involve their students in writing nature journals as an extension of their reading/writing workshop classes. The combination of notes and visual displays provides a fascinating record of students' observation as well as their research (see Figure 6.5).

Other interesting book formats can provide models for student work. Students wishing to explain how something is done through a nonfiction book can use instruction manuals as models. *Cat's Cradle: A Book of String Figures* (Johnson, 1993) teaches the basics of making string figures like Jacob's ladder and

Facts About

Crickets

FIGURE 6.4. Second grader's "Facts About Crickets" book cover.

cat's whiskers using detailed instructions and illustrations. Titles like *Swimming with Sea Lions* (McGovern, 1992) suggest other book formats. The author provides information on Galapagos sea lions through a series of diary entries.

Another interesting, easily imitated book design could be described as an "album format." In *Children Just Like Me* (Kindersley & Kindersley, 1995), children from around the world tell their own stories through text and photographs of their homes, schools, hobbies, and friends. Teacher Bonnie Stadtlander's third graders created a class biography using this format. Each child created a page for the "album," incorporating photographs and text the children composed themselves.

In addition to finding interesting formats for their writing, students need minilessons designed to help them make their writing as effective as it can be. These lessons can focus on writing effective leads, learning to show not tell, and developing a "voice" that allows the reader to hear the person behind the writing.

Students in Judith Hendershot's class wrote nonfiction books after an entire year of studying nonfiction literature. The topics of their books ranged from World War II to a biography of the rock group NSYNC. Many students found ways to provide information using a conversational tone not unlike that of the best nonfiction authors. Consider this excerpt from a book by a sixth grader entitled "Learning to Hunt." In his discussion of "Dressing for Hunting" he stated:

> People seem to think that if your feet are cold, you should add more socks. The truth of the matter is that the more socks you jam into your boots, the colder

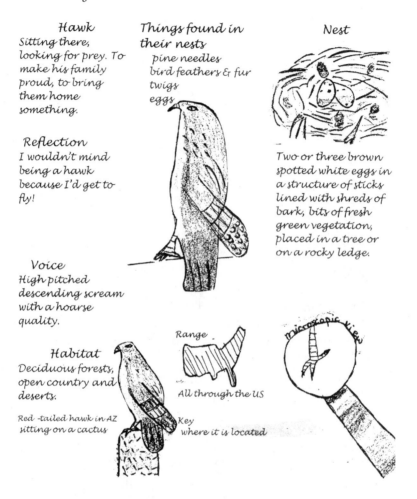

Red Tailed Hawk
I sighted it sitting on some wires looking for some prey for supper that evening!

Hawk
Sitting there, looking for prey. To make his family proud, to bring them home something.

Reflection
I wouldn't mind being a hawk because I'd get to fly!

Voice
High pitched descending scream with a hoarse quality.

Habitat
Deciduous forests, open country and deserts.

Red-tailed hawk in AZ sitting on a cactus

Things found in their nests
pine needles
bird feathers & fur
twigs
eggs

Range
All through the US
Key
where it is located

Nest

Two or three brown spotted white eggs in a structure of sticks lined with shreds of bark, bits of fresh green vegetation, placed in a tree or on a rocky ledge.

microscopic view

FIGURE 6.5. Fourth-grade student's nature journal.

your feet will be. Your feet need room to breathe. The better they breathe, the warmer they will be. The tighter your boots, the faster your feet will get cold. Wear a thin Thermax liner with a wool sock. Both of these will take away the moisture (sweat) from your feet and keep your feet warmer.

Clearly, this student obtained a great deal of knowledge over the school year about how nonfiction authors convey information in interesting, conversational ways. He uses the conversational "you" in his writing and clearly but simply provides readers with the information they need to know about dressing for hunting.

SUMMARY

Nonfiction trade books have the potential to enrich teaching in learning in every content area, including science, social studies, mathematics, art, and music. Nonfiction titles can help teachers meet the objectives of the curriculum in ways not possible through textbooks alone. They can enhance student learning of virtually every aspect of any content area.

Most importantly, the use of nonfiction trade books for inquiry study is essential if students are to be successful learners in the 21st century. Nonfiction trade books can help guide students through every phase of the inquiry process. They can support students as they pose inquiry questions, consider information sources, learn to locate information, and create their own products based on their research. The use of nonfiction trade books, coupled with the strategies described in this chapter, can empower students as they locate the answers to questions that matter to them. Nonfiction trade books can demonstrate to learners what it means to engage in research and help them to see the enormous potential for learning that inquiry projects can provide.

REFERENCES

Armstrong, J. (1999). Orbis Pictus Award acceptance speech. Available online: *www.jennifer-armstrong.com/flash/Speeches_and_Articles/Orbis_Pictus.htm* [retrieved October 11, 2001]

Duthie, C. (1996). *True stories: Nonfiction literacy in the primary classroom.* York, ME: Stenhouse.

Freedman, R. (2000). An author's perspective. In E. C. Stephens & J. E. Brown (Eds.), *A handbook of content literacy strategies: 75 practical reading and writing ideas* (pp. 8–9). Norwood, MA: Christopher-Gordon.

Freeman, E., & Person, D. (1998). *Connecting informational children's books with content area learning.* Boston: Allyn & Bacon.

Graves, D. (1989). *Investigate nonfiction.* Portsmouth, NH: Heinemann.

Harvey, S. (1998). *Nonfiction matters: Reading, writing and research in grades 3–8.* York, ME: Stenhouse.

Hoffman, J. V. (1992). Critical reading/thinking across the curriculum: Using I-charts to support learning. *Language Arts, 69,* 121–127.

Palmer, R. G., & Stewart, R. A. (1997). Nonfiction trade books in content area instruction: Realities and potential. *Journal of Adolescent and Adult Literacy 40*(8), 630–641.

Rankin, V. (1999). *The thoughtful researcher: Teaching the research process to middle school students.* Englewood, CO: Libraries Unlimited.

Sebesta, S. (1989). Literature across the curriculum. In J. W. Stewig & S. L. Sebesta (Eds.), *Using literature in the elementary classroom* (pp. 110–128). Urbana, IL: National Council of Teachers of English.

Short, K. G., Harste, J. C., & Burke, C. L. (1996). *Creating classrooms for authors and inquirers.* Portsmouth, NH: Heinemann.

Short, K. G., Schroder, J., Laird, J., Kauffman, G., Ferguson, M. J., & Crawford, K. M. (1996). *Learning together through inquiry: From Columbus to integrated curriculum*. York, ME: Stenhouse.

Tower, C. (2000). Questions that matter: Preparing elementary students for the inquiry process. *Reading Teacher, 53*, 550–557.

CHILDREN'S BOOKS

Aliki. (1983). *A medieval feast*. New York: Crowell. (3–6)
    Describes the sights, sounds, tastes, and smells of a medieval feast.

Allen, J. (1993). *What is a wall, after all?* Illustrated by A. Baron. Cambridge, MA: Candlewick Press. (2–4)
    Poetry describes the functions of walls and their varied locations.

Anno, M. (1999). *All in a day*. New York: Paper Star. (1–3)
    Ten artists illustrate children and their activities in eight parts of the world during one 24–hour day.

Armstrong, J. (2000). *Shipwreck at the bottom of the world: The extraordinary true story of Shackleton and the* Endurance. New York: Random House. (6–8)
    This Orbis Pictus Award-winning book describes the events of the 1914 Antarctic expedition of Ernest Shackleton, the subsequent disaster that befell it, and the crew's eventual rescue.

Arnosky, J. (1994). *All about alligators*. New York: Scholastic. (1–3)
    This book uses description to provide easy-to-read information about alligators.

Baines, F. (1995). *Castles*. New York: Watts. (2–4)
    This simple text provides basic information about medieval castles and those who lived and worked in them.

Brewster, H. (Ed.). (1996). *Anastasia's album*. New York: Hyperion. (4–6)
    Using the visual format of a family album, describes the life of Anastasia, youngest daughter of the last czar of Russia, Nicholas II.

Burleigh, R. (1991). *Flight: The journey of Charles Lindbergh*. Illustrated by Mike Wimmer. New York: Philomel. (1–4)
    Lindbergh's transatlantic flight is described through text and vivid illustrations.

Chang, I. (1991). *A separate battle: Women and the Civil War*. New York: Dutton. (5–6)
    Describes the roles women played as nurses, spies, and combatants in the Civil War.

Cole, J. (1983). *Cars and how they go*. Illustrated by G. Gibbons. New York: Crowell. (K-2)
    This simple explanation of how cars work is ideal for young children.

Cone, M. (1992). *Come back, salmon: How a group of dedicated kids adopted Pigeon Creek and brought it back to life*. San Francisco: Sierra Club Books. (4–6)
    The inspiring story of how children and teachers in Everett, WA, cleaned up Pigeon Creek so that salmon could once again spawn there.

Conrad, P. (1991). *Prairie visions: The life and times of Solomon Butcher*. New York: HarperCollins. (5–6)
    Photographs and text describe frontier photographer Solomon Butcher in Nebraska at the turn of the 20th century.

Dorling Kindersley. (1992). *Eyewitness visual dictionary of flight*. New York: Author. (5–6)
    Traces the development of flight from balloons to supersonic jets.
Earle, S. (1999). *Dive!: My adventures in the deep frontier.* New York: Scholastic. (5–8)
    The author, a marine biologist, describes her experiences exploring the under-
    sea world.
Freedman, R. (1980). *Immigrant kids.* New York: Dutton. (5–6)
    Freedman chronicles the lives of immigrant children in the late 1800s and early
    1900s.
Freedman, R. (1987a). *Indian chiefs.* New York: Holiday House. (5–6)
    Describes the lives of six Indian chiefs in the West in times of crisis.
Freedman, R. (1987b). *Lincoln: A photobiography.* New York: Clarion. (5–6)
    This 1988 Newbery Medal winner describes the life of America's 16th President.
Freedman, R. (1994). *Kids at work: Lewis Hine and the crusade against child labor.*
    New York: Clarion. (5–6)
    Freedman describes how Lewis Hine's photographs led to the enactment of
    child labor laws.
Garelick, M. (1997). *Where does the butterfly go when it rains?* Illustrated by N. Wilton.
    New York: Mondo. (1–3)
    This text for young children details where various animals go when it rains.
Gibbons, G. (1993). *Whales.* New York: Holiday House. (1–3)
    Using her trademark accessible format, the author provides information on
    whales in general and on specific species.
Giblin, J. C. (1994). *Thomas Jefferson: A picture book biography.* New York: Scholastic.
    (3–5)
    Details the facts and foibles of Jefferson's life in a format accessible for young
    readers.
Gibbons, G. (1996). *The reasons for seasons.* New York: Holiday House. (1–3)
    Gibbons explains the seasons, the solstices and equinoxes in simple text and
    pictures.
Grolier. (2001). *Plants and plant life* (4 vols.). New York: Author. (5–6)
    This multivolume set uses photos, illustrations, maps, charts, and diagrams to
    provide an easy-to-understand introduction to botany.
Johnson, A. A. (1993). *Cat's cradle: A book of string figures.* Palo Alto, CA: Klutz Press.
    (2–5)
    This activity book provides directions for making a variety of string figures.
Kindersley, B., & Kindersley, A. (1995). *Children just like me.* New York: DK Publishing.
    (2–5)
    Describes the homes, food, school, and hobbies of children throughout the
    world.
King, C. & Osborne, L. B. (1997). *Oh, freedom!: Kids talk about the civil rights move-
    ment with the people who made it happen.* New York: Knopf. (5–6)
    Children interview 31 friends, family members, and neighbors who each tell
    the story of the civil rights movement from their personal perspective.
Knowlton, J. (1988). *Geography from A to Z: A picture glossary.* Illustrated by Harriett
    Barton. New York: HarperCollins. (1–3)
    This simple glossary describes geographic terms like *glacier*, *marsh*, and *zone*
    with simple text and clear illustrations.

Langley, A., & Dann, G. (2000). *Eyewitness: Medieval life*. Photography by Geoff Dann & Geoff Brightling. New York: Dorling Kindersley. (5–6)

    Readers learn of homes, clothing, tools and weapons in medieval times.

Lasky, K. (1992). *Surtsey: The newest place on earth*. New York: Hyperion. (5–6)

    Briefly outlines the history of Surtsey, an island formed from a volcanic eruption of the coast of Iceland in 1970.

Lasky, K. (1994). *The librarian who measured the earth*. New York: Little, Brown. (2–5)

    A picture book biography of the life of Eratosthenes, an ancient Greek who developed an ingenious method for measuring the earth's circumference based on geometry.

Levine, E. (2000). *Darkness over Denmark: The Danish resistance and the rescue of the Jews*. New York: Scholastic. (5–6)

    This title describes how the Danish people resisted the Nazis and prevented the annihilation of Danish Jews.

Macaulay, D. (1977). *Castle*. Boston: Houghton Mifflin. (5–6)

    The author meticulously details the building of a medieval castle through pen and ink drawings.

Marcus, L. S. (2000). *Author talk*. New York: Simon & Schuster. (5–6)

    The author profiles the life and work of 15 authors through interviews with each.

Marsalis, W. (1995). *Marsalis on music*. New York: Norton. (5–6)

    Wynton Marsalis teaches the fundamentals of music and jazz improvisation in this book that is accompanied by a CD-ROM.

McGovern, A. (1992). *Swimming with sea lions*. New York: Scholastic. (3–5)

    The narrator describes her adventures in the Galapagos Islands through diary entries.

Miller, B. M. (1995). *Buffalo gals: Women of the Old West*. Minneapolis, MN: Lerner. (4–6)

    This excellent title describes the hard lives of American frontier women.

National Geographic Society. (1994). *Exploring your world: The adventure of geography*. Washington, DC: Author. (3–6)

    Describes a variety of geography-related topics through photos and text.

Peacock, L. (1998). *Crossing the Delaware: A history in many voices*. Illustrated by W. L. Krudop. New York: Scholastic. (4–6)

    The author describes the travails of Washington and his troops during the Revolutionary War.

Pluckrose, H. (1987). *Crayons*. New York: Watts. (3–5)

    Suggests ways to use common materials along with crayons to create magical products.

Pratt, K. J., (2001). *Salamander rain: A lake and pond journal*. Illustrated by K. J.Pratt. Nevada City, CA: Dawn. (4–6)

    This field guide/nature journal reawakens learners to the joys of the world around us.

Pringle, L. (1990). *Global warming*. New York: Arcade. (5–6)

    This title the greenhouse effect, assessing its impact on the world.

Rand McNally. (2001). *Rand McNally children's millennium atlas of the world*. New York: Author. (5–6)

An up-to-date world atlas designed specifically for upper-grade children.

Reid, B. (1988). *Playing with Plasticine*. New York: Morrow. (2–4)

This book encourages children to create pictures using the clay-like substance Plasticine. (3–5)

Simon, S. (1990). *New questions and answers about dinosaurs*. New York: Morrow. (4–6)

Presents the latest theories about dinosaurs and their habits.

Singer, M. (1995). *A wasp is not a bee*. Illustrated by P. O'Brien. New York: Holt. (2–4)

Compares and contrasts characteristics of 12 similar but different animal pairs.

Waters, K. (1993). *Sarah Morton's day: A day in the life of a Pilgrim girl*. Photography by Russ Kendall. New York: Scholastic. (2–4)

This historically accurate photoessay traces a day in the life of a young girl living in 1627.

Waters, K. (1996a). *Samuel Eaton's day: A day in the life of a Pilgrim boy*. Photography by Russ Kendall. New York: Scholastic. (2–4)

This photoessay focuses on the life of a young Pilgrim boy eager to help with the harvest.

Waters, K. (1996b). *Tapenum's day: A Wampanoag Indian boy in Pilgrim times*. Photography by Russ Kendall. New York: Scholastic. (3–5)

This photoessay, a companion to the aforementioned books by Kate Waters, describes a day in the life of a young Wampanoag boy living in Plymouth, MA, in 1627.

Webb, S. (2000). *My season with penguins: An Antarctic journal*. (4–6)

Webb's book describes the summer she spent studying penguins in the Antarctic.

APPENDIX.

Orbis Pictus Award-Winning Books

Starred books indicate award winners. Others listed are honor books or notables.

2000

** Bridges, R. (1999). *Through my eyes.* New York: Scholastic. (All ages)

  The powerful memoir of 6-year-old Ruby Bridges, the first black student at the all-white William Frantz Public School in New Orleans in 1960.

Jenkins, S. (1999). *The top of the world: Climbing Mount Everest.* Boston: Houghton Mifflin. (3–5)

  Beautiful collage illustrations accompany a step-by-step account of a climb to the top of Mount Everest.

Johnson, S. A. (1999). *Mapping the world.* New York: Atheneum. (4–6)

  A well-illustrated, brief chronological history examines how mapmaking has developed over the centuries.

Montgomery, S. (1999). *The snake scientist.* Boston: Houghton Mifflin. (4–5)

  Full-color photographs document the reemergence of tens of thousands of Red–Sided Garter Snakes and the scientist studying them.

Myers, W. D. (1999). *At her majesty's request: An African princess in Victorian England.* New York: Scholastic. (5–6)

  The dramatic true story of an orphaned African princess saved by an English naval officer from ritual sacrifice and given to Queen Victoria as a gift.

Reich, S. (1999). *Clara Schumann: Piano virtuoso.* New York: Clarion. (5–6)

  This thoroughly researched book about piano prodigy Clara Schumann draws on a variety of primary sources.

1999

**Armstrong, J. (1998). *Shipwreck at the bottom of the world: The extraordinary true story of Schackleton and the* Endurance. New York: Crown. (5–6)
The incredible, dramatic survival saga of Antartic explorer Ernest Shackleton and his crew.

Burleigh, R. (1998). *Black whiteness: Admiral Byrd alone in the Antarctic.* New York: Atheneum Books for Young Readers. (4–6)
This stunning picture book recounts the events of Admiral Richard Byrd's successful 6-month solitary Antarctic encampment in 1934.

Holmes, T. (1998). *Fossil feud: The rivalry of the first American dinosaur hunters.* Parsippany, NJ: Messner. (5–6)
This book examines the life stories of two 19th-century American dinosaur paleontologists and gives details of the bitter feud that existed between them.

Jenkins, S. (1998). *Hottest, coldest, highest, deepest.* Boston: Houghton Mifflin. (2–3)
This world record book of natural history uses striking colorful paper collage illustrations to identify and describe outstanding places.

Lobel, A. (1998). *No pretty pictures: A child of war.* New York: Greenwillow Books. (5–6)
The author's personal gripping memoir of surviving the Holocaust.

1998

**Pringle, L. (1997). *An extraordinary life: The story of a Monarch Butterfly.* New York: Orchard Books. (3–6)
The miraculous story of the Monarch Butterfly's migration from Massachusetts to Mexico and then to Texas.

Dorros, A. (1997). *A tree is growing.* New York: Scholastic. (2–4)
A picture book introduction to trees traces the growth of an oak tree over the course of a year.

Giblin, J. C. (1997). *Charles A. Lindbergh: A human hero.* New York: Clarion. (5–6)
This sympathetic account is an excellent introduction to Lindbergh.

Hampton, W. (1997). *Kennedy assassinated! The world mourns: A reporter's story.* Cambridge, MA: Candlewick. (4–6)
A novice United Press International reporter's account of the day President John F. Kennedy died.

Stanley, J. (1997). *Digger: The tragic fate of the California Indians from the missions to the gold rush.* New York: Crown. (4–6)
This book chronicles the lives of Native Americans of California from 1769 through the 1850s.

Wick, W. (1997) *A drop of water: A book of science and wonder.* New York: Scholastic. (3–6)
The author illustrates the properties of water using close-up photography.

1997

**Stanley, D. (1996). *Leonardo da Vinci.* New York: Morrow Junior Books. (4–6)

    This beautifully illustrated biography follows Leonardo da Vinci's life from birth to death and includes many of his extraordinary achievements.

Blumberg, R. (1996). *Full steam ahead: The race to build a transcontinental railroad.* Washington, DC: National Geographic Society. (5–6)

    This book describes one of the most ambitious construction projects of modern history.

Freedman, R. (1996). *The life and death of Crazy Horse.* New York: Holiday House. (5–6)

    A riveting account of the life of the great Sioux warrior who defeated General George Armstrong Custer at the Battle of the Little Big Horn.

Osborne, M. P. (1996). *One world, many religions: The way we worship.* New York: Knopf. (4–6).

    The author presents an accessible and well-crafted volume that introduces young readers to the world's seven major religions.

1996

**Murphy, J. (1995). *The great fire.* New York: Scholastic. (5–6)

    A compelling account of the Great Chicago Fire, combining personal accounts and historical documents.

Colman, P. (1995). *Rosie the riveter: women working on the home front in World War II.* New York: Crown.(4–6)

    Photographs and other visuals illustrate an account of the women who replaced men in the workplace during World War II.

Pringle, L. (1995). *Dolphin man: Exploring the world of dolphins.* New York: Atheneum Books for Young Readers. (5–6)

    This book focuses on a marine biologist and his work with the dolphin community of Sarasota, FL.

1995

**Swanson, D. (1994). *Safari beneath the sea: The wonder of the North Pacific coast.* San Francisco: Sierra Club Books. (4–6)

    The plant and animal life of the Pacific Northwest coast is described in an easy-to-understand text.

Dewey, J. O. (1994). *Wildlife rescue: The work of Dr. Kathleen Ramsay.* Photography by Don MacCarter. Honesdale, PA: Boyds Mills Press. (4–6)

    A day in the life of veterinarian Kathleen Ramsay and her National Wildlife Center as they rescue animal patients.

Freedman, R. (1994). *Kids at work: Lewis Hine and the crusade against child labor.* New York: Clarion. (5–6)

    Photobiography of photographer Lewis Hine, using his own photos of children working that prompted passage of child labor laws.

McKissack, P., & McKissack, F. (1994). *Christmas in the big house, Christmas in the quarters.* New York: Scholastic. (5–6)

    A narrative describing Christmas preparations that contrast those of the plantation owner's family and those of the slaves.

1994

**Murphy, J. (1993). *Across America on an emigrant train.* New York: Clarion. (5–6)

    An account of Robert Louis Stevenson's 12-day journey from New York to California in 1879, interwoven with a history of the building of the railroad and the settling of the West.

Brandenburg, J. (1993). *To the top of the world: Adventures with Arctic wolves.* New York: Walker. (5–6)

    A compelling chronicle of a wildlife photographer's experience living close to an Arctic wolf pack.

Brooks, B. (1993). *Making sense: Animal perception and communication.* New York: Farrar, Straus & Giroux in association with Thirteen/WNET. (5–6)

    This volume examines how animals perceive sensations and communicate with others.

1993

**Stanley, J. (1992). *Children of the Dust Bowl: The true story of the school at Weedpatch Camp.* New York: Crown. (4–6)

    This title traces the history of the Weedpatch School, set up at an emergency farm labor camp.

Cone, M. (1992). *Come back, salmon: How a group of dedicated kids adopted Pigeon Creek and brought it back to life.* San Francisco: Sierra Club Books. (4–6)

    This story describes how schoolchildren in Everett, WA, worked with their teachers to clean up Pigeon Creek and reclaim it as a salmon spawning ground.

1992

**Burleigh, R., & Wimmer, M. (1991). *Flight: the journey of Charles Lindbergh.* New York: Philomel Books. (1–4)

    This picture book depicts 25-year-old Charles Lindbergh's solo flight from New York to Paris.

Conrad, P. (1991). *Prairie visions: The life and times of Solomon Butcher.* New York: HarperCollins. (4–6)

    A collection of photos and stories about photographer Solomon Butcher and Nebraska at the start of the 20th century.

Myers, W. D. (1991). *Now is your time!: The African-American struggle for freedom.* New York: HarperCollins. (5–6)

    A history of the struggle of African Americans for freedom and equality, beginning with the capture of Africans in 1619 and up to contemporary times.

1991

**Freedman, R. (1990). *Franklin Delano Roosevelt.* New York: Clarion. (5–6)

    A well-researched biography tracing FDR's early life through his presidency.

Ekoomiak, N. (1990). *Arctic memories.* New York: Holt. (3–5)

    This story describes scenes from an Inuit childhood in both English and Inuktitut.

Lauber, P. (1990). *Seeing Earth from space.* New York: Orchard Books. (4–6)

    Text and photos taken from space depict our planet from the astronauts' perspective. (4–6)

1990

**Fritz, J. (1989). *The great little Madison.* New York: Putnam. (4–6)

    An engaging biography of James Madison that vividly describes the problems facing the new nation in its infancy.

Blumberg, R. (1989). *The great American gold rush.* New York: Bradbury Press. (5–6)

    Describes the emigration of people to California in pursuit of the dream of discovering gold.

Lauber, P. (1989). *The news about dinosaurs.* New York: Bradbury Press. (3–6)

    A beautifully illustrated explanation of many of the new theories about dinosaurs.

Index